Walk to Jerusalem

£2

Walk to Jerusalem

In Search of Peace

GERARD W. HUGHES

Darton, Longman and Todd
London

First published in 1991 by
Darton, Longman and Todd Ltd
89 Lillie Road, London SW6 1UD

© 1991 Gerard W. Hughes

British Library Cataloguing in Publication Data
Hughes, Gerard W.
 Walk to Jerusalem.
 1. Palestine. Christian pilgrimages to Jerusalem –
 Biographies
 I. Title
 248.463092

ISBN 0–232–51917–X

Phototypeset by Input Typesetting Ltd, London SW19 8DR.
Printed and bound in Great Britain by
Courier International Ltd, Tiptree, Essex.

To all those I have met
on the road to Jerusalem
and on the way through life.

Contents

Maps

Acknowledgements

I thank the following who kindly commented on an early draft of this book: Ursula Burton, Graham Chadwick, John Coventry, Mary Rose Fitzsimmons, Isabel Gregory, Aileen Ireland, Valerie Kent and Donald Nicholl. I also thank Teresa de Bertodano, formerly of Darton, Longman and Todd, for encouraging me to write it, Sarah Baird-Smith and Mary Jean Pritchard for continuing the encouragement and Olive Peat, who worked so carefully on the copy-editing. Finally, I thank Father Jock Earle, the Jesuit Provincial, who allowed me to take time off for the pilgrimage and who encouraged me on the way.

August 1990   GERARD W. HUGHES

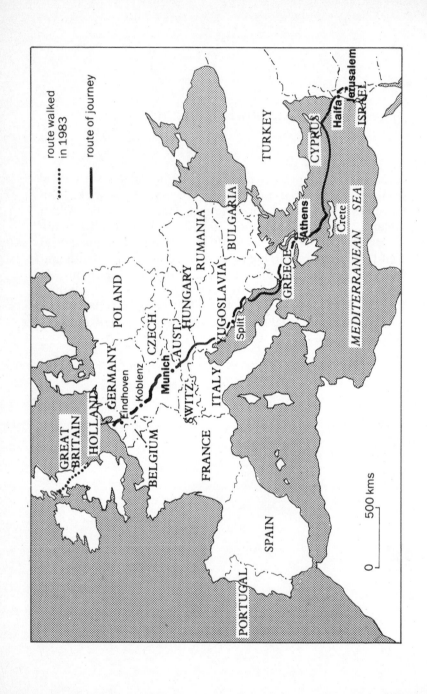

Prologue

In 1975, while on foot from Weybridge to Rome, I thought of someday walking from Skelmorlie, Ayrshire, where I was born, to Jerusalem. It remained a thought until July 1983, when I spent a two-week summer holiday in walking from Skelmorlie to Hull. This was the first leg of the pilgrimage to Jerusalem, which I then hoped to complete in 1984. But circumstances prevented me from going any further until 1987, when on February 21 I took a ferry from Hull to Rotterdam to continue on the road to Jerusalem.

After the walk to Rome I wrote *In Search of a Way*, using the physical journey through France and Italy to reflect on the inner journey which we all have to make, beginning at conception and ending in death. It was to find direction in the inner journey that I undertook the outward one.

Walk to Jerusalem is also about two journeys, the physical journey through Holland, Germany, Austria, Yugoslavia, Greece and then by ship to Haifa, and the inner spiritual journey through life. Both journeys had a particular focus. The physical journey raised funds for Pax Christi, a Christian organisation founded after the Second World War, initially to work for reconciliation between Germany and the allied nations and later expanding into all areas relating to justice and peace. The outer journey therefore was to help Pax Christi, the organisation; the inner journey was a search for Pax Christi, the peace of Christ.

While walking through Germany in March 1987, I met a Jesuit with whom I had studied thirty years earlier. I told him that on my way I had met some priests who were less than welcoming when I introduced myself as a Jesuit priest on a peace pilgrimage to Jerusalem on foot, a walk which was being sponsored to raise funds for Pax Christi. In reply

1

my friend advised me, 'You would be wiser not to volunteer the information that you are a Jesuit priest, because wandering priests with haversacks and dressed as you are, raise suspicion. Nor should you say that you are walking for peace, because many will then consider you to be either a communist sympathiser or a communist dupe. Above all, do not mention Pax Christi, which some priests consider a leftist and subversive organisation.'

If the human race has a future, Church historians will look back in amazement at the second half of the twentieth century and ask, 'Why were the Christian churches so slow to see and understand that the nuclear defence question was central to their Christian faith? Why did the majority of Christians consider the survival of the human race to be a merely political question, so few see it as an ethical question, and so very few see it as the most fundamental and important theological question which has ever faced the Church, because it affects every aspect of life and the very survival of life itself?'

Few people have the leisure, money, physical energy or inclination to make an outer journey on foot to Jerusalem, but every individual has to make the inner journey through life. The details of the outer journey are of interest to few and are important only in so far as they throw light on the inner. The inner journey is of interest to everyone and of importance, not just for the individual, but for the whole human race, because each of us is not only in this world, but we also contain the world within us. 'When a baby throws its rattle out of the cradle, the planets rock.' We are minuscule parts of a vast interlocking system dancing through space, affecting and being affected by everything around us. Our partners are not only all other human beings, animals, plants and inorganic particles of our world, but also all the stars and planets of the heavens. Whether or not we believe in an after-life, whatever our belief or disbelief in a theology or ideology, the world, as long as it exists, will always bear the imprint of our journey through it, for better for worse, for richer for poorer, for its health or its sickness, its life or its destruction. And death cannot cancel out the change which our living effects.

There is a spirit that is in my heart, smaller than a grain of mustard seed, greater than the earth, greater than the heavens, greater than all these worlds.

(Chandoya Upanishad 800 B.C.)

Each of us must make our own unique inner journey. Your journey will be different from mine, but we belong to one another and affect one another, whether we are aware of it or not. I do not want anyone to follow my route, but I hope this book offers hope and direction to other staggering pilgrims and helps them to find their own direction. The signpost to follow is appreciation of our own worth. It is because we do not value ourselves that we undervalue one another and our world, threatening its extinction in the name of security and defence. On the inner journey we find our own signpost, which points beyond ourselves and beyond our false values. The heart recognises the signpost; it reads: 'You are precious in my eyes. You are honoured and I love you' (Isaiah 43:4).

On the journey to Jerusalem I reflected often on nuclear deterrence. I had finished a draft version of this book before the dramatic changes happened in Eastern Europe at the end of 1989, changes which have lessened the immediate danger of nuclear war. I have not redrafted the book because my purpose in writing it was not to study the arguments for and against nuclear deterrence, but to examine the nature of our Christian spirituality. I give attention to nuclear deterrence because our support of such a method of defence reveals the fractured nature of our spirituality, which affects every aspect of our lives.

Even if all nuclear weapons were to be destroyed, unless our minds and hearts, which have considered nuclear deterrence to be a legitimate means of defence, undergo a radical transformation, our spirituality will remain fractured and we shall find other means of destroying our enemies, ourselves and our world. It is the roots of peace and violence which concern me in this book, and which must concern every human being.

1

I Go Because I Must – Preparation

To know Thee is the end and the beginning.
Thou carriest us and Thou dost go before,
Thou art the journey and the journey's end.
(Boethius)

Before planning the pilgrimage to Jerusalem in any detail, I first had to test my legs to know if I were still capable of walking fifteen to twenty miles each day carrying 34 pounds, the weight I had carried to Rome in 1975. Apart from a 250-mile walk in the summer of 1983, I had done no long-distance walking in the previous eleven years and my joints were beginning to creak.

In July 1986 I walked for six days in the west of Ireland beginning in Connemara and following the coastline north. I was carrying the haversack I had used for the Rome walk, including tent, sleeping bag and cooking utensils. After the first two hours walking I was sitting by the roadside when a farmer passed at walking pace on his bicycle. He wished me the time of day, stared at my haversack and dismounted. Just recently, he told me, he had seen a gentleman with a haversack just like mine, but he was not bearing it on his back. He had it in a little cart drawn by an Irish wolfhound.

I walked 100 miles in six days and although I was tired, and had sore muscles and slightly blistered feet at the end of it, I was confident that I could still walk long distances. On the last evening I pitched my tent on a deserted campsite by the sea about six miles from Killeary harbour. As I ate my supper the dark clouds rolled in from the west and the wind began to freshen. Soon the rain began in earnest and the wind strengthened. As I tried to get to sleep the wind was gusting, the wet outer cover of the tent flapping against the inner and I could feel the irregular raindrops on my face. Around midnight the tent collapsed, enfolding me in its wet embrace. I felt for the entrance zip and stuck my head out into the Atlantic gale. As my sleeping bag was still dry on the inside, I wrapped it inside my cagoul and made a dash for the only open shelter in the campsite, the toilets. After a sleepless night, I collected the sodden tent at dawn, packed the haversack, which now felt twice its weight, and walked breakfastless into what the guidebooks describe as one of the most beautiful stretches of coast in Ireland, now covered in heavy, drenching mist.

As I walked that day through heavy rain under the weight of the sodden haversack, I began to waver about the Jerusalem walk, but after a sleep and a meal, and when the sky cleared and I could dry my clothes in the sun, I thought of the gentleman with the Irish wolfhound. I realised that to walk to Jerusalem with the haversack on my shoulders would be so physically demanding that the pilgrimage would become an endurance test, which was not the object of the exercise. I could walk with a lighter load by dispensing with the tent, sleeping bag and cooking equipment, but this, besides being much more expensive, would also be very restricting, for I would have to plan each day's walking in such a way that I could ensure finding a bed for the night, and for meals I would be dependent on cafés and restaurants. I preferred the heavy load and independence.

In 1975, before walking to Rome, I heard from an Edinburgh man, Ian Tweedie, who told me that he had walked a few years before from Aldershot 'where I had served in arms for my sins' to Rome, drawing his haversack behind him on an aluminium frame fitted with pram wheels. It had served him well and he offered to construct a similar machine for me. I declined his offer then. Eleven years later I was less contemptuous of pram wheels. In the autumn of 1986 I wrote to Ian again asking if he still had the haversack on wheels. He asked me if I would like to give the machine a name. A few weeks later I collected it, decorated with a St Andrew's flag, 'lest they make the dreadful mistake of thinking you are English', a carved Jerusalem cross and a red plastic

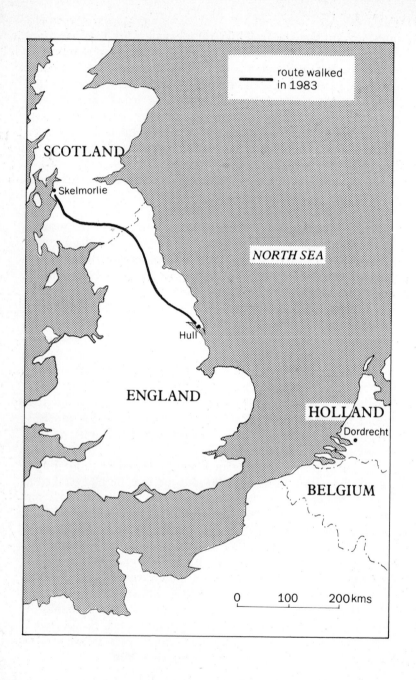

route walked
in 1983

SCOTLAND

• Skelmorlie

NORTH SEA

Hull

ENGLAND

HOLLAND

Dordrecht
•

BELGIUM

0   100   200 kms

nameplate bearing the name 'MUNGO'. The red haversack was fitted to an aluminium frame and so sprung that with a strap over one shoulder and a steering stick, which could fit into either side of the frame, the pram wheels could take most of the weight. On an even level surface I could walk with relative ease and on downhill stretches Mungo would give an encouraging push.

I chose the name Mungo for several reasons. Mungo, also called Kentigern, was a Celtic saint, and Celtic spirituality was very aware that creation itself is a sacrament, a sign and an effective sign of God's presence in all things, a spirituality which we desperately need today. Mungo, too, founded the church in Glasgow, where I had lived as a child and later worked as a priest. From Glasgow he went to North Wales and founded a monastery, later called St Asaph, in memory of one of its early abbots. Mungo, seeing a resemblance between the Clyde valley which he had left and the valley to which he had come, named the Welsh valley 'Clyde', which in Welsh became 'Clwyd'. I had spent twelve years in the Clwyd valley in a Jesuit house called St Beuno's. Beuno was another monk from Mungo's monastery. When Beuno's niece, Winifred, rejected the advances of the wicked prince Caradoc, he cut off her head. Uncle Beuno put her head back on again and we had a stained glass window in the St Beuno's chapel illustrating the miracle. The Celtic monks, too, were great travellers by land and sea. According to a ninth-century account, the motive for St Brendan's voyage to America was not to save souls, but 'to wonder at the glory of God's creation'. My final reason for choosing Mungo was the pun on his name. In Scots 'mun go' is 'must go' and I felt I must attempt this walk to Jerusalem.

In preparation I began to do some more regular geriatric jogging, but after one jog in the snow in January 1987, I felt jagged pains in my right knee which later began to swell. Forty years earlier I had a cartilage removed, the surgeon warning me that the operation could cause arthritis later. The knee had served me well and, apart from a twinge on the first day of the walk to Rome, it had given me no serious trouble. I decided on no more jogging, a decision easily kept, and both pain and swelling subsided.

Early in February I visited my sister Edith, who was living
in Largs, Ayrshire, where I spent five days practising walking
with Mungo fully packed with all that I would need for
Jerusalem. Jim and Pauline Gallacher, who had accompanied
me over a stretch of the Rome walk in 1975, drove me to
Wemyss Bay and I gave Mungo its first testing over the five
miles from Wemyss Bay to Largs. I had gone only a few
yards when the machine keeled over, leaving me literally in
a twist, for I could not get free of the shoulder strap until the
machine was righted. The road runs along the shore of the
Firth of Clyde, a narrow road, most· of it without pavement.
The traffic was heavy and I felt unsafe with the unstable
Mungo and the oncoming traffic, especially as the evening
light was fading. After two miles there is an alternative hill
route into Largs, longer but traffic-free. It was already dark
when I reached the top of the hill and I could see through
the trees the lights of the Isle of Bute across the Firth. It was
a euphoric moment and I felt great delight at the prospect of
this long walk through Europe with plenty of time 'to wonder
at the glory of God's creation'. Then there was a loud crack
and Mungo keeled over for a second time. When I left St
Beuno's in North Wales in 1983, I had been presented with
a walking stick mounted with a bronze labrador head with
'Beuno' inscribed on a plaque beneath it, a memorial to a
lively dog I had there. The walking stick was now in two
pieces, the lower part immovably lodged in the left-hand side
of the aluminium frame. I transferred the top half of the stick
to the right-hand side of the frame, but it was uncomfortably
short, so that I was walking with one hand behind my back.
At Edith's house I tried to extract the broken stick but only
succeeded in lodging it more firmly into the frame.

I began the training with a 25-mile walk without the haversack over the hills from Largs to Greenock, returning by the
shore road, and wearing not boots, but trainers, hoping they
would be easier on my feet. They were not, so next day I
walked in shoes and did 14 miles with Mungo fully packed.
When I took off my shoes in the evening, one little toe was
bleeding, the blood stain seeping through the shoe, where it
remains to this day and no amount of polishing can remove
it. On the fifth day I walked 24 miles with a fully packed
Mungo and my feet were pain-free at the end of it. For the

last three days of training, instead of thick socks I had worn a pair of very thin woollen socks which I rubbed with soap and sprinkled with foot powder every morning, covered them with a pair of thin cotton socks and walked in shoes, not trainers. This method served me well and I had no serious foot trouble until I left Munich, where I had the shoes fitted with special mountain soles and heels.

Reassured after the practice walk that I was fit enough to do the pilgrimage, and that Mungo would also be, once fitted with a metal rod to replace the broken walking stick, I began planning the route. My first plan was to go to Jerusalem via Istanbul, proceeding through Hungary, Bulgaria, Rumania and to Ephesus in Turkey, where I could take a boat to Israel by way of Rhodes. I did not even consider going overland through Turkey, Syria and Lebanon into Israel, assuming it would not be possible, and even if it were possible, reckoning it would be suicidal. At the end of the pilgrimage, on my last day in Jerusalem, I met a 63-year-old Frenchwoman, Henriette Tommy-Martin, who had walked on her own from Paris to Jerusalem the year before, her route taking her through Syria and Lebanon. She told me that in all her journey the warmest welcome and most generous hospitality she experienced was in Lebanon.

In the end I decided on a route via Athens, because walking through Yugoslavia and Greece seemed a more attractive prospect than walking through Rumania and Bulgaria. Besides, I could visit Turkey on the return journey. I drew a straight line on a small-scale map from Rotterdam to Athens and then worked on large-scale maps to plan a detailed route avoiding main roads as far as possible. It was relatively easy to plan routes through Holland, Germany and Austria, but detailed maps of Yugoslavia and Greece were unobtainable. On a rough reckoning the distance from Rotterdam to Athens was about 3000 km with another 190 km for the route Haifa–Nazareth–Jerusalem. I planned to begin walking on March 1st and to reach Athens by June 30th. On paper this planning was very easy!

It was on the road to Rome in 1975 that I had first dreamed of one day walking to Jerusalem, but it had remained a pleasant dream for many years. Now that I had committed myself to it and thought about the details, I began to feel apprehensive and to doubt the wisdom of attempting such a pilgrimage, doubts which continued the whole way to Jerusalem. Once the pilgrimage was over I was glad that I had not given in to the doubts, and in living with them I was much helped by Jesus' image of the Kingdom: 'The kingdom of heaven is like the yeast a woman took and mixed in with three measures of flour till it was leavened all through' (Matt. 13:33).

A few months before starting on the pilgrimage I had learned how to make bread and began to understand the parable much more vividly. When warm water and brown sugar are mixed with the yeast, it begins to bubble and froth. This was a very good image of my state of mind when I dreamed about a walk to Jerusalem from the comfort of an armchair, bubbling with enthusiasm. When the bubbling yeast is poured into a bowl of dry flour, it disappears into the mass and when I began to knead, most of the grains of flour resisted my attempts to bring them into contact with the yeast, finding refuge on the periphery of the bowl. I could imagine the grains saying to one another, 'Not bloody likely, I don't want to lose my personal identity and independence by getting mixed up with that lot.' The resistant grains of flour represented all those elements in me which were resistant to the walk and of which I was not aware until I had made the decision to go. I was instructed to keep kneading until the whole mass was no longer sticky and it began to squeak. I imagined that the squeaks represented the sense of peace and strength which we experience when our whole being is in harmony with a decision. By the time I reached Jerusalem I was squeaking!

Friday, February 20

I set off from Manresa House, Birmingham, where I was living, took a train for Hull and caught the overnight ferry to Rotterdam. Brother Willie Jordan, one of the Manresa community and a man of many gifts, had extracted the broken walking stick from the haversack frame and replaced it with an aluminium rod with a plastic handle, which fitted exactly and served me well, bent but unbroken, until I reached Jerusalem. I celebrated Mass before leaving Manresa and prayed that Christ's peace should be in me, in all my family and friends, in all the people I have ever worked with, especially the little groups of bruised peace and justice workers. I prayed, too, for faith in the power of God working through our weakness and able to effect infinitely more than we can think or imagine, a faith which can preserve us from the despair which threatens when we look at the complexity and apparent intractability of justice and peace questions.

Before catching the ferry, I visited Mary Featherstone in Cottingham, near Hull. She had been matron at Stonyhurst college for twenty-five years and had retired in 1967. While still at Stonyhurst she had become a legend, based on the fact of her extraordinary intuitive gifts, not only in medical diagnosis, which had saved the lives of some of her patients, but also in her detective skills, which made Miss Marple seem a plodder in comparison. If some crime had been committed in the school, 'Sister' would know the culprit long before the authorities, a gift she used solely to defend the innocent, never to incriminate the guilty. I have great trust in her wisdom and powers of intuition and had she advised against the pilgrimage, I should have felt I was tempting providence by going. She approved, which was most encouraging. Her approval, however, did not spare me from many practical warnings and apprehensions, on the dangers of sleeping on damp ground or in a damp bed, the care to be taken with food and drink, especially in foreign countries, in walking the roads and looking both ways before crossing, ensuring that my wallet was kept in a safe place, and so on. As her vivid imagination conjured up possible dangers, the peace I had felt during Mass at Manresa began to ebb. While Mary was in the kitchen preparing an excellent lunch, I glanced at her *Daily Telegraph*, which included a leading article on a peace conference in Moscow to which Mr Gorbachev had invited representatives from East and West. The writer poured scorn on the meeting and praised President Reagan's Strategic Defence Initiative. The glib and polished style of the article contained the seeds of violence, because it presented as sound common sense one of the most destructive of human attitudes, distrust, which nurtures fear and so fuels violence. The writer proposed for our defence and security a massively expensive and unprecedented lethal first-strike system, which would threaten ourselves as much as threaten the enemy. The article acted on me like adrenalin, drove away imaginary fears and confirmed me in what I was doing.

I stood on the deck of the overnight ferry from Hull to Rotterdam, watched the sun go down in a glorious red sky and then went below to look at maps and study a Dutch phrase book before dinner.

Saturday, February 21

I slept on a lounge bench and awoke early with the beginnings of a cold. From Rotterdam I took a train to Delft, where I had planned to spend a week in a Jesuit house, to visit peace groups in Holland and the Pax Christi headquarters in Antwerp.

Almost all the Jesuit community spoke such excellent English that I never needed the phrase book. One of them, Father Kes Hillenaar, had been teaching at Stonyhurst in 1950, when I was also teaching there, and I had not seen him since. He took me on a tour of the beautiful old city criss-crossed with canals, with its picturesque market square, flower market and rows of shops displaying Delft china. In the evening I was invited to attend what was called 'an informal Mass' in the large chapel adjoining the house. The Mass had been prepared with great care and was celebrated in a small side chapel, attended by about thirty people, mostly elderly or middle-aged, with a few younger women but no younger men. This 'informal Mass' had begun in the 1960s, when the main chapel could not contain the vast numbers of young people who wanted to attend. The drastic fall in numbers was indicative of what has happened generally in Holland. Dutch Catholics were traditionally very loyal to Rome, jealous of their identity as Catholic, with their own schools, radio stations and organisations. I read somewhere that their separatism even included a Catholic goat-breeders association!

Before the Second Vatican Council in 1962, under the leadership of Cardinal Alfrink but with the co-operation of all the Dutch bishops, all parishes were encouraged to join in preparation for the Council and were invited to express their views on the need for renewal in the Catholic Church. At the Council itself the Dutch bishops played a leading part because they were in touch with their people and had listened to them carefully. After the Council, Catholics studied its documents in their parishes and tried to put them into practice with an enthusiasm which was sometimes excessive, excesses which were to be expected in a Church which had for so long been restricted by what one bishop described as 'triumphalism, clericalism and legalism'.

Everywhere I went in Holland almost everyone with whom I spoke told the same sad story of the excitement and enthusiasm of Dutch Catholics during and immediately after the Council and of the gradual disillusionment which followed as Rome, becoming nervous at what was happening, began to appoint more 'conservative' bishops. They certainly succeeded in slowing down the innovations, but the policy has also emptied the churches. What is left is an ageing and divided Church, divided between those who support the more conservative bishops, reckoned to be about 30 per cent of church membership, and those who do not. I was not in Holland long enough to begin to assess these generalisations, which may well be too pessimistic, for the faith and future promise of a Church can never be measured statistically. In a Scottish Catholic newspaper in the late sixties I read an article in which the writer encouraged his readers to pray that Scotland should be delivered from the excesses of the Dutch Church, a prayer which was imposing no great burden on God at the time. One of the Scottish bishops returning from the Council had assured his flock that there was no need to worry as nothing had changed.

We need to find a new vocabulary in the Church with which to describe the divisions within it, because the current labels 'conservative', 'progressive', 'traditionalist' are misleading. All these labels should be applicable to every bishop within the Church. It is essential that the Church should have conservative, traditionalist bishops – that is, bishops who do preserve, nurture and cherish the radical message of the Gospel, who are in touch with the 2000-year tradition of the Church and of its Hebrew origins, aware too of the variety of ways in which it has succeeded in handing on the Gospel message to different people of very different cultures at different times, as well as being aware of the ways it has failed to do so. But that is not the meaning of our current usage of 'conservative' or 'traditionalist', terms often used to mean exactly the opposite. I read of a recent appointment of a bishop whom the writer labelled 'conservative', and added in justification of this label that the new bishop had stated that 'praying the rosary is a more effective way of promoting world peace than taking part in peace demonstrations', that he considered Aids to be a scourge of God, and that he was noted for his extreme anti-communism. I know nothing of the bishop in question, who may not be guilty of the attitudes ascribed to him, but such attitudes should not be graced with the word 'conservative'. Statements like 'Saying the rosary is a more effective way of promoting peace than taking part in peace demonstrations', can be taken to mean, and is so understood by many, that as long as we recite our prayers for peace, then nothing else can be expected of us. This encourages a spirituality which absolves us from the cost, the risk and the pain of facing the violence of the facts in which we live, a spirituality which, in fact, denies the truth of the Incarnation. 'Aids is the scourge of God' is, I believe, a blasphemous statement, because it presents God as unforgiving, ruthless, vindictive and merciless, a God who scourges babies at birth. Such an attitude of condemnation can encourage a selective moral self-righteousness, blinding those who hold it to the violence of their own attitudes and justifying them in their lack of compassion. Extreme anti-communism encourages individual and national paranoia and spiritual blindness, because the attitude externalises evil and projects it onto another, causing the real enemy, which is within each person's mind and heart, to be ignored and so allowed to continue its destructiveness. A bishop who encourages his flock to pray for peace while at the same time discouraging them from involving themselves in political and social action for peace, who denounces Aids as a scourge of God, and who is fiercely anti-communist would be a welcome ally in any fascist or tyrannical state and would be very unlikely to suffer the fate which Christ promised for his followers, 'You will be dragged before governors and kings for my sake to bear witness before them' (Matt. 10:18). Such bishops are much more likely to be honoured, approved and decorated by governors and kings. If 'conservative' as applied to a bishop means a timid labourer in the Lord's vineyard, whose knowledge of tradition is limited to his own childhood, and who is afraid of anything that grows, unable to distinguish the healthy from the diseased, and who cuts down both, emptying the churches of most of its youth, then no such person should be appointed as bishop. Similarly, if 'progressive' signifies a man who has little knowledge or love of tradition and who is intolerant of those who do have it, he, too, should not be appointed as bishop. On the other hand, if 'progressive' signifies a man who struggles to communicate the Gospel message in a language which people can understand and who can show the relevance of Christ's message to every aspect of life – including the political, social and economic structures in which we live as a nation and which determine our relationship to other nations – then this is a quality which should be required in every bishop. Our terms 'conservative' and 'progressive' are signs of the fractured nature of our spirituality. It is not without significance that bishops labelled 'conservative' will usually be supporters of nuclear deterrence.

Sunday, February 22

Next day Father Kes Hillenaar took me with him to a country church where he celebrates Mass every Sunday because there is no longer a parish priest. The liturgy was very sober with not a trace of the excesses against which we had been encouraged to pray in Scotland – perhaps in answer to Scotland's prayers! However, there was a very confident altar girl in charge of a very diffident altar boy, who took his many orders meekly from her. During the week the laity take charge of the parish and use the presbytery as their headquarters. The parish was in the heart of greenhouse land and on the way home we visited one of the tomato-growing parishioners. The greenhouses were about 100 metres long and 50 metres wide with automatic sprinklers, windows opening by thermostatic control when the temperature became too high, automatic fertilising, the whole complicated procedure regulated by computer. The tomatoes had been planted in January and would be cleared by June, when the greenhouse would be used for lettuce growing. When I saw this, I could understand better the desolation I have seen in Lanarkshire, Scotland, the acres of broken little greenhouses where farmers once grew tomatoes but can no longer compete against Dutch efficiency.

The Jesuit community in Delft were most welcoming, interested in what I was doing and very encouraging, which was important to me at this time when I was feeling very apprehensive about starting the pilgrimage. Most of the community were teaching in a Jesuit college. I was impressed with their calm and simple life-style. They had lived through the crises of the Dutch Church and although they must have been hurt and disillusioned, they were plodding on in difficult circumstances, their hope in a kingdom which grows most vigorously when everything seems hopeless.

Monday, February 23

I took a morning train to Antwerp to visit the Pax Christi headquarters, my cold now in full spate. I had packed four handkerchiefs for the five-month trip, relying on paper handkerchiefs for day-to-day use. Paper handkerchiefs were quite useless for this cold and I travelled to Antwerp with four soaking linen ones. At the Pax Christi headquarters I met Valerie Flessati, who had been in charge of the Pax Christi office in London, where I had worked briefly as an office boy three years before. She was doing research on the history of Pax Christi and told me of interesting documents she had been allowed to study in the Westminster Cathedral archives on the activities of a Catholic peace group in England in the 1930s, inspired by some Dominicans, especially those in Blackfriars, Oxford. They had received no official encouragement from Westminster. I also spent time with Étienne de Jonghe, who is in charge of Pax Christi international, who advised me to visit a joint Catholic and Protestant peace centre in Antwerp known as IPIS.

16

Before visiting IPIS I went hunting for a shop which sold handkerchiefs. Spotting a likely shop across the road, I obeyed Mary Featherstone's instructions, looked carefully both ways and crossed. On reaching the other side I was stopped by a policeman on a motor cycle, who gave me a severe dressing down for crossing the road when the traffic signal was still at red. My explanation in broken French that I had looked carefully both ways did not impress him and he brought out his notebook. I added that in Britain, whence I came, it was not an offence to cross a clear road on foot even if the lights were at red. He did not accept this excuse, told me that he would not book me this time, but that I must realise that I was no longer in Britain, 'for now', he added, 'you are in civilisation'. I found a shop and bought a dozen handkerchiefs, which were all soaking by the end of the day.

IPIS was a very large centre with a library on peace and peace-related questions, but here, as elsewhere, I could find very little on the theology and spirituality of peace. The Churches in Holland and Belgium, both Catholic and Protestant, were much more involved in the peace movement than in Britain, their peace groups more highly organised and more politically active and influential. In Holland they had almost succeeded in influencing the government to refuse to have U.S. Cruise missiles, but then failed. When I visited the Pax Christi office in The Hague next day, they were still struggling with this disappointment, which was forcing them to reflect more on the roots of peace and violence and leading them to turn their attention to building up contacts between East and West. When I asked, both in Antwerp and in The Hague, about the spiritual training offered to peace activists, I heard no clear answer. The peace movements were supported by the young, who were disillusioned with their Churches and suspicious of spirituality, which they understood as meaning saying lots of prayers, singing hymns and holding back from any political action. Some of the Dutch bishops had invited all their parishes to express their views on nuclear disarmament, but the more 'conservative' bishops did not welcome discussion on what they considered to be socio-political issues.

Tuesday, February 24

When I returned from Antwerp on Monday night I went to bed early, hoping to sleep off the cold, but I awoke in the night bathed in sweat and suspected 'flu. I have had 'flu only once in my life, in 1967, and it left me weak for the following two months. I had intended spending a week in Holland visiting peace groups, in particular a group of Franciscans who were living at a nuclear base. In Europe, among Catholic religious orders, the Franciscans were the most active and energetic in promoting peace. I also wanted to spend more time in the Pax Christi library in Antwerp and in The Hague, but I was afraid that if I lingered the 'flu might develop and I would be a burden to the Jesuit community. I was also afraid that it might lead me to abandon the pilgrimage before I had really started. In spite of the bad night, I felt slightly better, visited the Pax Christi office in The Hague in the morning and decided to start the walk next day, Wednesday. I spent Tuesday afternoon reading a book which I found in the Jesuit common room, and this confirmed me in my decision to start the next day, for I knew that if I lingered the 'flu would probably develop. The book was called *The Ending of Hunger* (published by Praeger Studies, CBS International Publishing, New York). I made notes on it in my diary, which was soaked through in the course of the pilgrimage, but the legible jottings included the following:

> 80% of the world's trade, 93% of its industry and 100% of its scientific research is controlled by the industrial rich nations of the world.

> According to the World Bank report of 1980, about one billion people live in relative poverty, mostly in developing countries, and about 800 million are malnourished.

> In 1961 there were about 6,000,000 people in the world's regular armed forces. In 1981 there were 25,000,000. Including the reserves, paramilitary forces and civilians engaged in the military industrial complex, there are about 100,000,000 involved.

> The world trade in conventional arms tripled between 1960

and 1980. By 1982 the world was spending about 1,000,000 dollars per minute on arms.

In a square made up of 6,000 dots, each dot represented three megatons, the total firepower expended in World War II. The 6,000 dots represented the firepower of the world's current nuclear stockpile. One hundred of the dots would be sufficient to destroy all the large and medium-sized cities of the world.

The U.N. set .7% of the gross national product as the standard amount which each developed nation should give in overseas aid. U.K. was contributing .27%.

Wednesday, February 25

On my first day's walking, I experienced the first of the striking coincidences which recurred frequently during the pilgrimage. Before setting off, the Jesuit community invited me to celebrate Mass in English. The first reading was from Ecclesiasticus and included the lines,

> For though she [wisdom] takes him at first through winding ways, bringing fear and faintness on him, plaguing him with her discipline until she can trust him, and testing him with her ordeals, in the end she will lead him back to the straight road and reveal her secrets to him.

I prayed that she would reveal the secrets while going easy on the ordeals. The Gospel was from Mark, chapter 9, in which John says to Jesus, 'Master, we saw a man who is not one of us casting out devils in your name, and because he was not one of us we tried to stop him.' But Jesus said, 'You must not stop him; no one who works a miracle in my name is likely to speak evil of me. Anyone who is not against us is for us.' These words were also encouraging, like an injection of life and hope. So much of the sorry story I had been hearing of the Catholic Church in Holland was because we do not believe 'anyone who is not against us is for us', but assume instead that anyone who does not subscribe to our particular notion of God, of the Church, of particular doctrines or moral teachings, must therefore be against us, as though God can

19

only work within the narrow limits of our blinkered vision. God is at work in all things and in every human being. Our task as human beings is to discover him at work in each one, but we can only discover him if we trust. I once read of a religious superior whose communities were always happy and in harmony. His biographer commented 'The goodness of his subjects existed at first solely in his pious imagination.' If we can learn to trust the goodness of each one, the trust brings the goodness to birth.

Trust is at the roots of peace: distrust is at the roots of violence.

After breakfast, accompanied by one of the community, I walked to the station to catch a train to Dordrecht on the outskirts of Rotterdam, choosing Dordrecht because the route from Delft to Dordrecht was so criss-crossed with canals that I despaired of finding a direct route which would avoid major roads. Mungo keeled over twice in the short distance from the house to the station, which was alarming. I still had a heavy cold, but was free of the shivers of 'flu. The temperature during the nights in Holland had been −10°C, rising to −4°C during the day. It was the coldest winter they had had for years. Fortunately, I did not know that it was also to be the longest within living memory and that there would still be snow in Munich when I arrived there at the end of March.

2

Healing Colds and Other Ills – Holland

Fullness to such, a burden is,
That go on pilgrimage;
Here little, and hereafter bliss,
Is best from age to age.
(John Bunyan, *Pilgrim's Progress*)

Wednesday, February 25 (continued)

Dordrecht lies 12 miles to the south-east of Rotterdam. Once through its suburbs I was in flat, open country, the thin covering of snow sparkling in the sunlight, the sky a delicate blue. I crossed the Nieuwe Merwede by ferry and walked along its southern bank to Werkendam, where I arrived at 1.00 p.m., having walked fast for three hours without stopping, apart from the ferry break. In walking to Rome, I used to stop for ten minutes after every hour and, at the beginning of the walk, I removed boots and socks at each stop and bathed my feet, if I could find water. I intended the same break after each hour on the road to Jerusalem, but on this first morning it was so intensely cold, with a temperature of −4°C, that I would have frozen had I stopped and my hands were too numb to undo shoe laces. Before setting out from England I had thought about taking gloves, but thinking spring was near, I had left them behind, a decision I was now regretting. I frequently changed Mungo's steering stick from one side of the frame to the other so that I could put the exposed hand in my pocket before it became too frozen.

The general principle in packing a haversack is to abandon anything which is not strictly necessary, but like all other clear principles it becomes complex when put into practice. I was carrying a tent, sleeping bag, maps and phrase books, a Bible and notebook, a minimum amount of equipment for celebrating Mass, one change of clothing and six pairs of thin socks. Without the tent and sleeping bag I should have had to arrange each day's walking so that I could be sure of finding lodgings at the end of each day, and without cooking equipment my freedom to move would have been even more restricted, but my definition of 'necessary' was very arbitrary. What I considered necessary, others would reckon superfluous luxury. A few years ago I had read a fascinating book called *Peace Pilgrim*, the biography of an American woman, who had spent the last thirty years of her life walking the length and breadth of the United States in the cause of peace, covering the southern states in the winter and the northern states in the summer. Her only luggage was a toothbrush. She followed the Gospel precept literally, 'Provide yourselves with no gold or silver, not even with a few coppers for your purse, with no haversack for the journey or spare tunic or footwear, or a staff' (Matt. 10:9), but she did wear a pair of trainers. She carried no money, did not beg and kept to a vegetarian diet. The book included photographs, one taken when she first began walking, the other taken shortly before her death. Her vitality breaks through the blurred black and white photographs. Her name was unknown. She called herself 'Peace'. The book was written by friends who had met and been influenced by her on the way. She slept rough and ate when food was offered. In all her thirty years of walking alone she had only once been attacked. She practised non-violent resistance and her attacker, a psychopath, desisted. She also claimed that in thirty years of walking without begging, the longest period without food had been three days. The first part of the book tells of her travels and her teaching: the second part is made up of tributes to her memory from people who had met her on her way. As she became known, schools, colleges, universities, radio and TV stations would invite her to speak and for these engagements she would accept lifts. On her way to one such appointment she was killed in a car crash.

After returning from Jerusalem I heard about a Brother of Charity (a member of the male branch of Mother Teresa's congregation) who had walked from Paris to Jerusalem and back without money or haversack. I realised that Mungo and I were on a luxury trip in comparison, but this thought did not make it any easier to resist the cold.

At Werkendam I stopped for a meal of two enormous and very tasty sausages buried under a mound of chips covered with mayonnaise, a mixture I had never tried before and found far superior to HP sauce. From my seat in the café I could see the ships and barges sailing by. There is something very peaceful about watching slow-moving barges, so I took a 5 km detour from my planned route to have longer walking by the river, then turned south to Almkerk, where I had planned to stop for the night. The walking had been easy on the first day, for the roads in Holland are flat, the main roads have cycle tracks and the minor roads, to which I kept all day, are well surfaced.

Camping was out of the question in this freezing weather, so I decided to look for a church spire and ask for a bed or floor space at the nearest presbytery. The church had a presbytery adjoining, an indication in Britain that the church is Catholic. I rang the presbytery bell and the door was opened by a woman with kindly eyes but not a word of English. She looked bewildered as I practised my Dutch phrases, signalled to me to wait and then returned with a man who could speak English. I introduced myself and he, the Protestant minister, without any hesitation or request to see my passport or papers, invited me in, showed me to a room which belonged to his son, who was away at theological college, and told me that I had arrived on a good evening because his wife had just prepared a special meal to welcome another son, a long-distance lorry driver, who had arrived home unexpectedly. It was an excellent meal and at the end of it the pastor produced the family Bible, read a passage in Dutch, commented on it, paused for a period of silent prayer and then ended with a final prayer and a hymn. After dinner, while the pastor had to meet with a group in the church, I took a short walk to look at the bright night sky and reflect on the day. Wisdom had been very kind to me today, guiding me safely along straight and winding roads and bringing me to this haven where I was so kindly and warmly welcomed and invited to join in the family prayer. To my amazement, the fierce cold bordering on 'flu, which I had reckoned would take at least a week to clear, had disappeared. Fast walking in sub-zero temperatures was the most effective cure I had ever experienced.

Thursday, February 26

Next morning, breakfast was followed by another Scripture reading and prayer. My hosts refused to accept anything for my board and lodging but asked to be remembered in my prayers on the road. They came to the garden gate to see me off on the next 38 km stretch to Oisterwijk. I thanked God for the pastor and his wife and for the kindness they had shown me. The weather was slightly warmer, although still freezing, and my road was through farmland, all neatly plotted and ploughed, but bare. Now that my cold had gone I could smell the countryside, spread liberally with organic fertiliser. I was grateful for these flat roads at the beginning of the walk and never found them boring, because they either ran through forests, which felt friendly and protective, or along waterways which somehow help the walker to glide along with them, or through open country with views stretching to the horizon on every side, as though one were walking on the top of the world. The countryside spoke peace to me, reflected in the faces of the people, a serenity expressed even in the leisurely way they rode their very solid-looking bicycles, mothers sometimes riding with one child in the front pannier and another at the back. Their houses, like the fields, have a cared-for look and I never saw a house without its window display of plants and flowers. In most countries dogs bark, growl and strain on their leads as a stranger goes by. In Holland I was pursued by only one dog, which was noiseless and stopped to sit up and beg whenever I looked round.

I crossed another river, the Bergse Maas, and as I was the only passenger, the ferryman chatted with me. When I told him I was walking to Jerusalem by way of Athens, he told me that the journey would be worth it if only to see Athens, which he had visited the previous summer. I ate lunch sitting in the sun by the roadside; it was the last time I was able to sit outside and eat in comfort until I was south of Munich. Later in the afternoon, pausing to rest by the roadside, I spotted something black lying in the snow-covered ditch. It was a motor cyclist's gauntlet, very damp but in good condition with fur lining on the inside. It was a most welcome find and protected me from chilblains all the way to Yugoslavia, giving more warmth to the steering-stick hand than to the hand in my pocket.

At 5.30 p.m. I was in Oisterwijk, hoping that wisdom would continue to be as kind as yesterday and find me somewhere to stay for the night. Wisdom evidently reckoned she had done enough and I had my first experience, to be repeated many times, of a long search for accommodation at the end of the day. There was a town map on display and I noticed a street called 'Canisius' with a church marked on the road. Peter Canisius was a Dutchman, who became a Jesuit in the sixteenth century, shortly after the Order was founded. He became a famous theologian of the counter-Reformation and was the author of the catechism, a synopsis in question-and-answer form of the Catholic faith incorporating the decrees of the Council of Trent, inflicted on Catholic children for generations. Canisius himself was a most gentle character whose sound principle in discussion with the reformers, later unfortunately forgotten, was always to concentrate on the points of agreement rather than on the differences which separate. On the way to Canisius Street I found another church and, as it was already dark, I tried there for accommodation. The parish priest was not at home and I was referred to a large pastoral centre across the road. It was a large, well appointed building with notices on its windows welcoming any who might be in distress. Inside there were four members of staff ready to attend to my needs. In elemental Dutch I introduced myself and my need for shelter for the night. Years of pastoral experience did not enable the helpers to understand my Dutch nor cope with my request, so they referred me to the tourist bureau nearby, which gave me the address of the nearest bed-and-breakfast place, fortunately not too far away. The other evening problem was finding something to eat. Restaurants were usually open till late, but my budget would not stretch to a restaurant every evening as well as lodging, so I learned to shop every evening before 6.00 p.m.

Fortunately the place where I stayed was excellent and relatively cheap, but before going to sleep I was doing mental arithmetic on my finances and wondering whether the search for accommodation was going to be equally difficult every evening. I had begun the pilgrimage hoping to keep within a budget of £30 a week, but I soon realised this would be impossible if I was going to sleep in comfort and eat enough to have the energy to walk each day. The 38 km I had walked was tiring enough, but the hour and a half search for accommodation at the end of it was exhausting.

Friday, February 27

Most of the *pensions* at which I stayed in Holland, Germany and Austria provided excellent breakfasts of rolls, cheese, boiled eggs, cold meat and real coffee. It was such a breakfast that enabled me to face cheerfully the morning drizzle and begin the third day's walking. I planned a route along minor roads through farmland and forest to Nuenen, a town on the outskirts of Eindhoven 36 km away.

Before setting out each day I used to look at the Mass readings, read a few psalms and a chapter or two of one of the Old Testament prophets. From these readings I would find a word or phrase, hear it spoken to me during the first hour's walking and keep bringing my wandering mind back to it. The phrase acted like an anchor to my drifting thoughts, so that when I found my mind moving to self-preoccupation with some worry or anxiety about my survival on this walk, or to memories of past hurts and disappointments, I could bring the dark mood into touch with the chosen phrase. That day the phrase was, 'Open my eyes that I may consider the wonders of your law.' The phrase was like the opening of a door, allowing me to step beyond the prison of my own preoccupations, helping me to see them in perspective.

For the second hour I would pray for peace, using some image or word to focus my mind. The most helpful image was the scene in St John's Gospel in which Jesus appears to his disciples on Easter Sunday evening and says to them, 'Peace be to you,' and shows them his wounded hands and side, an image which speaks volumes on the nature of peace – that it is risky, costly and demands vulnerability. In Holland and Germany, if ever my mind strayed, it never took long before a screaming, low-flying plane reminded me of what I was about.

In the third hour I prayed for healing, my own healing and for the gift of healing. Years before I had read the story of a Church of Scotland minister who, noticing in his Scripture reading the New Testament emphasis on healing in Jesus' ministry and also in the accounts of the early Christian Church, felt that healing was a much neglected ministry in the modern Church and began to pray for an hour every day, from 11.00 till midnight, for the gift of healing. Two years later he discovered, to his surprise, that he had a gift for physical healing, a gift he exercised until his death. Before reading about him, while I would have agreed that Jesus' ministry was a healing one, I also had an instinctive suspicion of any minister or lay person who claimed to be a healer, reckoning they were probably charlatans. I have seen something of the damage which fake healers can do, intensifying the sufferings of those they claim to be helping by assuring them that their illness was really a sickness of soul from which they could not be cured until they turned to the Lord Jesus, the way of healing being prescribed by the healer and demanding a complete break with their past lives. The unfortunate victims of these undiscerning healers would then try to make such a break, would deny their own past, cut themselves off from their own deepest self and so block the very source of their healing. But while my suspicions were justified in some cases, they had blinded me to the truth that healing is Christ's ministry and that every Christian is called to be an instrument of his healing.

I also began to see that my notion of a healing ministry had been far too narrow, for I thought of it in terms of physical healing from incurable and terminal illness. Jesus had said, 'My peace I give you, not as the world gives peace,' and I began to see that his healing, too, is not always healing as the world understands it. A person suffering from terminal illness may experience great inner healing. This inner healing

27

may, or may not, bring with it a physical healing. Death is not disaster, but is birth into a new life. In death life is changed, not ended. The healing is in coming to accept death in peace, tranquillity and hope, and the healing affects not only the person who dies, but their relatives and friends and, I believe, every human being; and the healing gift continues after their death. Many people have the gift of healing but are unaware that they possess it, the kind of person, for example, who can enter a room, perhaps say nothing, but by their very presence can defuse a tense situation. The gift of being a good listener, a gift which requires constant practice, is perhaps the most healing gift anyone can possess, for it allows the other to be, enfolds them in a safe space, does not judge or advise them, accepts them as they are without desiring to change them, and communicates that support at a level deeper than words. One way of discovering our own gifts of healing is to ask ourselves, 'What is it you look for in another person when you are down in the depths?' Then try to be such a person to another in need of healing. In this way we can get in touch with our own healing gifts. They are latent in all of us and do not need ecclesiastical appointment. God lets us be, and a sign of his action in us is that we should let others be.

During the fourth hour which was usually after the lunch break, I prayed the rosary. The rosary is centuries old, a simple way of recalling the Incarnation, Passion and Resurrection of Christ, called the joyful, the sorrowful and the glorious mysteries. Each mystery is divided into five parts, called decades. The joyful mysteries, for example, are divided into the annunciation to Mary that she is to conceive a child, the visitation which Mary makes to her cousin Elizabeth when she hears the news, the nativity of the child in Bethlehem, his presentation in the Temple, and finally, the finding of the child in the Temple at the age of twelve. Each decade consists of one 'Our Father', ten 'Hail Mary's and one 'Glory be to the Father'. In my own family we used to recite the rosary together every night, a practice I disliked. I used to hope my mother would forget to have the rosary, which she never did, or I tried to speed up the prayers to get through them as soon as possible. I could concentrate my mind neither on the words we were uttering nor on the mystery which we were meant to be contemplating, and I fell to daydreaming while muttering the words. It was on the walk to Rome that I rediscovered the rosary, for I discovered its value as a rhythmic prayer, reciting a word or syllable in time with my step. This practice has a stilling effect on the mind and I found I could keep my mind on one mystery for one hour's walking. If I try praying the mystery while I am still, I can hardly keep my mind on it for ten seconds. I am sure that the rosary, like so many other forms of repetitive prayer, began as a pilgrim prayer. It is said that there are places in the country parts of Spain where the distances between villages are measured in rosaries!

In the fifth hour I would let my memory drift to family, friends and acquaintances, try to visualise them, thank God for them and pray for his blessing on them. As I continued on the road, as I shall describe later, this form of prayer developed and included the dead as well as the living.

By the sixth hour of walking I was usually tired and just looked at the trees and the fields, the rivers and the sky, and asked them to do the praying for me. I tried to keep to this plan every day I was walking, but it never turned out as neatly as I have described it. Sometimes, especially at the beginning when the weather was so cold and an east wind was blowing from Siberia, all my energy was concentrated on keeping one foot moving in front of the other. Lines from the canticle of Daniel were always a great help, 'And you, showers and dew, O bless the Lord. And you, frost and snow, O bless the Lord. And you, frosts and cold, O bless the Lord. And you, frost and snow, O bless the Lord. To him be highest glory and praise forever' (Dan. 3).

As I walked I began to recover what had become so clear to me on the Rome walk, a sense of wonder at nature and a feeling of at-one-ness with it. The bleak, bare, frozen countryside became comforting, especially if I were feeling tired and low in spirit, because I knew that under the bleak surface new life was preparing to break through in Spring and that although my consciousness felt wintry, there was a life greater than my consciousness, a life-giving Spirit hovering over the chaos of my thoughts. But this awareness of at-one-ness with nature, sacrament of God's presence, made the presence of low-flying planes screaming over the peaceful countryside the more painful.

I reached Nuenen around 4.30 p.m. and began the hunt for accommodation. At the first church the parish priest was away, but his housekeeper directed me to St Clement's, where the parish priest himself answered the door. He was a nervous, elderly man, who looked very worried as I introduced myself. He asked to see my passport, which was a perfectly reasonable request, but I felt uncomfortable to be at the receiving end. He retired with the passport and then returned with another priest, a visiting White Father, who spoke fluent English, and when he translated my request into Dutch, the parish priest's face changed from anxiety to welcome. He not only offered me a bed and supper, but also invited me to meet all the other priests in the house over a dram of whisky, the last dram before Jerusalem. The parish priest showed great interest in my pilgrimage and spent a long time poring over my maps. The visiting White Father told me the story of two boys who ran away from home to join the Foreign Legion but were rejected because they were under age. They took refuge with the White Fathers and eventually joined them instead; both later became bishops.

Nuenen was the home town of Vincent van Gogh, who was considered a disgrace to the town in his own lifetime. The parish priest of St Clement's preached against him, warning his congregation that they should have nothing to do with him. However, the church sacristan befriended Vincent, who presented him with one of his paintings. A friend of the sacristan wanted to buy the painting. The sacristan consulted his wife, who advised against the sale for anything less than 10 guilders (about £3)! St Clement's now has a memorial plaque to Vincent van Gogh. While we were talking I could hear the sound of fireworks and music in the street outside, the beginning of carnival time which would end on Shrove Tuesday. At 2.00 a.m. I was still trying to sleep in the carnival noise.

Saturday, February 28

The next day's route included a two-mile stretch along the Suid Willemsvaart canal, a dull, cold, wet day, but the roads were flat and well sufaced and I reached Nederweert, about 35 km from Nuenen, around 5.00 p.m. A very busy but friendly priest gave me lodging and, when his work was finished, sat chatting until late into the night, telling me about the divided church in Holland, how the 'conservative' bishops tended to be silent on peace issues, supporting neither Pax Christi nor the ecumenical peace movement, selecting for their seminaries only those young men who they considered to be uncontaminated with modern ideas, and refusing to accept candidates who had attended schools of which their lordships did not approve. The parish priest was no wild radical and in his own parish he tried to cater for all, wherever they might be on the theological spectrum. At one of his Sunday Masses, which I attended next morning, he was catering for those to the right of centre, for it was a very sober celebration with a women's choir, all dressed in black, massed behind the altar.

Sunday, March 1

As I set off in cold drizzle on Sunday morning for Roermond, I thought on the previous evening's conversation, on this false division between 'conservatives' and 'progressives' in the Church. Dorothy Day, founder of the Catholic Worker movement in the U.S.A., could be labelled 'conservative' as far as her devotional practice was concerned, but she was also a radical and light-years away in her thought and lifestyle from those to whom the label 'conservative' is normally given. She became a Catholic in the 1920s at great personal cost, separating from the man she loved and whose child she bore, and dedicated her life to the promotion of peace and justice. She produced a newspaper *The Catholic Worker*, founded houses of hospitality throughout the States and opposed nuclear arms, suffering insults, injury and imprisonment for her public protests and slanders from her own Catholic brothers and sisters, bishops and priests. She refused charitable status for her organisation, because she did not want to be in any way beholden to the state she was opposing, putting her trust instead in God's providence. The thought which dominated her life was St Paul's vision of the Church as the Body of Christ, and she believed that the whole human race was called to share in this life. She saw Catholic social teaching as an application of this truth to our times and this was the theme of her newspaper. It was her consciousness that we are the Body of Christ which made her so uncomfortably radical, refusing to comply with the nuclear air raid practices in the 1950s, deliberately sitting in Central Park in New York when she should have been in a shelter, a refusal which others began to imitate until nuclear air raid practices were abandoned.

The parish priest at Nederweert had complained of one particular bishop who ended every discussion with an appeal to Rome's authority, his central article of belief being the phrase 'Roma locuta est, causa finita est,' 'Rome has spoken and that is the end of the matter'. But this same bishop was selective in his obedience, paying little or no attention to the social encyclicals, which have been described as 'the best-kept secret in the Catholic Church', while emphasising the encyclical 'Humanae Vitae' as though it were a central teaching.

Roermond was only 24 km away from Nederweert, but I took a wrong turning when within 8 km of Roermond and ended walking along an elevated motorway, an offence soon brought to my notice by the hooting from many cars. Car drivers become the most self-righteous upholders of law and order when they spot an erring pedestrian. The road led straight into Roermond and the hard shoulder was an excellent surface for Mungo, but my courage failed at the constant hooting, so I put Mungo on my shoulders and tried to negotiate the steep bank of the motorway to a path below. I found a minor road later which eventually merged onto the motorway, now providing a special cycle track leading over the complex waterway system bordering the west side of Roermond. I enjoyed this last hour's walking with the sea birds circling overhead against a wintry sky, the waterways busy with a variety of small craft. I also enjoyed the last hour because I knew it was the last stretch of walking for the next few days.

Monday, March 2 — Tuesday, March 3

In Roermond I had arranged to meet Eileen Opiolka at the main post office of the town. Eileen had been a student at Glasgow University when I was chaplain there. She was involved in many of the chaplaincy activities, but there was a long period during which she did not appear. When I asked her where she had been all these weeks, she replied that she had been busy with her German. Later, I met her German friend, Peter Opiolka, and two years later I celebrated their wedding in Scotland. Eileen and Peter now live in Düsseldorf with their three children, Evelyn, Vivien and Colin. I stayed with them in Düsseldorf until Ash Wednesday morning. Although I had only been five days on the road, it felt much longer and I appreciated every minute of my stay in the warm atmosphere of their home, chatting with Eileen and Peter and playing with the children, who are bilingual, their Scots origin coming through in their accent. With the children we visited the park where the deer were so tame that they could be fed by hand, an experience which thrilled me as much as the children, for although I had seen hundreds of deer on the Scottish hills, I had never been closer than 50 metres. Peter showed me a copy of the *Guardian Weekly* which contained Gorbachev's speech at the Moscow peace conference, derided by the *Telegraph* leader-writer. He seemed to me to be the only world statesman able to grasp and communicate the magnitude of the nuclear threat and to show willingness to take the practical steps to lessen the tension. Peter also showed me a copy of the comic strip, 'Where the Winds Blow', a black satire on H.M. government's booklet *Protect and Survive*, advising the citizens of Britain on the measures to be taken in the event of nuclear attack. I knew that Eileen had seen nuclear deterrence as a faith question for years, but in her experience of the Catholic Church in Germany she found little attention given to the question.

Ash Wednesday, March 4

The weather worsened while I was resting in Düsseldorf and
it was snowing as Eileen drove me back to Roermond on Ash
Wednesday morning. In Düsseldorf I had been able to buy
more detailed maps for my route through Germany and Austria. As I began the 10 km stretch to the German border, my
mind was a jumble of memories, memories of wartime Britain
1939–45 and also memories of 1956–59 when I studied theology at the Jesuit college of Skt Georgen in Frankfurt, where
I was ordained priest in 1958.

I was born and spent the first five years of my life in
a village in Ayrshire, called Skelmorlie, built on a hillside
overlooking the Firth of Clyde. I still have some clear memories of those years, of my first day in the village school where
we learned to write and do sums on slates, each pupil having
a little tin box containing a sponge with which to wipe the
slate clean. I can still see the blue tin covered in rust marks
and smell the rotting sponge. This was my first and last
experience of ecumenical education for twenty-two years,
until I went to Oxford in 1951. In Skelmorlie everyone knew
everyone and everyone's business, and I remember finding it
strange when we moved to Glasgow that people did not greet
every passerby on the street. We were one of the few Catholic
families in the village. On Sundays we went to Mass in
Wemyss Bay, the village at the foot of the hill. On our way
home from Mass, as we climbed the hill, the Presbyterians
were coming down on their way to the Church of Scotland
service. As we met, greetings were different from ordinary
weekdays, more formal, a slight nod of the head, no words
spoken. Childhood memories are fascinating and the memories which linger are always worth attention, for they usually
reveal a way of perceiving which remains with us and charac-
terises our perception, reactions and attitudes for the rest of
our lives. I like to think that my interest in ecumenism began
with those Sunday morning encounters.

After Skelmorlie, and apart from a chemistry master during
my secondary schooling whose classes we used to interrupt
at midday telling him that we must now recite the Angelus,
I was never taught by anyone who was not a Roman Catholic

until I went to Oxford to read Mods and Greats. The first five terms there were given to Latin and Greek literature, the remaining seven terms to philosophy, ancient and modern, and ancient history. The first ancient author who forced me to think beyond the parameters of Catholicism, as I then understood it, was Lucretius, who lived before Christ and dedicated his life to ridding human beings of religious belief, convinced that this was the greatest service he could render humanity.

Lucretius believed that fear was the most powerful and the most destructive of human emotions. He also thought that belief in an after-life intensifies fear and causes people to act inhumanly towards one another, because they are afraid that if they do not obey the prescriptions of the gods as made known to them by the religious authorities, then they will live in torment for all eternity. As an instance of this inhumanity, he tells the story of Iphigenia, Agamemnon's daughter. Agamemnon, sailing to Troy to rescue Helen, was becalmed at the island of Aulis. He consulted his seer, his holy man, who told him that he must sacrifice his daughter Iphigenia to the winds. Lucretius describes the death of this innocent girl and ends with the thundering lines, 'Tantum religio potuit suadere malorum.' 'O religion, what crimes are committed in your name.' At first, it was the beauty of his poetry which attracted me and the cleverness of his argument, based on the idea that belief in immortality is an illusion and that we, and every other part of creation, consist of a mass of bombarding particles. When the particular configuration of particles, which we consider to be 'I', disintegrates, then there is no longer any 'I' to worry about. Later, it was the truth of the lines, 'O religion, what crimes are committed in your name,' which engaged me.

When I first went to Oxford I was so rooted in my Catholic education that I found it difficult to imagine how any intelligent and sincere Christian could fail to see that the Roman Catholic Church was the one true Church, but I kept meeting intelligent and sincere Christians who did fail to see it, and it was this experience which aroused my first conscious interest in ecumenism. At this time I still thought of Church unity as meaning that all Christians were eventually to become Roman Catholics.

Immediately after Oxford I went to Heythrop College, the

Jesuit house of philosophy and theology, then in Oxfordshire. Father Maurice Bevenot SJ, a patristic scholar with a particular interest in St Cyprian's treatise, *De Unitate*, and whose theology course was on the nature of the Church, encouraged me in my interest in ecumenism and kept referring me to books and articles which were pouring out of Germany. As I could not read German, I asked if I might spend a summer vacation there to learn the language. The dean of studies, Fr Bruno Brinkman, a man of great thoroughness, suggested that I make a proper job of it and spend the remaining three years of theology in Germany, studying at Skt Georgen, the Jesuit college, in Frankfurt/Main. I readily agreed, but after a few months there I was regretting my decision.

Germany was in its period of post-war recovery. Skt Georgen was a new barracks-like building set in a wasteland of allotments a few miles from the city centre. Its method of study was the antithesis of Oxford. While in Oxford lectures were few and voluntary, the main work being reading for and writing two essays each week, which were then read to tutors, who commented on them and then set the subjects for next week's essays, in Skt Georgen there were four lectures a day, to be attended by all, no essays and no private sessions with tutors, which in Oxford had been the most valuable part of the course. In Oxford too, although the philosophy we had to study included Plato and Aristotle, the emphasis was on linguistic analysis, an emphasis which bored me at first, until I began to see its importance when applied to our religious statements about God and learned to keep asking the question, 'What does it mean?' In Skt Georgen massive, unintelligible concepts were hurled at us four times a day in lectures, re-presented to us in reams of closely typed notes and I could not understand the meaning of their meaning. Some of my German companions had a touching faith in the value of these notes, believing that if learned well they would be invaluable to them in their later apostolic work. One, in particular, fascinated me. He had a box of coloured pencils with which he underlined his typed notes in different colours. One of the pencils was white, which intrigued me. On mentioning this phenomenon to a friend, he said, 'O, that's for underlining the unimportant bits'! I gained little from the lectures apart from a fascinating course on church history, including a history of the Reformation, when, for the first time, I heard a Catholic lecturer speak in praise of Luther.

Although I never took to the lecture system at Skt Georgen, I began to appreciate the lecturers as my German improved. I also began to read Karl Rahner, who was then lecturing at Innsbruck; some of his typed notes found their way to Frankfurt and the first of his *Theological Investigations* were just being published. I struggled through his tortuous German, feeling like a mole burrowing into deepening darkness, popping up occasionally to the surface, and realising that although I was back in the same place, everything seemed different. He helped me to see clearly that ecumenism, the movement towards church unity, was not a question of all other Christian denominations becoming Roman Catholic, but that each denomination should be open to the Holy Spirit, source of all unity, open to the Word of God in Scripture, and that each denomination should also be true to its own tradition. What the Church is to become is a mystery: something we cannot predetermine, because God is always greater than his Church. All that we can say about the future of the Church is that whatever form its development may take, it will be consistent with its origins. There were most interesting ecumenical developments going on in Germany at the time, while in Britain most Catholic and Protestant clergy limited their contact to polite bows across four centuries if they happened to meet in the street. They did not meet for prayer together, and in at least one Catholic diocese in Scotland, Catholics were forbidden even to recite the Our Father together with Protestants. In Germany, opposition to the Nazis had brought Christian denominations together with an urgency which the Churches in Britain had never known. In the post-war devastation, 2,000 churches in West Germany were being shared by Protestants and Catholics, and official conversations were being held between Catholics, Evangelical and Lutheran Churches in which they were, at last, following the St Peter Canisius' principle of concentrating their attention on points of agreement, rather than on the differences which separated them.

The three years in Germany were useful not only for the theology I learned, but also for the experience of living together with men who had been through the trauma of Nazi Germany and who had fought in the war. Many of them had been members of the Nazi youth movement and I was ordained with two former SS men. When I first arrived in Germany, almost my only knowledge of Germany and Germans was derived from British wartime propaganda. I had deep, but unacknowledged, prejudice against all that was German. My three years in Frankfurt helped to break down the prejudice and taught me the folly and destructiveness of generalisations about nations, races, classes, ideologies and religions. But it was a slow process, which is still continuing, and the learning came not through lectures or reading, but from informal conversations and holidays together. I soon began to see how different Germans could be one from another. I also saw something of the guilt burden under which they were labouring as a result of Nazi atrocities during the war. Why had the Catholic Church, so strong in numbers and in influence in Germany, failed to speak out clearly and strongly enough against the evils of the holocaust and of the pernicious ideals and doctrines of the Third Reich? Why was it that so few were able to discern what was happening and why did those who were able, and who did resist, receive so little support and arouse so little protest when they were sent off to the concentration camps or executed? One of the clear voices of protest was the Austrian peasant, Franz Jägerstatter, who refused to serve in the army because he considered the war to be unjust. He was opposed by his bishop and clergy and he was beheaded for his convictions.

This experience in Germany taught me that what happened to Germany under the Nazis could befall any nation, including Britain. Violence and destruction are latent in every individual and in every nation. When violence erupts, it infects. Nazi violence soon infected the Allies, who adopted measures in the course of the war which would have been unthinkable before war began: carpet-bombing German cities, a tactic deliberately undertaken to break enemy morale by killing their civilian population, in some cases avoiding the destruction of military targets because these could be useful to the Allies later. The residential areas of German cities were deliberately destroyed, a crime against humanity, in order to force an unconditional surrender. The tragedy of Nazi Germany became the tragedy of the Allies too, and it was not only the Germans who had to weep and make reparation.

Talking with Germans, and later in reading about the rise and fall of Nazism, I saw more clearly how the evil had at first been hidden under the appearance of good. For Hitler seemed to promise the revival of a demoralised nation and soon won support from the majority of German people, who were deceived by the apparent respectability and high moral tone of the Nazi propaganda. Even during the war itself this high moral tone continued, and the administrative building of Dachau bore an inscription. 'There is one road to freedom. Its milestones are obedience, diligence, honesty, order, cleanliness, temperance, truthfulness, sacrifice and love of one's country.' I read, too, of the deliberations of the Catholic hierarchy during the 1930s. Although a few of the bishops were totally opposed to the regime, others felt they should co-operate as far as they could, encourage Catholic youth to join the Hitler Youth movement so that they could act as a leaven in the mass. The president of the bishops' conference was an elderly man who could remember the loss of two thousand Catholic parishes under Bismark, and he feared a similar loss through open opposition to the Nazi regime. It is easy to condemn with hindsight, but condemnation achieves nothing except a glow of self-righteousness which blinds us to our own state. As a nation, we in Britain are just as prone to the iniquities of a Fascist state as were the Germans, and as Christians we are just as likely to be taken in by seductive appeals to nationalism and by specious government propaganda, which can erode freedom in the name of national security, when it is presented in a high moral tone and under the appearance of good.

As I walked from Roermond to the German border, it was not only snowing, but there was also a biting east wind, which grew fiercer and colder on the following days and was still blowing when I reached Frankfurt a week later. Fortunately, I had bought a cagoul and trousers for the journey which were windproof, waterproof and, best of all, free of inner condensation. Eileen Opiolka had also presented me with a pair of woollen gloves to supplement the motor cycle gauntlet, so I rarely felt cold while I was walking, even in the worst weather.

3

'Aus Welchem Grund?' – Rhineland

> As often as the elements of the world
> are violated
> by ill treatment,
> so God will cleanse them.
>
> God will cleanse them
> through the sufferings,
> through the hardships
> of humankind.
>
> (Hildegard of Bingen)

At the German border a friendly official waved me through without even asking to see my passport. Near the border was a British military base with children playing in the school playground, which bordered the main road. Looking in the direction of the noise, I almost stepped into a dugout where a guard was lying on the ground, his hand at the trigger of his gun.

At Wassenberg I stopped at a gasthaus for lunch, empty except for one red-eyed customer with several empty bottles beside him, who was continuing the carnival celebrations into Ash Wednesday. He stared hard at me and at Mungo, which I trailed in behind me. 'What are you doing with that?' he asked. 'Walking to Jerusalem', I said. He blinked and shook his head in disbelief, took another drink, then asked, 'Aber aus welchem Grund?' Perhaps he was a philosopher who had fallen on hard times, for he did not ask 'Warum', the German word for 'Why', but literally, 'Out of what ground?' In German unpractised for nearly thirty years I tried to explain, but the sentences disintegrated as I uttered them and my friend looked even more puzzled. After twenty minutes he was still asking, 'Aber aus welchem Grund?' and I am still trying to answer his question as I write this book.

'Out of what ground?' Like everyone else, had anyone ever asked me, 'Are you in favour of peace?' I should have answered, 'Yes, of course.' We all want peace. The question is how we are to achieve and sustain it, a question so complex and emotionally charged that it is better avoided in polite company. In Christian churches, while we regularly and readily beseech God to bring peace to all the world's trouble spots, we rarely and very reluctantly dare examine the question more closely. When we pray for peace, for what are we asking, and what does the prayer demand of us? Christians are divided: some believe that prayer alone will bring about peace and that the prayer would be contaminated if combined with any form of political action, while others believe that prayer for peace which does not lead to some form of political action is ineffective. This difference in belief about the relationship between prayer and action is deeper and more destructive than our denominational differences and it cuts across them. It raises the most fundamental questions about the nature of Christian faith, about the nature of God whom we worship, how he relates to us and we to him, how and where we are to find him. Focusing on peace reveals the fundamental divisions and flaws in our Christian spirituality. Perhaps that is why we prefer not to examine the peace question too closely.

I can understand the attitude of those who, while not accepting the extreme view that prayer alone is effective, nevertheless believe that it is possible to take religion seriously without considering questions of peace and justice to be of the essence of faith, because this was my own attitude for the first thirty-seven years of my life.

I began to take prayer seriously for thoroughly selfish reasons at the age of sixteen. I was at a Jesuit school, Mount St Mary's near Sheffield, which offered an annual scholarship covering school fees for two years. I began to study for this exam and thought that prayer might improve my chances, so I recited many extra 'Our Fathers' and 'Hail Marys' each day. I failed the exam, but prayer had become attractive.

Mount St Mary's, when I arrived in 1937, was struggling for recognition as a public school. A condition of recognition

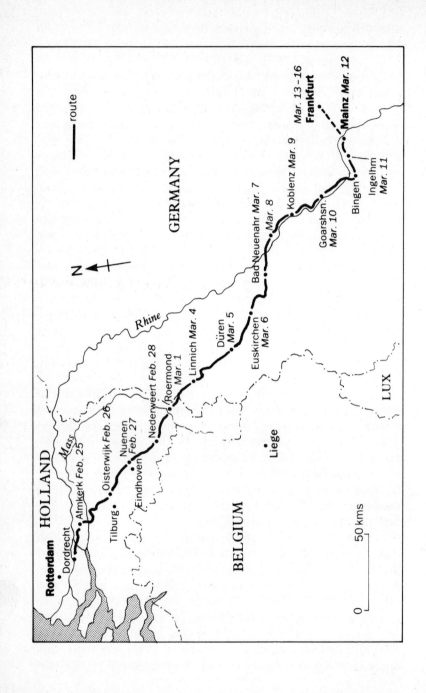

was an Officers' Training Corps (O.T.C.), providing basic military training for its pupils, and I arrived as the O.T.C. began. Annually, the school celebrated the Feast of Corpus Christi with a solemn High Mass in the morning and, in the afternoon, a procession of the Blessed Sacrament through the school grounds, the procession led by a group of small boys bearing baskets containing flower petals which they strewed on the ground. Following them came four canopy-bearers, and beneath the canopy a priest held the Blessed Sacrament in a golden monstrance. Behind the canopy came all the other priests in the community wearing vestments, then the choir, followed by the rest of the school. With the advent of the O.T.C. there was an addition to the Corpus Christi solemnities. A guard of honour, dressed in military uniform of the 1914–18 war and bearing rifles with fixed bayonets, flanked the outside of the canopy, proceeding at slow march and presenting arms at the beginning and end of the ceremony as the priest held up the monstrance in blessing. It was in 1940, the year I had begun to pray, that I was appointed to the Corpus Christi guard of honour. For days beforehand we practised the slow march and the presenting of arms in the playground. Although not an O.T.C. enthusiast, I felt honoured to be appointed to the guard of honour, marched alongside the Blessed Sacrament with my rifle and fixed bayonet and prayed occasionally as I went. It never crossed my mind that there was anything incongruous in what I was doing, and had anyone suggested that there was, I should probably have suspected them of being cowardly 'conchies' (conscientious objectors).

At that time I was intending to become a medical doctor, but the following year I had thoughts of priesthood, and later I thought of becoming a Jesuit. I prayed to know whether I should join the R.A.F. or the Jesuit noviceship. The R.A.F. was the more attractive alternative with its glamour, excitement and call to heroism, and it seemed to me that I could give as much praise and glory to God by shooting down Germans as I could by enduring the rigours of a Jesuit noviceship. Eventually, I went to the Jesuit noviceship, but not for any pacifist reasons, which I should then have considered cowardly.

Twenty years later, having finished my Jesuit training, I

was teaching at another Jesuit school, Stonyhurst, in Lanca-shire. Stonyhurst also had an O.T.C., its name now changed to C.C.F., Combined Cadet Force, an institution for which I was initially grateful, because it occupied the boys for two afternoons a week in marching up and down the playground or conducting mock battles in the college grounds. I never questioned the morality of having a C.C.F., accepting the ancient Roman dictum, 'To preserve peace, prepare for war,' until Easter Sunday morning in 1961.

If Easter fell early, the college did not break up for the vacation until Easter Monday. The boys were expected to attend the full Holy Week services, which in those days were interminably long, all celebrated in Latin, culminating on Easter Sunday morning with a solemn High Mass. The boys attended the Easter Sunday Mass dressed in military uniform because the Mass was immediately followed by a military parade in the playground, with the Rector standing on a raised dais and taking the salute at the march past.

Early on Easter Sunday morning 1961, I was passing the playground door when I met an enraged colonel. During the night some boys had been at work, removed the raised dais and daubed the unilateral disarmament sign in white paint on a wall in the school playground and the message, 'March begins here. No children please.' The suspects were the boys at the top of the school. As I was in charge of them, I was therefore expected to lead the criminal investigations. I was an inept detective, did not have enough firm evidence to charge anyone, and let the matter drop. It was only later that I discovered what I had suspected, that the brain behind the operation was the school atheist, who had come close to expulsion a few months before for producing a cartoon in the boys' school magazine which was considered blasphemous. Three years ago I celebrated a requiem Mass for this 'atheist', Eric Kemmet, who died of a heart attack at the age of 43. I had kept in touch with him from time to time ever since he left Stonyhurst. He was very gifted, sensitive, intelligent, and a tortured searcher after truth. I thanked God for his life, his humour and his integrity. I regretted that I had never told him before his death of my gratitude to him for his Easter Sunday prank, because his prank was one 'ground reason' for my peace pilgrimage to Jerusalem.

It all began with the merest whisper in the recesses of my mind. 'Is it not a blasphemy to encourage children to celebrate the feast of the Resurrection with the weapons of death?' At first I could easily dispel the whisper with loud assertions to myself. The Church had developed a Just War theory over 1500 years and who was I to question it? Stonyhurst was proud of its military tradition and the boys' refectory was decorated with the portraits of seven Old Boys who had been awarded the Victoria Cross. I had never heard any of the Jesuit staff, who were almost all older, wiser, holier and more experienced than I, question the existence of the C.C.F. I knew the goodness and integrity of so many people who had served in the armed forces and fought in the war, some of them giving their lives. But the whisper continued and refused to be silenced by all my counter-arguments.

Besides teaching Latin and Greek, I was also teaching sixth-form religion, spending hours of preparation in an effort to overcome the boredom of the majority with any religious topic. The disbelieving Eric might show occasional interest, but the believers studied the classroom cobwebs, examined their finger nails, or snoozed. I began reading more widely. Teilhard de Chardin's *Phenomenon of Man* and *Le Milieu Divin* had just been published in English. In 1962 the Second Vatican Council began, and its documents were coming through, bringing excitement to some and shock to others. I also began reading extracts from a few of the classical atheists, Auguste Comte, Feuerbach, Nietzsche and Albert Camus. Of all this reading, the author who impressed me most was Camus, especially the address he gave to French Dominicans at the end of the Second World War, in which he pleaded with them to be true to the Gospel and to join with those who, although unable to share the Christian faith, had dedicated their lives to the promotion of justice. It was the atheist Camus who sent me back to the Old Testament prophets, and a flood of uncomfortable questions broke on my mind. Does the notion of God impoverish human beings, as the humanists claimed, keeping them in a state of servile fear, a prey to the power lust of those who, in the name of God, hold them in subjection? If God's ways are not our ways, and his thoughts are not our thoughts, then how can we be certain that the God whom we worship is the one true God, and not some idol?

The Old Testament prophets condemned all forms of worship which did not proceed from hearts reflecting Yahweh's special love of the poor and the oppressed. 'I cannot endure festival and solemnity. Your New Moons and your pilgrimages I hate with all my soul. . . . You may multiply your prayers, I shall not listen. . . . search for justice, help the oppressed, be just to the orphan, plead for the widow' (Isaiah 1:13–17). Albert Camus sounded much more like the Old Testament prophets than the writers of many theological treatises with which I bored my religion classes. What had begun as a whisper, questioning a military parade on Easter Sunday, had now become a roar in my head, raising questions which were very threatening to me as a priest, a Jesuit and a Catholic. At first, I could keep them at bay, because the daily life of the school was so busy that I had neither the time nor the energy to give them serious attention. Whenever I did attend to them, they shook my foundations. These questions then are 'the ground' from which I eventually appeared in the gasthaus in Wassenberg to be questioned by the drunk philosopher. How I tried to answer them comes later.

On Ash Wednesday evening, March 4th, I reached Linnich, about 32 km from Roermond. This had been one of the very few days when the walking was dull, much of it through built-up areas and, although I kept to minor roads, the traffic was heavy and the roads were narrow, so that much of my attention was absorbed in manoeuvring Mungo to avoid oncoming lorries. My prayer plans were reduced to a very simple, 'Lord save me or I'll perish.' There was no answer at the presbytery door in Linnich, so I found a *pension* for the night. In Germany and Austria I became expert at assessing a *pension* within seconds of entry, and discovered a *pension* law of inverse proportion: the larger the form to be filled in on application, the more expensive the tariff, the poorer the quantity and quality of the food, the more uncomfortable the bedroom and the colder the temperature. At Linnich there was no form to be filled in; the lodging was cheap and excellent, and a breakfast of schwarzbrot, cheese, eggs, cold meat and real coffee fuelled me for the next 32 km.

Thursday, March 5

My route lay along the east bank of the Ruhr, following minor roads. One of these roads indicated a cycle track alongside the river bank, a beautiful stretch at first, the surface hard-frozen, the river swollen and flowing fast to Holland and the sea. But after a few kilometres the track disappeared into the swollen river, and I had to retrace my steps to the road. Earlier in the day a disaster befell me: the zip on my walking trousers was irretrievably broken, so when I reached Düren that evening, having first called at a presbytery where the housekeeper told me the parish priest would not be back for two hours, I went in search of trousers. Düren had a plentiful supply of shops selling elegant and expensive trousers. As I was walking with a pair of waterproof trousers over the broken zip, and because the weather was likely to be cold for the next week, there was no immediate urgency and I was going to abandon the search when I saw a shop advertising a sale of jeans. I have never worn jeans in my life and have always thought they must be very uncomfortable for walking or climbing, besides looking a bit ridiculous on anyone over forty. But my prejudices crumbled when I saw that they cost less than half the price of the cheapest pair of trousers I had seen in Düren so far, and I bought a pair several sizes too big for me to ensure maximum freedom of leg movement.

It was dark and several degrees colder when I returned to the presbytery to meet the parish priest. He answered the door himself, led me to an office and then took up a position behind his desk, asking me to be seated. The atmosphere was chilly. While I was introducing myself he pulled out a little box containing small squares of paper in a variety of colours, and selecting one, he began to make notes. He then looked up and asked for my passport and 'celebret', which is a document every Catholic priest receives from his local bishop, assuring whoever it may concern that the priest has not been suspended or excommunicated and may be allowed to celebrate Mass. Having studied both documents, he then asked, 'And where is the official document from your religious superior authorising you to go walking to Jerusalem?' I told him I had no such document, but assured him that I was travelling with my superior's permission. He found this reply very unsatisfactory, telling me that I should have an official document properly signed and sealed. He then pushed aside his piece of paper and began to lecture me on the subject of pilgrimage, about which he obviously knew little. 'In embarking upon a pilgrimage like this, you must make most detailed arrangements beforehand and notify well in advance those with whom you are going to stay.' It was like being back in a Skt Georgen lecture room. I began to seethe inside, for I knew exactly what I wanted to say, but I could not translate it quickly enough into German. 'How can I possibly predict each day the number of blisters and their degree of painfulness, the state of muscles, ligaments and joints, the state of the roads on which I travel and whether Mungo will follow obediently or keel over? How can I foretell whether rivers will remain within their banks and whether their paths will be submerged or not?' Instead I listened in sullen silence until he ended the lecture with, 'And where did you stay last night?' 'In Linnich', I replied. 'And the night before?' 'With friends in Düsseldorf.' 'And what is their telephone number?' I told him I could not remember but had the number in my notebook in the haversack. As I went to get it, he lifted the telephone and dialled a number. I suspected he was phoning the police, but on my return with the notebook, he gave me a piece of paper with an address and a diagram giving directions. It was the house of a religious congregation which offered me a room for the night. So we parted amicably and half an hour later I was kindly welcomed by the 'Fathers of the Eucharist'.

Friday, March 6

On a day of bright sunshine, clear sky and a bitter east wind, I walked 32 km to Euskirchen. The landscape was changing now from flat plains to pleasant rolling countryside with little villages perched on hilltops, their church spires pointing to heaven. It was idyllic scenery, but the silence was shattered every now and again by the scream of low-flying planes and an occasional army helicopter. I spent the last hour of prayer in petition for a night's lodging, and this time the prayers were well answered. A young priest at the presbytery led me to a newly built youth centre belonging to the parish, which included a kitchen and a mattress on the floor. He was very trusting, did not ask to see my papers and entrusted me with the keys. So I told him I would go shopping and would be delighted if he would join me for a meal, but he was too busy.

Each day's walking had its moments of peace and delight. That day it was the leisure of the evening, shopping, cooking, eating with an appetite sharpened by the east wind. I disliked eating alone in a café, but enjoyed eating alone if sitting by the roadside, or in a place which was temporarily my own. Later, I understood why this was so. In a café the presence of other people made me conscious of being alone, while in this centre, and especially when sitting by the roadside, I could become more aware of the reality in which we all live, that we are all interconnected and interdependent, and that loneliness, while it feels real and painful, is, in fact, an illusion, for if we could see the reality in which we are living, that we are a unity in Father, Son and Holy Spirit in whom all creation has its being, then we could never suffer loneliness. The answer to loneliness is solitude; the most lonely are those who are unable or unwilling to face solitude. The solitude of that evening was sheer delight and even the washing-up was enjoyable. I could glimpse the truth of Montaigne's saying, 'Have you known how to take repose, you have done more than he who has taken cities and empires.'

Saturday, March 7

This was the coldest day so far with the strongest east wind and, apart from a lunch stop, I kept walking all day. After lunch I went shopping, but it was already too late. The shops had closed at midday and would not open again until Monday and maybe not then, for in many places Monday is a *Ruhetag*, a day of rest, when most shops and restaurants are closed. The countryside was hillier now, through open orchards and, as I approached the Rhine, vineyards. Late that afternoon, exhausted after 32 km against the wind, I reached a fashionable spa near the Rhine, full of large, expensive-looking hotels. I made for a church spire and was directed to a presbytery some distance away, a large and roomy-looking house. Steps ran up to the front door where a woman was already waiting. She told me the parish priest would be back any minute. I stood, still harnessed to Mungo, at the bottom of the steps, my teeth chattering with the cold. A car drove in and the parish priest, hatted and gloved, passed me without recognition, let the woman in and closed the front door. I stood below for another two minutes until fear of exposure drove me to the bell. As I rang the woman emerged followed by the priest, who asked me my business. He listened impassively, then barked, 'Passport please.' In my frozen state it was a struggle to get it from my pocket. He snatched it from my hand and led me into a front room. After examining the passport he asked for my celebret, then said, 'It is dated 1985. This is 1987. You could have left the priesthood in between times.' I agreed that this was a possibility but assured him that I had not. I also explained that in Britain I had never renewed my celebret except when moving from one diocese to another and that I had come to Birmingham in 1985. I showed him details of my route, where I had stayed and where I intended staying. He was not impressed. Germany, he told me, was swarming with people pretending to be priests and collecting money under false pretences. He then left the room, returning with a diocesan news-sheet warning the clergy of a wandering Irishman masquerading as a priest. I told him I was a Scot, a distinction he did not appreciate. He showed me the door, relenting at the last minute to offer me some money. I told him I was not looking for money, or a bed, but floor space on which I could sleep for the night, or an address to which I could go for cheap lodging. He could not help. I left, collected Mungo at the bottom of the steps and wandered the town for half an hour searching for lodgings, my bad temper communicated to Mungo, who wobbled dangerously. I found a reasonable *pension*, where they told me of the Zeebrugge disaster, that 193 people had been drowned in a cross-channel ferry that morning. This news distracted me from my anger, for I could imagine vividly the horror of the scene.

Sunday, March 8

I went to Mass and discovered that the celebrant was the priest I had met the evening before. When it came to homily time, which I awaited with interest, he read a pastoral letter from the bishop, an exhortation to his flock to practise humanity during Lent. To illustrate his point, his Lordship quoted from a recent poll in which citizens were asked to state whether or not they enjoyed family meals on weekdays and at weekends. During the week 53 per cent enjoyed them, but on Sundays the percentage dropped to 7 per cent. The bishop concluded that idleness was the cause of the discontent and therefore suggested that all should make a special effort to practise humanity during Lent, especially on Sundays.

On the road to the Rhine my mind was jumping from the Zeebrugge disaster to the events of the previous evening and the bishop's pastoral letter, wondering whether cutlery and crockery were flying about behind the lace curtains of the prim houses I was passing. I thought, too, of my reception at the two parish presbyteries. I could understand the attitude of the two parish priests. They had a responsibility to look after their church and presbytery and to guard against theft, but I also thought about the implications of the security consciousness which theft and vandalism engender. Violence is infectious: it is also imitative, for the victim retaliates violently. Victims may retaliate successfully, but the retaliation inevitably does violence to them in the long run. As Christians, if we become security conscious, then we need to emend the Gospel texts, adding to 'I was a stranger and you sheltered me', 'having first established through the appropriate official forms, correctly stamped, sealed and dated, the identity of the stranger'. Security consciousness, a growing phenomenon both in individuals and in nations, imprisons and cuts its victims off from whole areas of life, restricts and deadens, entombs us in an impregnable fortress which not only keeps out the enemy, but keeps us in. On a national scale, emphasising national security is the quickest and most direct road to totalitarianism, and we fall victim to the very dangers against which we think we are defending ourselves. In Britain today, the current emphasis on national security is ominous, especially when combined with a naive belief in our own invincible love of freedom. We are no safer than any other nation and quite as likely to become a totalitarian state.

At Linz I crossed the Rhine by ferry and began the long stretch along the east side of the river. The first few kilometres were along quiet roads in brilliant sunshine but, as the sun went down in the afternoon and the temperature dropped, I reached a dull industrial stretch at Bad Honnigen. Before searching for lodgings for the night I stopped to look at a church with a large building next to it called 'House of Christ the King'. As I was examining the outside of the church, a nun came out and asked if I was looking for something. 'A room for the night', I replied. 'Try there', she said, pointing to a door. I rang the bell, made my request, was welcomed, given a towel and a cake of soap and told that the showers were downstairs. It was only then that I realised I was in a doss house with many other gentlemen of the road who, having showered, were now sitting waiting for supper in two hours' time. I then discovered how far I really am from having 'a preferential option for the poor'. I was very cold, had no food left, was tired after the day's walking, and I dreaded the thought of standing around till bedtime, then sleeping in a bunk bed in a dormitory. I tried to find a *pension* in the neighbourhood, but the only one was closed and I was trapped in the doss house.

It was a good experience. The men, in so far as I could understand their dialects, were friendly and some of them highly organised for the road, carrying little briefcases as though going to a board meeting, their cases including papers and maps on which were marked other doss houses along the Rhine. The dormitory where I slept had only one other occupant, a giant of a man, who slept by the open window in a night temperature of $-8°C$. I took the bunk furthest from the window, where I lay fully clothed inside my sleeping bag with additional blankets on top, and slept well. When I went to pay next morning, the Brother-in-charge told me that all residents were guests of the house. Later I learned that these houses of Christ the King had been founded by a remarkable priest, Max Joseph Metzger, hanged by the Nazis in 1944 because he was caught trying to smuggle peace plans into

Sweden. In my three years in Germany I had never heard mention of him, but thereby hangs a tale to which I shall return.

Monday, March 9

Before leaving the doss house I phoned London asking the Jesuit Provincial to send me authorisation papers to assure any reader that I was walking to Jerusalem with his approval and blessing. I also asked him to stamp the document with as many seals as he might have to hand and to forward it to me in Munich. He did so, but no one asked to see it during the rest of my journey.

Once clear of the industrial area, the walk down the Rhine was magnificent, past the hillside vineyards with their ancient castles. On Monday evening I reached the bridge leading to Koblenz and found the Jesuit house there. I recognised two of the community from my student days at Frankfurt, but they did not recognise me at first. However, a third member arrived, who did remember me and it was he who gave me the sound advice which I quoted in my Prologue. In the evening I strolled round the city and met a group of peace people who were holding a demonstration in one of the city squares. I introduced myself and discovered that some of them were members of Pax Christi. They told me the story which I had so often heard before and was to hear many times again, that they found little support for their peace efforts from the official Church.

Tuesday, March 10

From Koblenz I had planned to take a steamer to Bingen, but the river steamers were not yet running, which was fortunate, because the next two days' walking were most enjoyable, along the Rhine valley with its hillside vineyards and ancient castles, and with a clear sky and bracing wind. Although the scenery was so different, it gave me something of the mood which the West Highlands can induce. The trees clap, the rocks sing, running water laughs, the birds swoop in the sheer joy of living and I am caught up in it all. But there was also a discordant note as I thought on the Rhine mythology which the Nazis had exploited, the terrible beauty which culminated in mass destruction.

'Aus welchem Grund?' the drunk man had asked me. I thought more on this as I walked along the Rhine. One answer I could have given him was, 'Because I want to learn more about the roots of good and evil.' The *Spiritual Exercises* of St Ignatius Loyola are about discerning the forces of good and evil at work within us as well as outside us, but there is one meditation in particular, called 'The Two Standards', which deals specifically with this problem, and it was this meditation which helped me through the mental and spiritual confusion which followed the Stonyhurst Easter Sunday parade. Although it helped me through, it also raised further questions and difficulties which I had not considered before.

Inigo, as Ignatius was called before his conversion, was a sixteenth-century Basque nobleman, who had a conversion experience in his late twenties. Out of that experience he wrote his *Spiritual Exercises*, a series of Scripture-based, Christ-centred meditations and contemplations designed to enable exercitants to get in touch with their own deepest experience, to begin to distinguish what is creative from what is destructive in their own inner life and so discover God's will. The full *Spiritual Exercises* last about thirty days and are divided into four periods, called 'weeks', the first being on sin and repentance, the second on the life of Christ, the third on the Passion and fourth on the Resurrection. St Ignatius places the Two Standards meditation immediately before the contemplations on Christ's public ministry, and he asks the exercitant to spend four separate hours on this one meditation.

In the Two Standards Ignatius presents in very colourful imagery a truth about human life which is fundamental in all Christian teaching and in most world religions, namely that we are all of us caught up in a cosmic struggle which is not only outside us, but goes to the very depths of our spirit, the struggle between the forces of good, which he calls 'The Standard of Christ', and the forces of evil, which he calls 'The Standard of Lucifer'. There is nothing original in the theme: what is original is the way Ignatius presents it, encouraging exercitants to use our imagination so that we become conscious of the struggle inside us as well as outside, and know it in our guts as well as in our heads. He uses the name 'Lucifer', which means literally, the light-bearer, because the evil one attacks most effectively under the appearance of light. The petition for each period of prayer is that we should know and recognise the deceits of Lucifer in our lives and guard against them: know, too, the attractiveness of Christ's life and teaching and embrace it.

Ignatius presents the cosmic struggle in quaint imagery, seeing Lucifer sitting on a smoky throne in the plain of Babylon, surrounded by innumerable little demons to whom he gives security regulations for the defence of the realm. Lucifer scatters his demons throughout the world, 'so that no province, no place, no region, no individual should be overlooked'. The instructions he gives them for ensnaring human beings are very simple: they are to lead people from a love of riches to a love of honour, and then 'to overweening pride'. The temptations are subtle, because riches are attractive, necessary, a blessing. It is not possessions which are wrong, but the possessiveness with which they can infect their owners, corroding in them every other love in life: love of justice, of truth, of other human beings and of themselves. The riches become an idol, and idols devour their devotees.

The second step is love of honour which, like riches, is not wrong in itself. Love of honour affects a deeper part of the soul than love of riches. Those enamoured of honour displace their true worth and invest it in a title, a position, a particular responsibility, and consequently, when that position is threatened, they will fight for its retention as though they were fighting for life itself, reckoning their own life to be meaningless and unbearable without the honour. This idolatry leads to the supreme idolatry; being alienated from themselves, they become alienated from the very source of life, from God in whom they live and move and have their being. They become 'as gods', full of hubris, unloving and unloved, complacent, glorying in their power and blind to the truth that they are, in fact, pitiable, poor and naked.

Jesus, in contrast, is pictured on a plain outside Jerusalem, 'beautiful and attractive to behold', with his friends around him. He instructs them to travel the world winning men and women over to a manifesto which is the complete opposite of Lucifer's. They are to persuade people to a love of spiritual poverty, and even to embrace actual poverty if God should call them to this, then to desire insults, injury and contempt, because from these spring humility, which is the root of all other virtues.

At first sight, this message of Jesus is most unattractive. Imagine a politician saying to his electorate: 'I promise you poverty, and some of you actual poverty. This will bring you insults, injury and contempt. You will then reach the goal of our policy for the nation, that you should become humble, for out of humility every other good will follow.' He would certainly lose his deposit. This raises very important questions. Is Jesus' message, while attractive and appealing to the religious compartment of our minds, utterly useless and impractical for the real world? It is only when we ponder and pray Jesus' message that we can begin to see its attractiveness and discover that it really does correspond to our own deepest longings and desires.

We all want to be free; but there can be no freedom without spiritual poverty. Spiritual poverty is an attitude of mind and heart, so centred on God and reliant on him, that nothing created can serve as a substitute. A person who has the virtue of spiritual poverty may, in fact, have riches, but is in no way possessed by them. The riches are accepted as a blessing, but like all blessings, they are for sharing, not for hoarding, are to bring life to others, not to stifle it. The closer we can come to spiritual poverty, the greater our enjoyment of the gifts of creation. In the Sermon on the Mount Jesus says, 'Blessed (i.e. blissfully happy) are the poor in spirit, theirs is the kingdom of heaven.' Poor in spirit, possessed by nothing, we can possess everything.

'Actual poverty' does not mean destitution, which is an evil, but it means renunciation of the right to have personal possessions. Some are called to this, but actual poverty is not an end in itself; it is a means toward attaining spiritual poverty. Without some experience of living like a poor person, the spiritual poverty which we think we have attained may be illusory, the illusion becoming clear when our possessions are taken from us.

No sane person should desire insult, injury and abuse, and

to have such a desire could indicate a pathological state, but when the insults come unbidden, there is nothing more effective for breaking down the walls of our false, imprisoning self. Criticism of ourselves is always the more devastating the more it is true. To bear the pain and accept the truth of the criticism, without denying it and without hitting back, is a liberating experience which leads us to humility.

The Latin root of the word 'humility' is 'humus', meaning 'the earth'. So humility has something to do with earthiness, with having our feet on the ground, seeing things in perspective. Humility saves us from taking ourselves too seriously and from the illusion that our problems are greater than anyone else's and insoluble, even by God. It saves us, too, from illusions of grandeur, which are always comic in any individual, but tragic too, and very destructive. The Greeks called such illusions of grandeur 'hubris', a disease afflicting especially those in power, and which inevitably brings destruction, not only on the transgressor, but also to their unfortunate subjects. Humility is the root of all other virtues. Without humility other virtues, courage, resolution, self-discipline, intelligence, devotion to duty, love of one's country etc., can become means of destruction. Humility is the virtue of freedom, enabling us to enjoy creation without being possessed or enslaved by it.

The prayer at the end of the Two Standards meditation is a petition to be received under Christ's Standard in the highest spiritual poverty, and even in actual poverty, if that is what God is asking of us, and to have the strength to bear insults, injury and contempt so that we can be more like him. This prayer runs through all the contemplations of Christ's public life and Passion. The theme of the Two Standards is like the theme of a symphony, permeating the whole work, every part of it being an expression of this basic theme.

After four hours' prayer on the Two Standards, the day ends with a final meditation called 'The Three Classes' in which Ignatius considers three types of response from three men, all of goodwill and anxious to find peace with God, who have all come into a fortune. Their problem is whether, in order to find peace with God, they are to retain or to relinquish the inheritance. The first type of response is to postpone the decision till tomorrow and tomorrow, until the man dies still possessing the inheritance. The second type of response is less dilatory. The man realises he must make a decision about the inheritance, but he is so attached to it that he swings the will of God until it is aligned with his own desire and so persuades himself that its retention is God's will for him. It is a very useful exercise to scan our own past decisions in the light of this example, for it gets to the heart of the matter. A very sobering illustration of this second type of response is the fact that in the history of Christianity there has never been a war with Christians involved on both sides, in which the bishops of any one of those nations have declared unanimously the war to be unjust. It did not happen in the Second World War, nor in the Falklands War. Yet it cannot be that the bishops on both sides are right, nor can it be God's will that we should kill one another. Some of the bishops must have chosen national interests in preference to the will of God, swinging the will of God around until it favoured their own nationalism. In the third type of response, the man, aware of his own attachment to the fortune, prays to desire to relinquish it and lives meanwhile as though he had relinquished it, so that he can reach a decision uninfluenced by his own attachment to the money, accepting or relinquishing the inheritance solely because he sees the decision as God's will for him.

It was the framework of thought and feeling provided by the Two Standards and Three Classes which enabled me to face the torrent of doubts which had started as the merest trickle with the question, 'Is it not blasphemy to encourage boys to celebrate the feast of the Resurrection with the weapons of death?' I began to see that my doubts were not doubts against faith, but rather faith's promptings. But this raised further questions: 'Is it not possible that I, and others, are so attached to a particular way of life inspired, not by the Gospel, but by public school ethos, that we have swung the will of God into line with our own thinking?' Were we speaking a double language and living a double truth, speaking eloquently on the values of Christ's kingdom and the beauty of the Sermon on the Mount, on the value of humility and the glory of Christ's cross, celebrating these truths in the daily celebration of the Eucharist, yet speaking another and opposite language by our actions and attitudes, encouraging our pupils on the path to riches and honours, judging their worth and the value of our work for them by the examination results achieved, the Oxbridge successes won, the school's sporting triumphs, the position, wealth and influence of our Old Boys? I began to see my own attitudes and values in a new way, and I did not like what I saw. Was I as interested and did I give as much attention and respect to those who cleaned the school as I did to those who managed it? Did I respond and react to people because they were human beings, each a unique manifestation of God, or did I measure out respect on a scale measured by my advantage and regulated according to the status and importance of the person with whom I was talking?

At first, I applied the thinking of the Two Standards to my own life and immediate environment: later, I began to see that it applied to all human activity, both sacred and secular. As I walked from Koblenz to Goarshausen I was thinking of it in relation to the rise and fall of the Third Reich and in relation to the Church. The Church, the 'Light of the Nations' is true to herself only in so far as she does enlighten and so discern between good and evil. That is her role, her service to the world. The Church is beautiful, but she can also become a terrible beauty, exulting in herself, becoming so attached to her own power and influence that she ignores the cry of the poor and gives divine sanction to what is demonic. I worked once with a Jesuit, Augustine Duc Thu, who had been in Vietnam during the war there. His work had been the instruction of new converts to Catholicism. As in Britain, and most Western countries, such a task would not constitute a whole-time job, I asked him how many he had been instructing. 'About three hundred,' he said. He then told me something of the history of the Catholic Church in South Vietnam. It was very wealthy, influential and numerous. After the Second Vatican Council there were all kinds of renewal meetings and courses for Catholics, 'but', he said, 'nothing happened. Then came the Communists and we lost everything. Then we changed. Then the converts began to pour in.' It was so simple a story and so true to the Gospel. When the Church is poor, without influence, without official status, then she comes to life. When she becomes wealthy, powerful and influential in a country, then she is in danger of becoming infected, blind and deaf to the needs of the poor, complacent, self-righteous, defensive, nationalist and increasingly authoritarian, while keeping up the appearances of being true to her vocation.

Goarshausen was full of large hotels, mostly closed, and I spent another hour searching for lodgings before finding a room with a view over the river. I sat by the window watching the river and its traffic, a tune going round and round in my head. It was the music of a psalm setting, 'How our hearts rejoiced when we heard them say, "Let us go to God's house", and now our feet are standing within your gates, O Jerusalem'. After leaving Stonyhurst in 1967, I went as chaplain to Catholics at Glasgow University. One of the students, Frances Duffy, had the voice of an angel, and this was one of her favourite songs. I was happy to be on my way to Jerusalem, felt no doubts now about continuing the journey and looked forward to the next day's walking to Rudesheim, then by ferry across to Bingen.

Wednesday, March 11

Over eight hundred years ago a remarkable woman lived in Bingen, an abbess, who was also a scholar, musician and a mystic. She saw the whole of creation as being married to God, everything in relation to God, and so she was involved in politics. Towards the end of her life she was put under an interdict for purely political reasons. After her death she was forgotten, and most people have never heard of Hildegard of Bingen, whose writings have only recently appeared in English for the first time with their message both of warning and of hope. Hildegard saw all creation as a unity, 'Through this world God encircles and strengthens humankind.' One of her favourite phrases is 'the greening of God' by which she means God's creative power. One of her poems is a warning, eight hundred years old yet remarkably contemporary:

> Now in the people
> that were meant to green
> there is no more life of any kind.
> There is only shrivelled barrenness.

The winds are burdened
by the utterly awful stink of evil,
selfish goings-on.
Thunderstorms menace.
The air belches out
the filthy uncleanness of the peoples.

There pours forth an unnatural,
a loathsome darkness,
that withers the green,
and wizens the fruit
that was to serve as food for the people.

Sometimes this layer of air
is full,
full of a fog that is the source
of many destructive and barren creatures,
that destroy and damage the earth,
rendering it incapable
of sustaining humanity.

The mystic sees into the heart of things; her vision is not limited by time or space. Her awful vision is being realised in our own day. The roots of our destructiveness are in the human heart:

Thus
humankind does well to keep honesty
to keep to truth.

Those that love lies
bring suffering
not only to themselves
but to others as well
since they are driven to ever more lies.

Their lies are like the juiceless foam,
hard and black.
Lacking the verdancy of justice
it is dry,
totally without tender goodness,
totally without illuminating virtue.

As often as the elements of the world
are violated

by ill treatment,
so God will cleanse them.

God will cleanse them
through the sufferings,
through the hardships
of humankind.

Hildegard's writing is like the greening of God, life-giving, wholesome, affecting every aspect of life. It is not a fractured spirituality, which divides matter from spirit, body from soul, natural from supernatural, religion from life, intellect from emotion. Although she is acutely aware of the reality of sin and evil, she sees creation as fundamentally good, and evil as the misuse of what is good. I cannot imagine Hildegard agreeing for one moment with those who claim that it is right to defend any nation, or group of nations, with nuclear arms, which can threaten all life on the planet. Such a conclusion can only come from a fractured spirituality which has lost sight of the unity of all creation.

The scenery was so beautiful and the weather so ideal for walking that I continued beyond Bingen in the direction of Mainz, for I had decided to make a detour to visit Skt Georgen, in Frankfurt. The stretch of road beyond Bingen was miserable. The elements had certainly been violated by ill treatment and I walked for two hours through built-up areas, cold, hungry and very tired after 48 km. I tried a church near Ingelsheim, but there was a padlock on the gate leading to it. When I found the presbytery, my courage failed me, for I was in no mood for an interrogation session. In Ingelheim I asked a passerby if she knew of any cheap lodgings. She was a Quaker, who spoke excellent English, having spent most of her life in India. She directed me to a hotel. There were innumerable forms to fill in and, true to form, it was a wretched place, serving no evening meals, a meagre breakfast and a large bill at the end of it.

The evening before, at Goarshausen, I had been feeling euphoric. This evening, too tired to find a place to eat, I sat in my room eating bread and cake, full of doubts about the wisdom of this pilgrimage and apprehensive about the future course of it. Before setting out on the pilgrimage, I had read a book on liberation theology by Gutierrez with the excellent title *They Drink from Their Own Wells*, in which he describes the strength of basic Christian communities, which draw their energy and hope from their own experience of God at work in their everyday lives. I liked the phrase, 'Drink from your own well', and I saw that in my own swinging moods about this pilgrimage, I was drinking from two separate wells inside me, the Christ well and the Gerard W. Hughes well. Tiredness, cold, hunger and ugly surroundings, as in this hotel, drove me to the Gerard W. Hughes well, bringing gloom, uncertainty and doubt. When in good spirits, I was more ready to drink from Christ's well. My own well, I began to notice, was full of conventional thinking, brimful of the dull waters of common sense, water that has been subjected to so much analysis and treatment, that it has become not only tasteless, but poisonous. From this well came such questions as, 'What on earth do you think you are doing walking the roads with this ridiculous haversack on wheels, a menace to traffic and to yourself? What vanity and arrogance to think that this gesture can contribute anything to peace, when it is probably undertaken to satisfy some unconscious need which you are not facing, but escaping through walking.' There was no satisfaction in this well, no life from its waters, just endless doubts. When I turned to Christ's well, it did not give answers to the statements and questions of my well, but an inner assurance that it was right to continue, to keep walking, and to trust that if I ought to abandon the pilgrimage, he would make it clear, and the decision would be taken in peace, not in gloom and doubt.

4

Frankfurt Revisited

If Christians are serious about peace, they must be serious about Church Unity. (Max Joseph Metzger)

My original plan had been to skirt Frankfurt and have my first long rest in Munich, but as I walked down the Rhine memories of my three years in Germany thirty years before kept recurring, so I phoned Skt Georgen and asked if I might spend two nights there.

Thursday, March 12

I left the wretched hotel in Ingelheim early for Mainz. It was another bright cold day with a strong east wind, and the walking along a minor road through open orchard countryside dispelled the weariness of the previous evening. I had no detailed map of Mainz, but took a compass bearing on what appeared to be the main railway station and tried to make a bee-line for it. Bee-lines are not possible for the pedestrian in modern cities, encircled as they are with ring roads, and I had a maze-like walk through Mainz suburbia before I found the Hauptbahnhof. Most German railway stations provide excellent restaurants and in Mainz I had my first good meal for days before catching a train for Frankfurt. As I waited outside the Frankfurt Hauptbahnhof to catch a tram to Skt Georgen, I had very vivid memories of my first arrival there thirty years before.

In 1956, Skt Georgen looked like a fortress set in a desolate landscape of garden allotments. Inside the fortress over one hundred black-robed Jesuits moved like clockwork from rooms to chapel to lectures to refectory. Meals began and ended with a long and solemn Latin grace. There was an American student, Bill Bichsel from Oregon, who used to add to the grace a sentence of his own, 'And, dear Lord, please supply the vitamins.' It was not always easy 'to be truly thankful' for the meals provided. When I arrived this time, there had been so many extensions and alterations that it was difficult to recognise the original building. Near the entrance there was a magnificent new library. Like Heythrop, the Jesuit house of studies in London, which is part of London University, Skt Georgen was now part of Frankfurt University and open to lay women and men, Jesuit students forming only a very small minority of the student body. Life there was transformed, much less formal, and for the meals I could be 'truly thankful'. There was not a black-robed figure in sight; all were now dressed informally, including some of the eighty-year-olds, whom I had thought of as old thirty years before, but who were still working. Father Grillmeier, white-haired in the 1950s, who has produced authoritative volumes on the Council of Chalcedon, was still discussing at recreation the meaning of Chalcedon's definition on the relationship between Christ's divinity and his humanity.

Friday, March 13

Next morning I walked the three miles into the city to visit the Frankfurt Dom, where I was ordained on July 31, 1958. I sat for a long time, at first listening to an accomplished organist playing Bach to an empty church, then thinking back to the ordination day when Frankfurt's purgatory was briefly transformed into heaven. I thought of my family, my sister Edith and my brother Joe with his wife, Margaret, who had left their one-year-old son, Gerry, at home in Scotland and had driven in great discomfort to Frankfurt along with my elder brother, Ian, who is a Salvatorian priest, and my aunt Helen, my mother's younger sister, and of the large number of Jesuits ordained with me. I thought, too, of the intervening years, of the enormous changes in the Church and in society, of the pain of adapting to the changes and the greater pain of refusing to adapt. As I remembered all these, an image

65

came to me of a cork floating on a torrent, in the torrent but not submerged by it. It was a surprising image of the Church, very unlike the 'rock of ages' or 'the ark of salvation', but later I came across a quotation from von Hügel which brought to mind the cork image, 'The Church is thus, ever and everywhere, both progressive and conservative; both free-lance and official; both, as it were, male and female, creative and reproductive; both daring to the verge of presumption and prudent to the verge of despair.' The cork bobs up and down between the semicolons, in the torrent, but not of it. I prayed for a spirit of trust in bewilderment, for certainty in uncertainty, for a spirit of detachment which can preserve us all from over seriousness about ourselves, or about the institutional aspects of the Church, so that we can live in the freedom of the children of God, delighting in his creation and free to share its tears and laughter. I wandered through the Dom, looking at its statues and plaques, noticing the glorification of war and militarism, a characteristic of so many cathedrals, which I had never observed until I began to think on the nature of peace. There was one plaque dedicated to Charles, Count of Lameth, commander of the French armies, Knight of the Order of St Louis, who had died in 1761 at the age of thirty-nine. Underneath was written:

> Qui christianas et bellicas virtutes conciliari non posse iactitant, spectent, sileant et imitentur. (Let those who claim that warlike and Christian virtues are incompatible, look, ponder and imitate.)

From the Dom I went to visit the Pax Christi offices in Frankfurt, where I was given a most interesting potted history of Pax Christi's work in Germany. Immediately after the war, Pax Christi's main work was to bring about a spirit of repentance among the German people for the evils done and to make reparation. There were prayers, pilgrimages to concentration camps in Germany and Poland, and a special pilgrimage to Israel. Later, the movement became more conscious of world peace and of Third World problems and initiated a Friday fast day for the Third World, an initiative adopted by the German bishops, which led to the founding of Misereor, a Catholic charitable organisation for Third World projects.

In the 1960s Pax Christi, reflecting more on the roots of peace, was encouraging peace education and soon became involved politically in the questions of nuclear defence, disarmament, the right to conscientious objection, the need for a new approach to East Germany, involvements which brought the organisation into conflict with the German hierarchy. At present Pax Christi in West Germany has about 22,000 members. From its foundation the movement has emphasised the ecumenical character of all its work and is currently working with German Protestant Churches for an ecumenical council of all Christian Churches on the theme of justice, peace and the integrity of creation. Such a council was first advocated by Dietrich Bonhoeffer in the early 1930s, but Bonhoeffer thought of it as a council of Protestant Churches only; it was unthinkable at that time that the Catholic Church should be invited, or that it would accept any such invitation. In 1939 Father Max Joseph Metzger proposed a council of all the Churches and he wrote to Pius XII with this suggestion, proposing that it should be held at Assisi.

Max Joseph Metzger was born in 1887, ordained priest in 1911, served for a year as military chaplain in the First World War and then had to retire for health reasons. He later became general secretary of a charitable organisation, later named 'Christ the King'. Through his war experience and charitable work he became a pacifist, attending and speaking at fourteen international peace conferences between 1917 and 1929. From 1929 to 1938 he was engaged in building up the Christ the King organisation, an attempt at Church reform through the co-operation of clergy and laity, men and women. His first interest was peace, which led him to see the need for Church unity if Christian peace efforts were to be effective. In 1938 he founded the 'Una Sancta' movement, a call to Christian unity in which Lutherans were urged to become better Lutherans, Evangelicals better Evangelicals, Roman Catholics better Roman Catholics by being true to the Scriptures and to their own traditions, thus opening themselves to the Holy Spirit, source of all unity, leading us into a unity, the nature of which no individual or Church can determine beforehand. When I was studying theology, the Una Sancta movement was flourishing in Germany, which was ahead of the rest of the world in its ecumenical theology and was a major influence on Vatican II's decree on ecumenism. In his youth, Metzger's father had forbidden him to play with Protestant or with Jewish children! Metzger was sentenced to death in October 1943 because an informer had betrayed him to the authorities for attempting to smuggle peace proposals into Sweden, and in April 1944 he was hung for treason in Berlin, a year before Bonhoeffer. Why is it that such a gifted, far-seeing, religious and courageous man has received so little recognition within the Catholic Church in Germany and elsewhere? In my three years in Germany I had never heard mention of him; my first introduction to him was in this Pax Christi office. A few months before his death he wrote from prison:

Ich konnt im ganzen Leben nicht erfassen,
dass man bei notstand höflich sich entfernt
. . .
Geht euren Weg, ich sehe euch ohne Neid,
Ihr klugen Selbstversorger all, ihr Weisen.
Ich gehe den meinen; mögt ihr Narr mich heissen.
Mich tröstet meiner Seele Seligkeit.

(I have never understood how people can behave like ostriches in a crisis. Go your own way, I envy not your clever self-protection, your worldly wisdom. Call me a fool, if you like. My soul is comforted by bliss.)

On the day of his death he wrote a final letter in which he saw his death as an offering 'for world peace and the unity of the Church'. The irony is that Metzger was not recognised in his life because he was 'too political', as if in his efforts for peace and Church unity he was engaging in some dangerous fringe activity, not central to the Church's life. But the reason why the Catholic hierarchy did not make a clear stand against Nazism was not because it was too 'unpolitical', but because it compromised itself politically by recognising the Nazi regime in 1933. Metzger was never approved of by his bishop, Bishop Grober, who considered him wayward when he was a young seminarian, and never revised his opinion. Max Joseph Metzger had begun with peace, and from peace he came to see the need for Church unity. I had begun with an interest in Church unity, and from Church unity came to peace, but it was through work on peace that I came to a clearer understanding of the need for and nature of Church unity.

I left Stonyhurst in 1967 and spent the next eight years as chaplain to Catholics at the University of Glasgow. On most Saturdays during term time I used to go hill climbing with groups of students. On one Saturday we were sitting on a hillside overlooking a glen which runs into Loch Lomond. Across the glen on the hill opposite we could see Ministry of Defence buildings and tunnels cut into the hillside. One of our group said that the largest store of nuclear weapons in Europe was hidden in those hills, information which may well have been untrue, but it was the possibility of its truth which affected my imagination. At this time, 1969, I knew very little about the details of our nuclear defence policy, and although I had doubts that any war could be just, I still believed that the possession of nuclear arms could be justified as an effective means of deterring a potential aggressor, for the weapons were then being used not as a means of destruction but as instruments for the preservation of peace. My thinking began to change on that Saturday afternoon because I began to see nuclear defence from a new perspective, occasioned by the sheer beauty of the surroundings.

Born in Scotland, I am a prejudiced observer of its scenery. There is a beguiling quality in the Scottish hills. When walking them on my own I have never felt lonely, or even alone, for they seem friendly, yet speak of mystery. This experience helped me understand what the early Fathers of the Church meant when they wrote of creation itself as being a sacrament of God, sign and effective sign of his presence. Every bush is burning, if only we have the eyes to see.

Had I heard this student's comment about the nuclear arms store in a lecture, or read it in a book, it would probably have had little effect but, hearing it on this hillside, it had a lasting effect, for I could see in imagination this beautiful landscape reduced to a smouldering mass, the friends around me vaporised, leaving only shadows. For Roman Catholics desecration of the Blessed Sacrament is a hideous blasphemy. Why is it that we react with horror to such a desecration, yet pay taxes which pay for desecrating weapons without a murmur and consider those few who refuse to pay such taxes to belong to the lunatic fringe? Here I am simply recording subjective reactions to a remark passed on a Scottish hillside, not giving a reasoned argument against a nuclear defence policy. The experience on the hillside had changed my way of perceiving the question, for I was now seeing it in a sacramental perspective. Whenever Christians discuss the morality of nuclear defence they must ponder the question from this perspective, otherwise they are restricting God, confining him to a 'religious' realm, and so denying his immanence, his presence in all things. They are not letting him be God, Father of Our Lord Jesus Christ, in whom all creation has its being.

Towards the end of my eight years in Glasgow, I was walking alone one day along the shore of the Holy Loch, where the U.S. submarines are based. It was a glorious day in May, the forested hills reflected in the still waters of the Loch, disturbed only by a slight ripple, the periscope of a nuclear submarine. This scene later became my imaginative picture whenever I prayed the Two Standards meditation of the *Spiritual Exercises*. We are engaged in a cosmic struggle between the forces of life and the destructive powers, which disguise themselves under the appearance of good, of reasonableness, of common sense. On the surface everything may appear well ordered and peaceful, but under the surface lurks a destructive power capable of destroying the whole area, of murdering millions, maiming millions, destroying future generations. The beauty of the scene made the presence of the submarine the more horrifying. I asked myself, 'Where is the evil?' The evil could not be in the submarine, nor in its weapons, for machines in themselves are incapable of evil. The evil must lie within the human heart and mind, not only the mind of the captain and crew, not only in the chain of command which is prepared to give the order to fire if an emergency arises. The evil must lie in the mind and heart of all of us who, by our silence and our taxes, collude with the evil intention.

The violence and destructiveness of nuclear weapons are the outcrop of a vast network of ideas and attitudes which are not immediately recognisable by our conscious minds, but which lurk, like the submarine, beneath an apparently well-ordered, charming, friendly and peaceful exterior. If it is true that nuclear weapons are the fruit of a vast and invisible network of attitudes, ideas, values, thought patterns and ways of behaving in which we are all engaged and to which we all contribute, then this raises questions about the value of campaigns for nuclear disarmament and of international agreements on nuclear arms control. Even if nuclear arms were to be abolished tomorrow, next day the agreement could be broken. Einstein said,

> We must never relax our efforts to arouse in the people of the world, especially in their governments, an awareness of the unprecedented disaster which they are absolutely certain to bring on themselves unless there is a fundamental change in their attitudes towards one another as well as in their concept of the future. The unleashed power of the atom has changed everything except our way of thinking.

International agreements are welcome and necessary, but enduring peace is only possible if we labour and sweat at the roots of the problem of violence. The roots lie in attitudes of mind and heart which at first sight can appear to be good, reasonable, sensible, respectable and just. If we really desire peace we must set ourselves an agenda which goes far beyond the dismantling of missile sites; we must face the far more threatening and difficult task of dismantling our minds and hearts. In the Gospels this task is called 'metanoia' meaning a change of mind and heart, an individual and national call to repentance.

This recognition was one of the reasons which led me to ask if I could work in spirituality after leaving Glasgow University in April 1975, for spirituality is concerned with the roots of good and evil, of life and of destruction. From 1976 to 1984 I was at St Beuno's, a Jesuit house in North Wales, working at first with Jesuits in their final year of training, called a 'tertianship'. In 1978 I was asked to develop the house as a Centre of Jesuit Spirituality for the giving of the *Spiritual Exercises* of St Ignatius and also for training others to give them.

When Ignatius and his first companions began to give the *Spiritual Exercises*, which was their main ministry, they gave them, not to groups but to individuals, because each individ-

ual is unique, with their own way of perceiving and understanding, their own willingness and strength to do the Exercises, whose object is to enable the exercitant to become more
perceptive and responsive to the action of God's Spirit at
work within each one. One of the early Jesuits, Jerome Nadal,
who was reckoned to have the best understanding of the
Spiritual Exercises, was once asked, 'For whom are these *Exercises* suitable?' 'For Catholics, Protestants and pagans', was
his answer.

When we started the Spirituality Centre at St Beuno's
there were only three of us on the retreat-giving staff, Father
Michael Ivens, who was running a tertianship, Father Patrick
Purnell, who was also responsible for the material running of
the house, and myself, also running the tertianship, so there
was little we could do at first except talk and dream of what
St Beuno's might become if we had a qualified staff, who
were free to work in it. One problem was the fact that many
priests and most members of Catholic religious orders are
expected to make an annual eight-day retreat, and so we could
foresee that St Beuno's could be so engaged in answering
this demand that there would be no places left for Catholic
laywomen and men, nor for Protestants and pagans! One
evening as we were discussing plans, it was suggested that
we should introduce a points system, so that any of us asked
to give a retreat to a Catholic religious would receive -1, a
Catholic layperson would win $+1$, non-Roman Catholic
clergy or laity would have $+3$, the highest points being
awarded for a card-carrying Communist or a Roman Catholic
bishop. In fact, we had two card-carrying Communists before
we had a bishop!

Individual retreat-giving is very privileged work, revealing
the great spiritual wealth which is in each individual, but
also revealing the reality of the Two Standards meditation,
how the destructive spirit works in all of us under the appearance of good. But the most interesting thing I observed in
giving the *Exercises* was that those people, irrespective of
religious denomination, who were actively engaged in some
form of justice and peace work, developed spiritually more
quickly and more deeply than those who were not so engaged,
because the nature of their work forced them to ask questions
which they had not considered before. I also knew that the

majority of them had neither the time, nor the money, to come to a retreat house, and that many of them felt so alienated from the Church that they would never think of coming. For this reason I asked my Superior if, after leaving St Beuno's, I could work on spirituality with people active in justice and peace work. The Provincial agreed and I have been engaged in this work ever since.

After doing this work for a year, travelling to meet groups wherever I was invited, I remembered a catechism question which I had to learn by heart as a child. The question was, 'What are the marks of the one true Church?' The answer: 'She is one, holy, Catholic and apostolic.' There were then further questions: 'What do you mean by one? What do you mean by holy?' etc., the answers showing that these characteristics were to be found in the Roman Catholic Church and in no other. I remembered these questions because in the peace groups I visited and in the eight-day retreats I gave to peace and justice people of various denominations, I was seeing something of those marks of the Church.

The peace movement brought together the most disparate people, cutting across religions and religious denominations, races, classes and generations. It was a small thing, but significant, that whenever we had a full day's meeting, the food which each brought for lunch was laid out on a table and all shared together. The most striking experience of unity was in the eight-day individually given retreats which I organised in the summer months. For eight days and in silence, Roman Catholics, Anglicans, Free Church members and Quakers lived and prayed together, the retreat-givers including Roman Catholic and Anglican, clerical, religious and lay. In the evenings we used to meet together to pray for one another in silence. At St Beuno's, where initially the majority of retreatants were Roman Catholic, we used to make this prayer before the Blessed Sacrament, which was placed on the altar in a monstrance. Catholics believe that Christ is really and truly present sacramentally in the consecrated bread, a belief not shared by all denominations. I suggested to the peace retreatants that we should have this silent prayer before the Blessed Sacrament. Whatever our beliefs, we all accepted that God is love, the heart of the Universe, and so we could see the Blessed Sacrament as a symbol of this reality. At the end of each retreat almost all commented on the powerful sense of unity which they experienced in these evening half-hours of silent prayer.

The unity experienced in working for peace was not only a unity across denominations and between individuals and groups; individuals began to discover a growing unity within themselves. I had been involved in ecumenical work for almost twenty-five years before beginning work with people engaged in justice and peace work. I had attended many ecumenical meetings and services, but had never experienced a real unity so clearly as I did when working with people engaged in justice and peace work. This confirmed what I had noticed at St Beuno's, that if people are committed to peace and justice work in some form, they tend to develop spiritually more quickly and more deeply.

I have already mentioned St Peter Canisius' excellent principle of concentrating on points of agreement rather than on differences in his encounters with the reformers, but unity will never come about through discussions only. God is the source of all unity. As we move towards God, we come into unity within ourselves and with one another. God is a God of compassion, of justice and of peace. As we act out of compassion for justice and peace on earth, we are moving towards God. When Christians co-operate in doing this, they are drawn into unity, and when they pray together they experience the unity which binds them. This is a truth which most Christian parishes in Britain have not begun to understand, so they do not co-operate but continue to do separately what they could more effectively do together, limiting their co-operation to prayers together for unity one week in the year. Max Metzger was right; if Christians are serious about peace, they must be equally serious about Church unity. But it is also true that Christian Churches will only discover their real unity in so far as they focus their attention on questions of justice and peace, because the God whom they worship is in justice and peace. Worship which ignores the needs of others, whether church members or not, cannot be the worship of the God of Abraham, Isaac and Jacob, Father of Our Lord Jesus Christ, who said, 'As you do to one of these least, you do also to me.'

Holiness is not a quality one immediately associates with

people who are involved in justice and peace work. A leading personality in peace action once said to me after a peace demonstration. 'In the peace movement we have a lot to learn from the police. They were much more restrained, polite and courteous today than many of the peace demonstrators.' Justice and peace work can attract people with chips on their shoulders, who use the peace movement as a means of channelling their own aggressiveness by marching in demonstrations and shouting 'Maggie out: Reagan out', hurling insults at the police as they pass, believing that if only they shout loud enough nuclear weapons will disappear and then we shall all live happily ever after. In my experience, very few act in this way, but the few are enough for the media, which can then create the impression that all engaged in peace work are dangerous fanatics. I had read newspaper articles describing the Greenham women as 'raving harpies', 'anarchic lesbians', etc. When I later visited Greenham with some trepidation, I was amazed at what I saw and heard. I was treated courteously by the women, who were living under the most primitive conditions, sheltered from wind and rain with plastic coverings spread over tree branches, which they called 'benders'. There were about fifty women camping at this particular gate. Their kitchen was an open wood fire, their pantry three dustbins containing bread, vegetables and fruit. Some of them, including one grandmother, lived there all the year round, while others came for shorter periods. The early desert Fathers probably lived in greater comfort than these twentieth-century women, for they did not have to endure an English climate, nor suffer the harassment of police, bailiffs and hostile neighbours attacking them at night with air guns, nor were they slandered by the media. One of the Greenham women, an ex-magistrate, has been in prison several times because she will insist on saying her prayers inside nuclear bases. Whenever she goes to prison, she fasts for the duration of her sentence, on one occasion fasting for thirty days. When I first met her she was on a three-day fast outside Westminster cathedral, the fast coinciding with the bishops' Low Week conference. She was fasting and leafleting the bishops and the passers-by on Third World starvation and the Arms Trade.

The vast majority of people whom I have met in the peace

movement have discovered that their commitment to peace has been for them a form of education which has affected every aspect of their lives. Initially their commitment may have been naive, assuming that by going on demonstrations they could rid the world of nuclear weapons and that this was all that was needed for peace to reign. The ineffectiveness of their protests helped them to understand better the complexity of the nuclear arms question and that it cannot be considered in isolation from Third World hunger and debt problems, human rights, women's rights in particular, poverty at home as well as abroad, race relations, etc. They also began to see that the peace issue not only affects every aspect of social and political life, but it also affects personal life, raising questions about our own peacelessness and injustice in our relationships to ourselves and to others, about our own ingrained attitudes of mind and heart. The problems are so massive that they become overwhelming, afflicting people with a frightening sense of helplessness and powerlessness. For many this becomes the start of a religious conversion, for they know by bitter experience that without God they can do nothing, and that God alone is their rock, refuge and strength. They discover their need for prayer, find themselves attracted to a simpler lifestyle, gain strength through fasting, become more tolerant and compassionate, and although they become more involved in peace work, they do so with a lightness of heart and take themselves less seriously. St Paul, in his letter to the Galatians, lists some of the marks of the Spirit, the signs of holiness: '. . . love, joy, peace, patience, kindness, goodness, trustfulness, gentleness and self control' (5:22).

The third mark of the Church is that she is catholic, a Greek word which means universal, embracing everything and everyone. People who persevere in their commitment to justice and peace and who reflect on their experience, find they become increasingly conscious of their relationship with the rest of creation and they develop a sensitivity to the unity in which we all live. They feel for their brothers and sisters behind the Iron Curtain as they feel for their own family, and it is this sensing which strengthens them in their commitment and leads them to practise civil disobedience and to face the consequences with equanimity and without bitterness. They become more sensitive to all sentient things, to animal and plant life, the rivers and the oceans. Many become vegetarian, not primarily for health reasons, but to be more at one with the millions who do not have enough to eat. Living in this awareness is the real meaning of being catholic and it is what all Catholics are called to become. An exclusive, élitist, enclosed-within-itself Catholicism with a selective morality, an individual-centred and other-worldly spirituality, which does not concern itself with peace beyond praying for it, while ignoring the attitudes and activities which make peace impossible, is a travesty of the true meaning of 'catholic'. The more the Catholic Church commits herself to the problems of justice and peace – and there are promising signs that she is doing so – the more likely she is to appreciate and value not only her own tradition, but also to see and understand the revelation of God in other Christian denominations and in other religions.

The final characteristic of the Church is that she is apostolic, another Greek word, meaning 'sent', 'commissioned'. The apostles are called apostles because they are 'the sent ones', the missioners, sent to preach the Gospel to the whole world. To be apostolic is to have a sense of mission, to experience a call, have an inner urge to communicate the message of Christ. If most justice and peace people were asked, 'Do you consider yourself apostolic?', the majority would say they did not understand what that meant and the rest would probably say 'no'. Yet many of them have this characteristic. They may have started on peace and justice work with a naive enthusiasm, enjoying the company at meetings and the excitement of demonstrations, believing in the usefulness of their cause and the effectiveness of their method, but when their enthusiasm waned and their efforts seemed futile, many have wanted to abandon all involvement in peace movements, but then discover that they cannot. They find they are caught up in something which is much greater than they are, something relentless, which intrudes into every aspect of their lives, afflicting them with restlessness, with a dissatisfaction with their own past lifestyle and values, yet leaving them without any clear sense of direction or knowledge of how they should proceed. Those of them familiar with the Old Testament prophets recognise their pain in Jeremiah's 'We were hoping for peace, but no good came of it' (14:19) and, 'Why is my suffering continual, my wound incurable, refusing to be healed? Do you mean to be for me a deceptive stream with inconstant waters?' (15:18). Yet, in spite of all the pain of it, they do not want to abandon the search for peace and they continue preaching and practising the Gospel of peace. This is what it means to be apostolic.

Through involvement in peace and justice work I began to see more clearly that the Church will grow in unity the more it ceases to concentrate on unity as we so often understand it, namely that we should all be united in the same doctrinal beliefs and in forms of worship agreed to by all, and instead concentrates on praying together to Christ, Lord of all creation. If we really were united in Christ, the pagans would advance on their third-century statement, 'How these Christians love one another,' saying instead, 'How these Christians love and care for every human being and for every particle of creation!' That is why the proposed council of all the Christian Churches to consider peace, justice and the integrity of creation, is so important.

I had intended spending only one full day in Frankfurt and starting out on the road to Munich on Saturday, but on Friday afternoon I met Father Johannes Beutler, a Scripture scholar lecturing at Skt Georgen, who was also a member of Pax Christi. He invited me to accompany him that evening to a meeting in Frankfurt for a group known as 'Religious for Peace'. The meeting would include Mass together followed by a lecture on West Germany and the Arms Trade. On Saturday he had to attend an afternoon meeting of unemployed men and women theology graduates from Skt Georgen, followed by a meeting of 'Neuer Deutschland', a German Catholic youth organisation. The meeting would last until after lunch on Sunday, when Johannes was joining a prayer meeting outside an American missile base at Hasselbach. I readily agreed to postpone my departure until the Monday.

Saturday, March 14

The thirty theology graduates whom we met on Saturday were complaining of the impossibility of finding jobs either in schools or in parishes in West Germany. The churches in Germany are not poor, so the reason for their unemployment was not financial. Either the parishes did not see the need for teaching theology to the laity, or else they found the theology taught by academic graduates was not answering the needs of their people.

When I was teaching at Stonyhurst, the curate of a neighbouring parish came to see me to discuss ways and means of communicating the documents of the Second Vatican Council to his parishioners. He gathered a group of twelve men and women, and booked a room in a local pub on Thursday evenings. At our first meeting, after orders had been taken, I gave a brief outline of what had been happening at the Second Vatican Council and also showed them some books on the subject, which had recently appeared. At our next meeting they arrived with copies of the books which they had obtained through the excellent Preston county library. They studied the documents, discussed them and made links between the documents and what was happening in their own lives in society and in the parish. I first learned from this group what subsequent experience has confirmed, that there is an enormous wealth of spiritual and theological talent in the Church, but it has remained buried because poor theological training in seminaries has led clergy to believe that their function is 'to teach, to govern and to sanctify'; consequently, the laity's role is to be governed, taught and sanctified, thus forming them into 'God's frozen people', whose function is to obey, pray and pay. Later, especially at St Beuno's, I was to see much more clearly the effect of this stifling attitude when I worked on spirituality. Fortunately, attitudes are now changing in the Catholic Church in Britain, where a few parishes are benefiting from the ministry of lay helpers trained in theology and in spirituality, and an increasing number of laity are engaged in the ministry of retreat-giving and spiritual direction, to the great benefit, not only of the laity, but of the clergy and religious as well.

From Frankfurt, Johannes drove me for three hours to Neuerburg, near Biltburg, for the meeting with Neuer Deutschland, a youth organisation which had numbered

35,000, but its membership has dropped to 23,000 because the youngsters are finding it too rigid, both theologically and politically.

Sunday, March 15

On Sunday afternoon, we drove to a prayer meeting outside the U.S. missile base at Hasselbach, as grim and drab as the other missile sites I have seen, with their high barbed-wire fences and massive iron gates. There were about 150 people gathered, including a much higher proportion of men than are usually evident at British peace meetings. The service lasted forty minutes, while we stood by the gates in a howling wind and flurrying snow. When the prayers were over, little children on their fathers' shoulders placed placards, flowers and pictures on the barbed wire fencing, undisturbed by the military on the other side of the fence. In Britain, such actions are a criminal offence: the god of security does not like flowers. At the end of the ceremony each group was invited to present itself and to state where they were from. When I announced through chattering teeth that I came from Birmingham and represented Pax Christi in Britain, I was given a great cheer.

After the service, friends of Johannes, Beata and Clemens, both former graduates of Skt Georgen, invited us back to their house to thaw out and have a meal. Beata and Clemens, both Catholics and committed to peace, complained about the lack of support and encouragement from the official Catholic Church which they experienced in their peace work, contrasting this with the more vigorous support which the Protestant Church leadership provides for people active in peace and justice.

When I began work with justice and peace groups in Britain, whenever I was invited for a weekend meeting, I used to ask the group organiser to offer my services to the local Catholic Church for the Sunday morning, to celebrate Mass and preach. I preached on the readings of the day, but because justice and peace are at the heart of all Scripture readings and because all Scripture readings are the word of God spoken to our present condition, I always tried to point out the contrast between the readings and the society in which we are living. For example, if we declare in church 'Lord, you are my rock, my refuge and my strength', how does such a profession of faith relate to our nuclear defence policy? After the Mass, a few might complain that such questions should not be addressed from the pulpit, but the majority would say that they were glad to hear such questions being mentioned at last. Occasionally, the priests themselves would say, 'I'm glad you brought up that subject. I dare not, because it causes such division within the parish,' while others might say, 'I don't think the pulpit is the place for politics.'

Such statements are a frightening commentary on the state of our spirituality. We do not like to mention any topic from the pulpit which might cause division in the parish. But the Gospel is divisive, 'I have come to bring not peace, but the sword, to set son against father, daughter against mother, daughter-in-law against mother-in-law' (Matt. 10:34–5). We have replaced the Gospel of Christ commanding us to love God above all things and our neighbour as ourselves, including among our neighbours, our enemies, with a new Gospel which forbids us to say anything which might upset our little group, even if our silence is collusion in a plan to kill millions of innocents if those in authority consider that our national interests are in danger. The pulpit is not the place for politics and no priest or minister should ever use the pulpit for party political purposes, but politics in the broadest sense concerns the way we relate to one another as human beings within a nation and between nations. To declare that the pulpit is not the place for politics in this general sense is to deny God, Father of Abraham, Isaac and Jacob, Father of Our Lord Jesus Christ, who has become one of us and who identifies himself with every human being. It is through our relations with one another that we find God. There is no other way for us to find him. To declare that politics in the broad sense must never be mentioned from the pulpit is to relegate God to the outer ether, to refuse to allow him to be God, and is therefore sinful.

After the meal we were to have a musical evening, two of the company playing violins, a third the cello, and the fourth the piano. While they were practising, I went outside to inspect the weather. It was even more bitterly cold, snow falling gently, but the wind had dropped and there was a full moon. I shall always remember those few minutes as I gazed at the snow-covered, still and moonlit landscape, listening to a Bach quartet, as though the whole earth was an orchestra playing its delight in creation to God, while the missile site had been hell's orchestra of fear preparing to express its hatred of all that lives.

It was late that Sunday night when we set off for Frankfurt, the snow falling so heavily that the car was slithering on the country roads and visibility reduced us at times to walking pace, but once we reached the Rhine valley the roads were easier and we returned to Skt Georgen at 1.00 a.m. I packed Mungo before going to bed, including in the packing my trousers, now fitted with a new zip, which spared me from having to wear the jeans. After an early morning Mass and breakfast, I took a tram and then train to Darmstadt, a few miles south of Frankfurt, to pick up my planned route to Munich.

5

The Veil Grows Thinner –
Odenwald, Romantic Way, Munich

What are the roots that clutch, what branches grow
Out of this stony rubbish? Son of man,
You cannot say, or guess, for you know only
A heap of broken images, where the sun beats,
And the dead tree gives no shelter, the cricket no relief,
And the dry stone no sound of water . . .
I will show you fear in a handful of dust.
(T.S. Eliot, 'The Waste Land')

Monday, March 16

Darmstadt was snow-covered, the bright sun causing a painful glare. The temperature was well below freezing and I
walked warily on the thin covering of frozen snow. On my
first night in Frankfurt I had woken up with such painful
cramp in my calf muscle that I jerked my leg straight. When
the cramp passed, my leg was still very sore, leaving me with
a slight limp and the fear that I might have torn a ligament.
A few kilometres beyond Darmstadt all pain had vanished
and I was walking normally through the beautiful hilly and
wooded country of the Odenwald, glad to be on the road
again, thanking God for the beauty of his creation and for
allowing me to make this pilgrimage. Then the snow began,
a few swirling flakes at first, heralds of the storm to come. By
the time I had put on my cagoul and trousers the snow was
so heavy that visibility was reduced to a few feet and Mungo's
little wheels were below the snow surface, so that I was
hauling a miniature snowplough. The prayer of praise ceased,
all my energy concentrated on the next step. I remembered

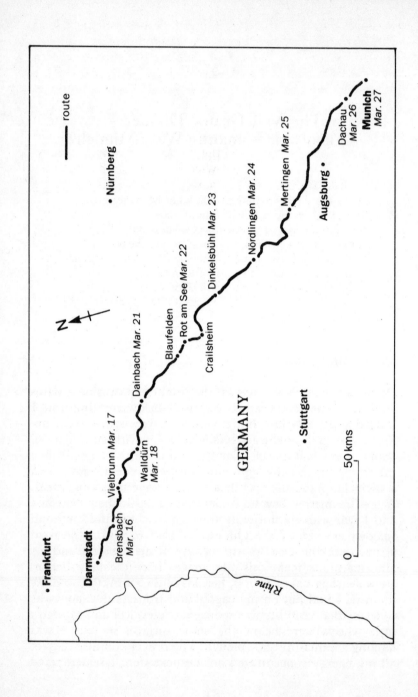

route

• Frankfurt

Darmstadt

Brensbach
Mar. 16

Vielbrunn Mar. 17

Walldürn
Mar. 18

Dainbach Mar. 21

Blaufelden

Rot am See Mar. 22

Crailsheim

Dinkelsbühl Mar. 23

Nördlingen Mar. 24

Mertingen Mar. 25

Augsburg •

Dachau
Mar. 26

Munich
Mar. 27

• Nürnberg

N

GERMANY

• Stuttgart

Rhine

50 kms

0

the story of an eccentric elderly Jesuit. Someone heard a loud crash in the library and rushed in to find him on the floor with step ladders athwart him, rubbing his head and groaning, 'Oh my God, why did you make me such a bloody fool?' As I staggered up the Odenwald hills dragging Mungo behind me, I was asking God the same question.

Thirty kilometres from Darmstadt I came to the village of Brensbach where I called in at a baker's shop for bread and to inquire about lodgings for the night. The woman gawked at me and Mungo, both snow-covered, ignored my order because she first wanted to know why in heaven's name I was walking in this weather with such a machine. When I explained that I was on my way to Jerusalem on foot, she took my order, but refused payment. I then asked her about lodgings in Brensbach and she told me there was nothing hereabouts, but why did I not try the 'Pfarrer', which can mean either the Catholic priest or the Protestant minister. I braced myself for an interrogation and rang the Pfarrer's bell. A cheerful-looking young man answered, listened to my request, did not ask to see any papers, but begged me wait a moment while he went to consult his wife upstairs. In a moment he was back again, welcoming me in for supper and offering me a bed for the night. Supper was an excellent meal, enlivened by the company of their three very chatty little children. Later that evening Christoph, the Pfarrer, and Claudia, his wife, sat talking till late telling me among other things of their experience of ecumenism in Germany today.

While studying theology in Germany, 1956–59, I had attended meetings of the 'Una Sancta' movement in Frankfurt, when in crowded halls Catholics and Protestants gathered together to listen to lectures on Protestant and Catholic theology of the Eucharist, on the sacrament of reconciliation, and on questions of papal authority, the lectures emphasising the points of agreement rather than the differences. During the war the Nazi regime, although it had caused splits within Catholic, Lutheran and Evangelical churches – some individuals within each denomination approving, or at least colluding by their silence with the government – the threat to basic Christian belief which the Third Reich imposed, brought many Christians together across the denominations. The post-war devastation in a divided Germany, and the fear in West Germany of attack from the communist East, continued to give support to the 'Una Sancta' movement and at least two thousand churches in West Germany were shared by Protestants and Catholics. After finishing theology at Frankfurt I stayed in Germany for another six weeks, at first working with a Dutch priest in giving missions in what was called 'the diaspora', the Protestant areas of Germany in which there were no Catholic churches, but which now contained large numbers of Catholics who had poured into these areas at the end of the war, mostly refugees from the Sudetenland. On one of these missions I celebrated the funeral Mass of a Catholic in a Protestant church, built as a Catholic church before the Reformation, and all the Protestants in the village attended. After the missions I spent two weeks at an ecumenical institute in Paderborn, where the director invited me to stay on so that I could attend the Evangelische Kirchentag in Munich and then have five days in a monastery in Bavaria where there was to be a meeting of Catholic and Protestant theologians to study the Eucharist together. I wrote back to England asking if I might extend my stay so that I could attend these meetings, adding that I would eventually like to return to Germany to do further studies on ecumenism to prepare me to work later on ecumenism in Scotland. I received a short sharp reply reminding me that there was work to be done in England and that I must proceed immediately to Preston to work in a parish.

On arrival at Preston, the parish priest, having welcomed me, added 'I don't know what we are going to do with you, but there will be a Mass to celebrate on Sundays and confessions to hear on Saturday evenings.' Ecumenism was not a priority in Britain at that time. A few months later I was invited to celebrate the wedding of my cousin, Anne Murray, a Catholic, to Henry Turner, a Protestant. The wedding took place in Scotland and I was given instructions the evening before from the parish priest, via his housekeeper, that at the wedding ceremony I was not to wear vestments, nor to bless the rings with holy water, nor to have the altar decorated with flowers, nor was there to be music. These regulations were not marks of respect for the Church of Scotland bridegroom, but signs of official Catholic disapproval of marriages across the denominations, a disapproval which had previously been expressed by refusing to have the marriage ceremony before the altar, so that it had to take place in the secrecy of the sacristy. I performed the ceremony as instructed, wearing a Jesuit black gown, omitting all blessings and sprinkling of holy water. At the end of the ceremony, a Church of Scotland minister, relative of the groom, approached me and said, 'May I congratulate you on such an excellent service, with none of those vestments, holy water, or incense, but just a good sober service conducted in a scholar's gown. John Knox would have been proud of you.' It was a sign of our mutual ignorance that what the Roman Catholic Church intended as a sign of disapproval, was perceived as a sign of approval, not only of a wedding across the denominations, but also of John Knox.

Even after the Second Vatican Council, the movement towards unity between the Roman Catholic and other Churches was very slow and hesitant, many clergy and laity feeling that any move towards other Churches must inevitably mean betrayal of the one, true, Catholic Church. When ecumenism reached Glasgow after the Second Vatican Council, there was a new cry heard from the Celtic end of the terraces at a match against their Protestant rivals, Rangers, 'Get tore intae yir separated brethren, Celtic.' Ecumenism had reached the Scottish shores and this was the manner of its coming.

After ordination in Frankfurt in 1958, I had asked my German Superior for permission to visit home in Scotland after ordination. He asked me why I wanted to go home, and I told him 'because it is home'. This, he told me, was not a satisfactory reason and that he could only allow me home if I had an academic reason, so I told him that I was interested in Scottish theology. He found this reason very acceptable. When I reached Scotland I thought I ought to do something about this Scottish theology, so I asked among the Jesuits I knew in Glasgow whether any were in contact with ministers of the Church of Scotland. They had no such contacts. I went to the Church of Scotland offices in the city and asked to see a directory of the clergy in the Glasgow area. Turning to the theology department at Glasgow University, I chose a name at random, John Macquarrie, then a lecturer in systematic theology, phoned him and was kindly invited to come along a few days later. I was with him for almost three hours that first evening, ending with supper with his wife and himself in the kitchen, and I had another long session with him before I returned to Germany. John Macquarrie was reading the Catholic theologians, was currently engaged in translating Heidegger, yet he had never in his life spoken with a Catholic priest and I had never in my life talked theology with a Church of Scotland minister.

Looking back in 1987 at the state of our ecumenical relations in Britain in the late fifties, it amazed me to see the progress which had been made, so I was very interested to hear of developments in Germany in the same period. According to Christoph and Claudia, relations between Catholic and Protestant Churches in Germany had worsened. Most West German Churches were now wealthy, so each denomination could build its own churches and there was no need to share. As a clergyman, Christoph noticed the problem especially in the pastoral care of people who married across the denominations. He said that the Catholic partner to such a marriage met with so many problems from the clergy, so much disapproval and so little support, that the majority gave up church-going altogether. In Britain, about 75 per cent of the weddings in which Catholics are partners are across the denominations. If the proportions are similar in Germany, the result of strained relations between the denominations will be devastating, not only in diminished church-going, but especially in the distress that such attitudes can cause within the marriage. Religion then becomes not a bond in marriage, but an obstacle to it.

It was sad to hear about the disunity of the Churches in Germany, which had held out such great promise to other Churches in the immediate post-war period. Because the Churches are now prosperous, they no longer need to share church buildings and can afford to be independent of each other. It is easier for a camel to pass through the eye of a needle than it is for a wealthy church to remain true to the Gospel. The Church needs wealth for her mission. It is not wealth which is wrong, but our attitude to wealth, when the wealth possesses us, becomes our security and determines what we do and what we do not do. Mother Teresa, on whose organisation thousands depend for their daily bread, refuses to accept any investments. Dorothy Day in the U.S.A., who founded the Catholic Worker movement and who had houses of hospitality throughout the United States, refused to accept charitable status for her organisation. Such a practice of poverty keeps faith and trust in God alive and flourishing.

Whatever the state of ecumenism in Germany today, the German bishops were instrumental in deepening the Catholic Church's understanding of ecumenism at the Second Vatican Council, offering from their own painful experience ideas and insights whose implications are still being worked out in the Catholic Church throughout the world. Enormous advances have been made in the last thirty years but, as in Germany so in other parts of the world, there is the constant temptation to retire back into the safety of our own denominational Churches, while still paying lip-service to the need for unity.

If we had really grasped the truth that God is the unity of Father, Son and Holy Spirit, and that the Church is God's sacrament, then striving for unity would be our first concern. Because God is mystery, therefore we cannot have a clear notion of what this unity would mean in practice. A life of faith is necessarily a life of risk. Working for the unity of the Churches is an essential part of faith and therefore it involves risk. One of the great obstacles to unity is our assumption, usually unacknowledged, that we know what unity means in practice, and so we refuse to co-operate in case we are led astray from our notion of unity. We confuse unity with uniformity, a confusion I once heard explicitly expressed when a celebrant at Mass invited the congregation, when exchanging the sign of Peace, to welcome one another with a handshake, 'sign of our uniformity'. God preserve us from uniformity! God's Spirit is a Spirit which delights in variety and holds together in unity brain cells and toe-nails, lions and lambs, elephants and fleas. Unity can never be found in uniformity. The heart of ecumenism is in prayer, because prayer is openness to the Holy Spirit, who prays within us. If our prayer is genuine, inevitably it will lead us into unity within ourselves and with other Christians, but it will also be a unity which wants to embrace the whole human race and all creation. Denominational loyalty which is not permeated and dominated by a desire for unity, fosters disunity and therefore cuts off its members from God, even although they may multiply their religious services, increase their membership, their church buildings and their bank balances.

If Christian Churches are serious about worshipping God, as distinct from worshipping their own spiritual security, if they are really more intent on mission than on maintenance, then they must combine and co-operate in whatever area they may find themselves, working for the good not only of church members, but of all the people in the area. In attempting to do this they will run into all kinds of difficulties, and the constant temptation will be to pull back, but this is to pull back from God. Once we begin to co-operate, in however modest a way, then we begin to see the truth of the statement, 'Act and you will understand.' We also begin to see more clearly the subtleties of the destructive spirit masquerading under the appearance of good and of half truths. 'We must proceed cautiously in our ecumenical work.' 'We must always be faithful to our own tradition.' 'We must not, in our attempts to be friendly, betray the Gospel.' All these phrases are true, but they are so often used to save us from the effort of going out to others, to protect us from demands we are unwilling to face. The language of prudence and orthodoxy can be used to disguise bigotry, love of power and control, narrowness of vision and lack of trust.

It was sad to hear that in Germany today couples who marry across the denominations meet, not with support, but with obstacles from the clergy, so that many, in consequence, leave the Church. There are problems in any marriage in which the partners do not share the same religious belief, and these problems would remain even if the clergy were models of understanding, but at present they are far from being so, and not only in Germany. St John says, 'God is love', and God does not appear to share the anxiety of his clergy, for men and women of different Christian denominations and of different faiths are drawn to live in marriage together. Real ecumenism today is being lived and practised within the Church of the family, and there the real problems of ecumenism are encountered. I know many couples, both committed Christians, but of different denominations, who have suffered agonies from the treatment they have received from unsympathetic clergy who cannot see further than a rule book. These couples do not feel they are listened to when they tell of their own experience and of the help they find in sharing in one another's church services, including sharing in the Eucharist, or when they express their desire to have their children brought up to be familiar with both denominations. Mixed-marriage couples need special pastoral care from the clergy of their respective denominations because they have chosen to live out together the unity of Father, Son and Holy Spirit to which the whole Church is bound and the Church has to listen to and be taught by their experience.

In 1982, while I was still at St Beuno's, someone sent me a book called *Holiness* by Donald Nicholl. I found the book fascinating, a study of holiness in major world religions, and in my 'thank-you' letter wrote that I was sorry to read that Donald Nicholl was in the U.S.A., for I would love to have met him. A few weeks later two men dropped in at St Beuno's on a casual visit, one of them a very tall and striking-looking man. It was Donald Nicholl, returned from the United States and on his way to take up a new appointment as Rector of Tantur, an ecumenical centre near Bethlehem, built after the Second Vatican Council as a place in which Scripture scholars of different Christian denominations could come for study and research. While showing Donald and his friend round the house I told him that I had been thinking of walking to Jerusalem sometime and that it was an amazing coincidence that he had come, for I had hoped to meet him and now discovered he was going to be living near Jerusalem. He replied, 'Nothing happens by chance,' a phrase I have never forgotten. I also told him that I was afraid I might not get permission to make the pilgrimage as some of my brethren did not consider it a useful way of spending a sabbatical. A few days later I had a card from Donald in which he suggested I ask not for a few months leave, but for three years to write a Ph.D. on 'Comparative views of Pilgrimage to Jerusalem from the fifth to the tenth century'! I heard nothing more from him until about a year later when the Jesuit Provincial was making his annual visit during which he sees each member of the community. A few minutes before I was due to go in and see the Provincial, when I intended asking if I might attempt Jerusalem on foot sometime, the post arrived, including a postcard from Donald showing the garden of Tantur and assuring me that there were plenty of trees under which I could pitch my tent when I reached Jerusalem. 'Nothing happens by chance', and this postcard confirmed for me that someday I must go to Jerusalem.

Tuesday, March 17

I was so tired when I went to bed after the conversation with Christoph and Claudia that I noticed little about the room in which I was sleeping. Next morning I looked at the many posters and pictures on the walls, one of them being a prayer, a German translation of a Celtic prayer attributed to St Patrick. I did not recognise the prayer, nor make a note of it at the time, but the gist of it was, 'May the sun shine on you and light up your heart, so that you become like a candle burning in the window of the house welcoming the stranger in from the storm. May you treat the earth gently, so that the earth may lie gently on you, as you make your journey from this mortal body to find your home in God.' It was Tuesday, March 17th, the feast of St Patrick. 'Nothing happens by chance.'

After breakfast with Claudia and Christoph and the three children, who treated me as though I were a permanent resident, I left Brensbach in a heavy snowfall which continued all morning until I reached Bad König, a popular spa, its streets almost deserted because of the weather and because Tuesday was 'Ruhetag' with most shops and restaurants closed. I wandered its streets looking for a place to eat, hauling Mungo, which now looked like a mobile snowman, behind me. At first, in Holland and Germany, I had always taken Mungo with me into restaurants, but at Bad König I was assured it would be safe to leave the haversack outside when I entered an empty pizza restaurant. I sat by a window able to keep an eye on Mungo gathering more snow outside. Before serving me the waitress brought a candle to my table and lit it. Nothing happens by chance. There is a unity in all things and love is at the heart of the universe, if only we can recognise it.

Iona is a small island off the west coast of Scotland, where Columba arrived in the sixth century, and from Iona, excellently placed for travel by coracle, he evangelised Scotland. It was on Iona that I first heard the phrase, 'the veil is thin here,' meaning the veil which separates earth from heaven, the veil which separates us from the vision of God, who is in all things and who plays and laughs, as well as weeps in all creation. On the road to Jerusalem I caught many glimpses of the thin veil. As I walked the roads I often thought of those Celtic monks, who wandered through Europe, wondering at the glory of God's creation, preaching the Gospel and founding monasteries. At first they were imaginary figures from the distant past, but they are in God, who is eternal, that is, always in the now, in the God who keeps my legs going along these roads, so those Celtic saints are as near to me as the living, in fact nearer. Why shouldn't St Patrick cheer me up on the road, just as the waitress cheered me by lighting the candle at the table? Following this line of thought, I found myself talking with these figures from the past and with my own dead relatives and friends, especially with my sister Marie, who had died forty years earlier. These conversations became very natural and they could be very helpful in decision making. I realise, even as I write, that this will sound as odd to some readers as it would have seemed to me before I tried it.

Provided the wind was not too cold nor the snow too heavy, I loved this walking through the snow-covered landscape in woods and farmland, through old villages where the farmyards abutted the main road, past wayside shrines of Our Lady. From Bad König the road climbed through forest and during the afternoon, with the snow still falling, I reached Vielbrunn. This was 12 km short of Amorbach, which I had hoped to reach by the end of the day, but I was too tired to continue. The gasthaus proprietor in Vielbrunn could not have been more kind. He welcomed me in, offering me cake and coffee on the house and he did not mind the puddle of water forming on his floor as the snow melted from Mungo and me. The gasthaus did not serve evening meals so I shopped in the village, bought what I thought at the time was an excellent supper and cooked it in my room on my camping stove. I was able to prepare a meal in less than five minutes, the time required to boil the water for packet soup, taken with large quantities of bread, with cheese or tomatoes. During this first course, the rice was cooking. When ready, I would mix in with it a tin of meat or fish, stew or pâté. On this occasion it was stew. The dessert course was fruit, preferably bananas and condensed milk, if I could find them. Meanwhile the water for coffee was heating, and the final course was bread or biscuits and cheese. As I ate supper I could hear the thaw. I slept well and woke to hear the birds singing and see the roads cleared of snow.

Wednesday, March 18

I could feel spring in the air and walked happily for the first three hours, mostly downhill and through forests, so that I was at Amorbach well before midday with only 17 km to go by main road to Walldürn, a famous pilgrimage centre, which was my destination for the night. As I was feeling energetic and in order to avoid the main road, I decided, without looking too closely at the map, to take a minor road to Walldürn. This would add another 7 km to the route but promised to be a quiet road through woodland. It was quiet and the road climbed steadily for the first 8 km. Then the wind rose, the snow began and suddenly I felt ill – a cold sweat and stomach pains, a raging thirst and slight dizziness. I knew it was because of the stew I had eaten the night before. At the summit there was a windswept village with no shops. At a closed restaurant, they did sell me from the back door two bottles of mineral water which I drank in the village bus shelter. The thought of food was nauseating. Beyond the village there were more roads than my map indicated and they did not have signposts. I stopped at a house to ask directions and had walked another 2 km when I found more unsignposted roads and not a house in sight. I went to take out my compass and discovered it was not in my pocket. I last remembered having it at the house 2 km back, so I retracked and found the compass lying beneath the snow on the ledge of the house porch.

The remaining 16 km into Walldürn were by far the most

difficult stretch of the pilgrimage so far. There was a fierce and cold headwind, driving snow, now covering Mungo's wheels, and I was feeling ill, weak and a bloody fool. My thoughts then took a very morbid turn.

I imagined I was walking in this kind of weather, but in the total darkness, day and night, of a nuclear winter. There would be no hope of finding food or shelter at the end of the day's walk, because all the towns and villages would be devastated. Paper money and travellers' cheques would be useless. I would be suffering not only hunger, cold and the results of last night's stew, but the loss of all my family and friends, my skin peeling off, wracked with pain, and fearful of meeting another human being because in their hunger and desperation they would rob me of anything I had, their self-preservation instinct blotting out every other consideration. I realised that these morbid thoughts were not fanciful and that this nightmare vision was also a glimpse through the thin veil of the reality in which we are living. We are a button's pressure away from the reality of a nuclear winter. A tiny percentage of our nuclear armament would be enough to destroy all life on earth for **ever**. **S**uch disaster could befall us without any deliberate act of aggression by any nation. There have already been hundreds of computer errors which have put the American Air Force on Red Alert by mistake. Such errors are concealed from the general public, who are assured that there is no need for alarm.

On the road to Walldürn I saw more clearly than ever the madness and horror of nuclear deterrence and the awful sinfulness of it. The evil is not just in the possibility that these weapons may destroy the earth; the evil is in the intention to use them. Imagining the darkness and terror of a nuclear winter, I also heard the reassuring voices of our political leaders and of some of our churchmen and philosophers. 'After all, we must remember that we are living in a real world, which really is sinful and includes enemies whose one desire is our destruction. In these sinful circumstances it is morally defensible to defend ourselves with nuclear weapons.' Hitler, were he alive, would thoroughly approve of these politicians, churchmen and philosophers, for he too believed that the only answer to terror is terror. Goering, in 1945, said, 'Why, of course, people don't want war. It is the leaders who determine the policy, and it is always a simple matter to drag the people along, whether it is a democracy, or a communist dictatorship. All you have to do is tell them that they are being attacked, and denounce pacifists for lack of patriotism and for exposing the country to danger. It works the same way in any country.'

As I walked through the storm, I heard the voice of Britain, as it has been so clearly expressed many times by Margaret Thatcher, 'It is unthinkable that Britain should ever renounce its independent nuclear deterrent.' She is not to be blamed for the remark as if she alone were responsible for it: she is simply expressing the majority view of the country. But what appalling arrogance the remark betrays. 'It is unthinkable . . .'; the statement, 'I cannot see how we can defend ourselves without nuclear weapons,' is turned into, 'It is unthinkable . . .'. My views, or my country's views, become for me the measure of all truth and set the limits to all thinking and imagining, so that the blinkered vision of one individual, or group, is presented as the standard of thinking and imagining for all peoples of all time. Every individual and every nation has a right to defend itself. What is in question is not the right to self defence; what is in question is a mode of defence which threatens the rights of other individuals and nations. Nuclear deterrence cannot be a legitimate means of defence, because of its nature it deprives other individuals and nations of their right to life. Nuclear deterrence can only deter because it includes a real intention not only of destroying the military forces of the enemy, but also of inflicting 'an unacceptable' loss on the enemy. 'Unacceptable loss' can sound quite respectable. What it means, in fact, is that the deterrent deters because it can destroy over one-third of the enemy's civilian population. No nation can defend its own values by nuclear deterrence without assuming that its values, and its values alone, are absolute, because the nuclear deterrent, of its nature, threatens all human life.

Those few kilometres in the storm on the way to Walldürn were among the most important to me of the whole pilgrimage. Imagining the nuclear winter showed me a meaning in what at some other times seemed a fruitless gesture – walking the roads to Jerusalem drawing the ridiculous Mungo behind me – and it kept me going when I was tempted to give up. The walk was a gesture of surrender to God, a way of protesting that as far as I am concerned, I do not want to be defended by nuclear arms and would prefer a life in prison or in a concentration camp rather than collude in the murder of innocents. At the moment of death and at the final judgement I do not want to face the millions who have died in agony, have been maimed for life, have been born deformed, these millions for whom Christ died and in whom he lives, and know that I supported, or silently colluded in this crime.

The devil is the father of lies. It is a lie that we can possibly defend ourselves with nuclear weapons. They will be the means of our own destruction. The policy of nuclear deterrence is rooted in pride, the sin which refuses to let God be God. Sin is national as well as individual. The Old Testament prophets were very clear on this point. They did not point out the sins of individuals; it was the sin of the nation which they castigated; individuals were only mentioned in so far as they were representative of the people. In our policy of nuclear deterrence we are caught up in national sin, and sin inevitably brings destruction unless there is repentance.

Why is it that intelligent, gifted, conscientious, kind people can support a policy of nuclear deterrence so strongly that no political party in the West stands any chance of being elected unless it endorses such a policy? Part of the reason is ignorance, and partly it is lack of imagination. Probably only a tiny minority of deterrence supporters have any idea of what it means, in fact. That is why in argument they almost always fall back on the question, 'And what would have happened if we had not defended ourselves against the Nazis in 1939?' The total firepower used in the Second World War was only a fraction of the total firepower contained in one Trident submarine, but our imagination cannot grasp this fact.

When Captain Cook first approached the Australian coast line in his ship, the natives took no notice and continued fishing by the shore, because such a ship was beyond their experience. But when the long boats were launched from the ship and the men began to row ashore, then the natives reacted. We are like those natives in our failure to recognise the meaning of nuclear deterrence. Ignorance and lack of imagination are as destructive as hurricanes and earthquakes.

In all the arguments I have read in favour of nuclear deterrence. I have never met any which make appeal to the imagination. Our culture, which divinises reason and dismisses emotion and imagination, leads us into a national schizophrenia, so that in the name of reason and common sense we can treat one another brutally. I would like to see compulsory courses in use of the imagination for all politicians and every parliamentary debate beginning with an imaginative exercise on the effect of the legislation which is being proposed. Those politicians who lack imagination would be placed in simulated situations for a period before they were allowed to speak. In debates among Christians on the morality of nuclear weapons, I have rarely come across any appeal to imagination or any obvious sign that the views being expressed have first been brought into prayer. I have attended many church services in which the congregation prays for peace, but I have never heard nuclear deterrence expressed as a prayer for peace. 'Dear Lord, inspire our scientists that they may invent yet more lethal weapons (to deter, Lord, not that we want to use them), preserve us from any unfortunate accident in their testing (lest we have something worse than Chernobyl in our own country), bless our economy that we may put these weapons into plentiful production (otherwise we cannot deter and so preserve peace), strengthen our leaders lest they waver in a strong defence policy, preserve them from being swayed by emotion or imagination, drive out from our midst any who, by thought, word or deed, threaten our national security, and grant us the protection of nuclear weapons now and for ever. Amen.' When our political, social and economic views are expressed in prayer before God, they begin to feel different and what we formerly held with great assurance and certainty, causes an uncomfortable feeling in our midriff so that we begin to realise that we must exclude not only emotion and imagination, but prayer as well, 'lest we waver in a strong defence policy'.

When we pray for peace, profess that God is our rock, refuge and strength, yet at the same time entrust ourselves to the protection of the most murderous weapons ever invented, we are living a lie, for truth is in deeds, not words.

As dusk was falling I saw Walldürn and its church spire

in the valley below. When I rang the presbytery bell a house-keeper answered and then summoned a nun. By this time I had a set formula of introduction, 'Good evening. I wonder if you could possibly help me. I am a Scot walking to Jerusalem and I should be most grateful if you could recommend some place in town where I could find cheap lodgings for the night. As I have a sleeping bag and mat with me, I can make do on a floor.' The nun, looked at me with obvious disapproval and said, 'I suppose you expect us to provide for your arrival without any preliminary notice?' I was too tired to be angry and just asked whether it was necessary to give preliminary warning at this presbytery before asking for information about lodgings in the town. She took this well, led me to a room where she began telephoning, explaining to her hearers that she had a Scot in the presbytery who could speak German, seemed honest, and was looking for lodgings for the night. She then summoned two youngsters to lead me through the snow to Frau Mairion's house. She was a kindly, elderly woman living in a house which was so clean and polished that it sparkled. She showed me to a basement room with a bed covered with the largest duvet I had ever seen. Although the request was for bed and breakfast, she offered to make me supper as all the shops were closed. I had not eaten since breakfast, but I still had no appetite and wanted only a hot drink before collapsing under the duvet. My tiredness vanished as I drank the tea and listened to Frau Mairion telling me about life in Walldürn under the Nazis and during the war. When she married in the 1930s, a relative, a Nazi official, had given her, as a wedding present, a copy of Hitler's *Mein Kampf*. (I later learned that this gift was given to all married couples under the Third Reich, which must have done wonders for Adolph's royalties!) When the American troops drew near to Walldürn at the end of the war she had burned her copy, and her Nazi relative became an ardent supporter of the Allied cause. Although she and her husband hated the Nazis and had both suffered much during the war, she still felt, over forty years later, that Hitler had been ill served by his subordinates and that he was not responsible for the atrocities of the Jewish holocaust and of the war.

She talked much of her husband, who had died a few years before, saying how present he seemed to her, how she talked to him and always consulted him about whatever she was doing. Then suddenly she became self-conscious and said, 'I have never told anyone I do this because they would think I am mad.' I told her I had been doing this with my own dead relatives and friends on the road to Walldürn.

Thursday, March 19–Friday, March 20

Because I was so tired, I asked if I might stay for two nights, hoping to spend the following day in writing an article for the English Catholic weekly, *The Tablet*, to which I had promised a series of six articles to be written on the road to Jerusalem. In fact, I spent most of the next day under the duvet and did not write a word. I could not remember ever having felt so tired. It snowed almost all day and the snow was so deep on the Friday that I stayed another night in Walldürn, doing some writing at last and also seeing something of the town.

Walldürn became a pilgrimage centre in the fifteenth century. According to a sixteenth-century account, its origins as a pilgrimage centre go back to 1330 when a priest accidentally knocked over the chalice while celebrating Mass. The spilled wine looked like blood and formed on the altar cloth a picture of Christ on the cross surrounded by a ring of pictures of Christ's crowned head. The priest was so frightened that he removed a stone from the altar, hid the blood-stained cloth and replaced the stone, telling no one of his action until he was on his deathbed. When the cloth was recovered the miracles began, and in 1445 Pope Eugene declared Walldürn to be an official place of pilgrimage. The pilgrims are still coming, including an annual group of walking pilgrims from Cologne. Frau Mairion entertained me one evening with stories of the pilgrims who had come to her house over the years, as varied and as colourful as in Chaucer's time.

Each morning at Walldürn I went to the 7.00 Mass in the main church. On the first morning I was puzzled by the congregation striking matches at the start of Mass and applying them to little metal boxes containing curled up tapers, which they kept burning throughout the service. Frau Mairion explained to me later that these tapers are burned by friends and relatives whenever an anniversary requiem Mass was being celebrated. Before leaving Walldürn I presented my unworn jeans, which I had been carrying since the day I bought them, for the use of some needy pilgrim.

Saturday, March 21

This was a day of brilliant sunshine and the beginning of another thaw. I had fully recovered from the effects of Tuesday's stew and walked 40 km to a village called Dainbach, where I found cheap lodgings in a beautiful house set on a hillside with a balconied room overlooking rolling, wooded countryside. The bedroom was spacious with large windows to the south and east. I was tempted to linger there, telling myself that it would be an excellent place in which to write *The Tablet* article, but I decided to push on to Munich.

Sunday, March 22

March 22nd was my birthday and the Gospel reading at Mass was from John, chapter 4, about the woman at the well of Samaria to whom Jesus said, 'The water I shall give you will turn into a spring, welling up to eternal life.' I thought about these words as I walked the 40 km from Dainbach to Blaufelden, a glorious stretch along country roads, meeting the occasional deer, the fields and forests snow-covered and sparkling in the sun. I remembered a spring I had seen in the Clwyd valley next to the ruin of a fifteenth-century church. The well was beautifully constructed in cruciform shape on the outside of one of the ruined walls. The clear water was still springing up in the centre of the well, but the edges were covered in dead leaves, moss and dirt. This well I have found a most useful image of the soul, for I imagined that one of the little specks of dirt, which I could see dancing in the movement of the spring, represented my human consciousness. Our conscious minds are only a tiny part of our intelligence and they can only grasp a minuscule fraction of what is going on within us and around us. Think, for example, of the intelligence of every cell in our body, and there are millions of them, each unique to us and as intricate in their construction as the galaxies. How do they know how to react to the coffee and toast we have for breakfast and ensure transportation and right distribution throughout the body, and how do they co-operate in turning this intake into energy, into thoughts, desires and longings? Yet in our arrogance we speak of 'I', as though the conscious 'I' was the whole of ourselves. I imagined the little speck dancing to the force of the spring and saying to itself, 'I am happy, I am delighting in life, I know that I am held in being and sustained by a power greater than I, welling up within me.' The speck feels God's nearness and experiences something of his presence. Then through the movement of wind and water the little speck moves to the side of the well and lodges among the dead leaves and slime. It then announces, 'Life is ghastly. My life is useless. I am a complete failure. Nothing makes sense any more. My previous delight in life must have been an illusion. This is the reality and there is nothing more to hope for.' My reality is far greater than my consciousness, which is necessarily very limited and narrowly blinkered. 'The water I shall give will turn into a spring inside you, welling up to eternal life.' This image of the well helped me to understand the strange saying of St Catherine of Genoa, 'My God is me, nor do I recognise any other me except my God himself.'

In Blaufelden I found a church, but no presbytery, inquired about lodgings and was told there were two hotels in the town. The first was fully booked and the second was closed. Near the church there was a gasthaus with large signs outside it advertising Guinness and offering cheap excursions to Ireland. I thanked the Celtic saints for this and ordered a Guinness before inquiring about lodgings in the area. The barman told me that failing the hotels, the only lodgings were 7 km away. It was already dark and I was too tired to go further, so I commended myself to the Celtic saints and began on the Guinness. A young man, who had overheard my inquiry at the bar, came to my table. 'Why don't you try the Pfarrer?' he asked and offered to take me there. The Pfarrer's wife answered the door, knew the young man, and invited us both in, taking us to a room with a table set in the corner. 'I am so glad you have come,' she said, 'because I invited two people for coffee and cakes this afternoon and neither of them turned up, so you must have it instead.' We sat down to a colosssal pile of cream cakes and coffee. Later, her husband arrived, a small energetic-looking man who rushed into the room like a whirlwind, listened to my story, then rushed out again. Within seconds he was back to say that he had found me accommodation and would drive me to the place 7 km away. When I went to pay the bill next morning, I was told that the Pfarrer had already paid it!

Monday, March 23

The veil felt very thin as I set off for Dinkelsbühl. Nothing happens by chance, and I thanked God for the birthday party and for Dekan and Frau Rhemalin, who had shown me such extraordinary kindness.

On Monday evening I reached Dinkelsbühl on the Romantic Way, a walled city of cobbled streets and medieval buildings, its east gateway dating from the thirteenth century.

Tuesday, March 24

Next morning I wandered through the town looking at its beautiful buildings and some of its magnificent churches before continuing along the Romantic Way to Nördlingen, an even larger walled city. There was a slight thaw. Patches of grass were appearing, but they were brown after weeks under the snow, and the occasional catkin was the only sign of spring. On the road to Nördlingen I met two tramps on the road, who stopped to admire Mungo and asked about the name plaque and whether such machines were mass-produced in Britain, so I told them Mungo was utterly unique and likely to remain so.

At Nördlingen I went to the Catholic church to inquire about lodgings. The presbytery was large, set in a spacious garden with a locked gate and a bell on the outside. When I pressed the bell a voice asked, 'What do you want?', so I gave my formula. The voice said, 'Try the police station,' to which

I replied, 'What a splendid idea. I hadn't thought of that.' I found a gasthaus round the corner which provided a bed and an excellent meal.

Wednesday, March 25

The Romantic Way had been heavy with traffic, mostly heavy lorries, which sent up showers of spray as they passed, so I took to country roads beyond Nördlingen and found myself on a forestry path which ended in a cul-de-sac. To recover the right road I had a most uncomfortable 3 km walking cross-country with Mungo on my shoulders, but it was worth the detour, for it brought me to a very long stretch of deserted road through a forest of tall pine trees, which provided a deep and friendly silence. In the late evening I crossed the grey Danube, flowing fast with melted snow under a leaden sky, but with light still breaking through in the west, as though the sun was sinking in tears. When I reached Mertingen, it was already dark and the lights were on in the church where the Mass of the Annunciation, March 25th, was being celebrated.

After Mass I was directed to lodgings in a gasthaus 2 km out of town. It was beginning to rain heavily as I arrived. All the visitors and the barman were sitting attentively at the T.V. screen watching a football match between Israel and West Germany. The barman told me there was no room, nor did he know of any place where I might find one, and he rushed back to the T.V. I sat contemplating a beer and a first night's camping in wet and freezing weather. West Germany won the match and the barman was in a much better mood, consulted his wife and told me that although it was out of season I could have a room, provided I did not mind a cold one.

Thursday, March 26

On Thursday I was back on the Romantic Way for a brief spell, had a good stretch on minor roads and then a miserable 12 km along a narrow main road with a constant stream of heavy rush-hour traffic. The road had no hard shoulder, the verge ending abruptly and a few inches higher than the churned mud which bordered it. Mungo was hard to draw through the mud and keeled over frequently while I was being showered with spray from the passing lorries. The Dachau concentration camp was a few kilometres off my route, but I decided not to go there as I had seen it thirty years before and had already walked 48 km that day. I found a *pension* on the outskirts of Dachau and made straight for Munich next day.

Friday, March 27

It rained heavily and continuously the whole way into Munich, where I arrived at the main railway station at 1.00 p.m. My thoughts matched the weather, for I remembered my visit to the Dachau concentration camp thirty years earlier and the effect it had on me.

In Frankfurt in 1958 we had a film one evening, a French documentary showing the German concentration camps as the Allies found them at the end of the war and including shots from film confiscated from the Germans and taken during the war. It was far worse than any horror film and did not spare the viewer in its gruesome shots of piles of emaciated corpses, of the gas chambers and incinerators. At the end of the film there was a stunned silence and most of the audience were in tears. After that film and a later visit to Dachau, the question which obsessed my mind was, 'How is it that such a gifted, intelligent and cultured nation, the majority Christian, and nurtured by centuries of Christianity, can sink to this level of evil?' At the time my own answer was that there must be some flaw in the German character and I was quite certain that such things could never happen in Britain. Thirty years later I think differently.

The lesson of Dachau and of the other concentration camps is a lesson not only for Germans, but for every nation, a lesson which is lost when made to apply to Germany only. Evil masquerades under the appearance of good, and the Nazi régime offered much that was good to a demoralised and divided nation, oppressed by the injustices of the treaty of Versailles, burdened with an impossible reparations debt, humiliated by France, with over 5,000,000 people unemployed and its small business people ruined, while the very wealthy grew richer on the misery of the many. National Socialism promised to redress the injustices following on 1918, to revive the economy and abolish unemployment, to curb, control and, if necessary, to destroy the large businesses and cartels working to serve their own greed rather than the good of the nation. It also undertook to encourage and support small businesses and private enterprise, reduce crime and restore law and order, to root out Communism and to restore Germany to its rightful place among the nations. The party also took a high moral tone, advocating hard work, cleanliness, temperance, truthfulness, self-sacrifice and loyalty. It tried to woo, rather than oppose, the large national institutions, including the Churches, and Hitler was careful to avoid anti-clericalism while coming to power. On coming to power the Nazis did reduce unemployment. They also encouraged private enterprise, restored the economy, reduced the crime rate and won massive support. The nation was united as never before, fasting together on one day a week, when all were encouraged to eat only a one-pot meal, the savings to go to winter relief for those still suffering the hardship of poverty. There was great emphasis on the physical health and hardihood of the nation and on cultural pursuits, music, art and literature. There was a plan, never effected but attempted, to have a library for every group of five hundred people. The cultural emphasis, like the emphasis on morality, was selective, to ensure that it fitted in with the narrow nationalism of the Third Reich. The Nazis were the enthusiastic inheritors, not the initiators of anti-semitism, so that their doctrine of racial purity found ready acceptance in the nation, and although some individuals and groups did not approve, the majority silently colluded.

It is easy to condemn with hindsight, but if the condemnation remains condemnation of the German nation and does not see that any nation can follow the same path, the condemnation is useless and the crimes of the holocaust will be repeated.

Hitler had known years of poverty and unemployment in

his own youth in Austria, had served in the German army during the First World War, rising to the rank of corporal and ending the war in hospital, blind as a result of a gas attack, to face more years of post-war unemployment. He seethed with resentment at his own past, his failure to be accepted at art college or as a student of architecture, seethed too against the German leaders, who had capitulated to the Allies and signed the armistice while the German army was still intact and undefeated. Hatred and resentment are powerful emotions which lodge deep in the soul, infecting every perception and reaction in the individual, who then communicates it to others and releases in them their own worst, meanest and most destructive emotions. Hitler was a demagogue of surpassing skill, who knew how to play on the meanest instincts of the masses, for he was so well in touch with his own. He also knew how to present his policies under the appearance of good so that he could win the support of thoroughly respectable people. Bishop Gröber, the diocesan bishop of Max Metzger, issued instructions to his diocese that all religious classes in schools were to begin and end with the greeting 'Heil Hitler'. Once in power, in the name of nationalism, national pride, law and order and national security, the nation was enslaved to its own idols, wreaked havoc in Europe, and infected its enemies with its own violence.

Among those who reflected in Germany after the war on the question, 'How did we allow this to happen to us?' the constant refrain was, 'We lacked discernment. Apart from a few exceptions who suffered imprisonment or death for their insights, we did not read the signs of the times in time.' The lesson of Dachau is for all nations and it cries out to us, 'Read the signs of our own times,' but we are not reading them in Britain and the majority of the population support, for example, our nuclear defence policy to defend what we are pleased to call our freedom and national values. Our freedom and national values are important and must be defended, but a nuclear defence policy is, in fact, a complete denial of those very values. Freedom won through terror, freedom which is freedom of choice for a few and oppression or annihilation for the many, is not freedom but tyranny. Nationalism, which is an appeal to greed and to the disregard of other nations and of groups within our own nation, is a pernicious, destructive doctrine which inevitably leads to disaster, not only for our enemies, but also for ourselves. In Britain, we are as much in danger of narrow nationalism as Germany was in the 1930s and the signs are clear for anyone with eyes to see and ears to hear. In the name of national security, there has been a steady erosion of civil liberties, each step justified in the name of law and order. The damage, for example, done by the I.R.A. is not only in the bombs they plant, but also the way they infect the British Government with their own violence, leading it to restrict civil liberties, to trials without jury, to the assumption of emergency powers, detention without trial, shooting without trial, increased media censorship, central control, introduction of new legislation – not as a protection of the nation's freedom, but to crush opposition. The destructiveness is not something which might happen in the future: it is something which is happening now, especially among the minority caught in the poverty trap and living in the inner cities in conditions of cold, hunger and misery, of which most of the population are completely unaware, so that a cabinet minister could declare in public that there is no longer poverty in Britain. The majority in Britain, as the majority in Germany in the 1930s, are prospering financially under our present regime and are therefore tempted not to look too closely at what is happening, while the poor become poorer and feel more helpless.

A month before I set out on the pilgrimage, I had planned to spend a few days at the Jesuit house of philosophy in the Kaulbachstrasse in Munich, to rest, do some sightseeing, meet peace groups, answer letters and write another article for *The Tablet*. In fact, I had arrived several days ahead of schedule. I was given a warm welcome and shown to a spacious room on the ground floor where, I was told, Father Karl Rahner had spent his last years. So I prayed for his help in writing *The Tablet* article and for the next stage of the journey.

6

Light in the Darkness – Bavaria, Austria

> We do not become enlightened by imagining figures of light,
> but by making the darkness conscious.   (Carl Jung)

Saturday, March 28

I had spent July 1957 in Munich, then the most beautiful
city I had ever seen, and I was an assiduous visitor of its
baroque churches, art museums, opera house. On one memorable Saturday evening I visited, along with a few thousand
other people, the Hofbraühaus, eating sausages and drinking
beer from the largest glass I had ever seen. It puzzled me
then, and it has puzzled me since, that it was in this beautiful
city and among these friendly, good-humoured and apparently easy-going people, mostly Catholic, the Nazi party had
begun after the First World War. In 1923 Hitler had come
near to effecting a *putsch* in Munich, which might have
brought him to power ten years earlier.

Of all the churches I had visited, the one which stood out
in my memory was the Michaelskirche, the Jesuit parish
church, set in the middle of the central shopping area. Whenever I visited it there were always crowds of people praying
at a side altar where Father Rupert Mayer s.j. was buried.
Father Rupert Mayer had come to the Michaelskirche in
1922, where he soon became well known as a preacher, con-
fessor and adviser, and was called 'Munich's helper in distress'. He believed in the need for collaboration between
clergy and laity in the Church and built up a body of laity,
nurtured on the Spiritual Exercises and called a 'Sodality',
until it numbered 8,000 members in Munich. He also helped
to establish a group known as the 'Sisters of the Holy Family'

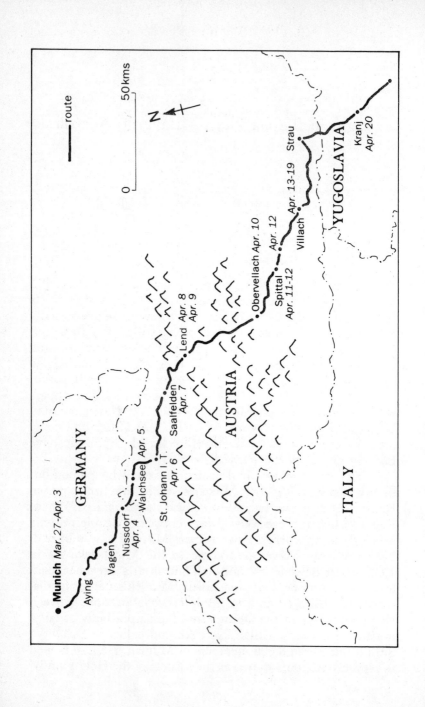

to answer the critical needs of the poor in Munich, especially of the large numbers of immigrants. He introduced a reception system for visitors and immigrant workers in the city's main railway station, and celebrated Mass there regularly on Sundays at 3.00 and 4.00 a.m.! He read the signs of the times and practised discernment of spirits on the Nazi regime, giving the results of his discernment to his Mass congregations in the Michaelskirche. His preaching was especially effective after 1933 when Catholic organisations and publications were systematically weakened and eventually forbidden by the Nazis. It was only a matter of time before he would be arrested. Informers attended his services and took notes, to be used later in evidence against him. On 5 June 1937 he was arrested by the Gestapo, convicted of being in violation of the 'Internal Treason Act' and of 'misuse of the pulpit'. As long as religion and spirituality were well insulated from everyday life, the Nazis were happy to tolerate it. Rupert Mayer's faith was not insulated, for he saw God in all things and in all relationships. Politics is about our structural relationships within a nation and between nations, and therefore those governments which maintain that the pulpit is no place for politics in the broadest sense are denying the God whom Christians worship, even although they may themselves be regular churchgoers. Father Mayer was sentenced to six months imprisonment and he was also banned from the pulpit. When, after his term of imprisonment, he reappeared in the pulpit with the permission of his superiors, he was again arrested in January 1938, released a few weeks later, but rearrested at the beginning of the war and sent to the Oranienburg concentration camp in November 1939. His health deteriorated because of malnutrition and the winter cold, and to avoid making a martyr of him, the Nazis ordered him to be confined in the Benedictine monastery of Ettal, where he remained until the end of the war. In May 1945, broken in health but not in spirit, he returned to what was left of Munich after the war. On 1 November 1945, while preaching on the feast of All Saints, he suffered a fatal stroke and died shortly afterwards. On 3 May 1987, Pope John Paul came to Munich and performed the beatification ceremony, giving him the title, 'Blessed Rupert Mayer', the penultimate step in the lengthy process of canonisation in the Catholic Church, naming him, 'the Apostle of Munich'.

On this visit to Munich I had no inclination for sightseeing, for I had some immediate practical jobs to do, such as getting new soles and heels fitted on my shoes, which had little heel left and very thin soles. Mungo's tyres were also very worn, and although I had a spare pair, I reckoned I would need a third pair before Jerusalem, and Munich was the most likely place to buy them. I also wanted to buy more detailed maps of Yugoslavia and, if possible, meet someone who knew the country and could advise me about routes and the possibility of walking through Albania. Pax Christi in Frankfurt had given me names and addresses of the Munich branch, which I wanted to visit. In addition, there were letters to answer, an article to write for *The Tablet*, and I wanted to have a good rest before starting on the most strenuous part of the pilgrimage through Austria and Yugoslavia.

Munich, 25 miles north of the Alps, has a plethora of shoe and boot repair shops, but after trying a few of them, the earliest date they could give me for the repair of my shoes, to be fitted with mountain soles and heels, was 2nd April, which would mean delaying my departure until Friday, April 3rd.

I asked where I could buy tyres for Mungo and was directed to an enormous wholesale tyre depot in the south of the city. There I joined a queue of well dressed businessmen, who, judging by the size of their orders, seemed to be representatives of multi-national transport companies. The gentleman taking orders on the other side of the glass did not think small was beautiful, nor was he amused, when I produced a replica of Mungo's tyre from my jacket pocket and asked if I might have a pair of them. He directed me back to a city centre store selling prams. The city centre store tried to be helpful, showed me their expensive prams, but told me they could not sell me tyres unless I bought a pram as well. I wrote to Ian Tweedie, telling him of my problem and asking him to send a spare pair of tyres to the Jesuit house in Split, Yugoslavia, where I would collect them. He was so prompt in despatching them that when a package arrived at Split, whoever received it did not know that I would be arriving in a month's time and returned the package to the Post Office to be returned to the sender. It never reached Ian, so the tyres may be a modest contribution from Scotland to Yugoslavia's ailing economy.

I visited the British consulate to make inquiries about Albania, was given an address in Paris to which I wrote explaining that I was a Scot walking to Athens and that my route lay through Albania, that I was looking forward to spending three or four days walking this beautiful country and would be most grateful for a visa for this purpose. There was a reply waiting for me in Split, telling me that I could only enter the country if I was with an officially recognised tourist organisation.

There are so many Yugoslav immigrant workers in Munich that they now have a Catholic parish of their own in the city, so I visited the parish priest, explained what I was doing and showed him my proposed route through the centre of Yugoslavia. He shook his head in disapproval, warned me against the dangers of travel in central Yugoslavia from wolves, bears, atheists, Muslims and Orthodox, and advised me to proceed as directly as possible from Ljubljana to the sea and to walk the beautiful Dalmatian coast, dotted with Franciscan churches, where I could always lodge for the night, so I returned to the Jesuit house and got busy with maps, planning a route along the Dalmatian coast to the borders of Albania. If I could not get a visa for Albania, I would take public transport from the coast to central Yugoslavia and risk the bears and wolves for the few days required before reaching the Greek border.

Sunday, March 29 — Thursday, April 2

On Sunday there was a Mass for English speakers in the Jesuit college where I was staying, and after Mass the congregation met for coffee. Among them were an Irish couple, Kevin and Bridgene Devine, who were very interested in my walk, not because it led to Jerusalem, but because my proposed route along the Dalmatian coast would bring me near to Medjugorje, a mountain village about 90 km from Split, where, it is claimed, the Blessed Virgin Mary has been

113

appearing daily to a group of children since 24 June 1981. Millions of visitors from all over the world have been visiting this tiny village, where thousands claim to have seen the sun dancing, where some have claimed extraordinary physical cures and many more have experienced an inner change which has transformed their lives, bringing peace where there was formerly anxiety, dispelling their sadness, giving them a desire for prayer and fasting, and leading them to adopt a simpler lifestyle. Before setting out on the walk I had seen a BBC Everyman programme on Medjugorje, which had impressed me by its objective reporting of the phenomenon. I had also met Christopher and Mary Campbell-Johnston, brother and sister-in-law of Michael Campbell-Johnston, the Jesuit Provincial. They had also urged me to visit Medjugorje because their own lives had been profoundly affected by a few days in the village. There was a letter from Christopher waiting for me when I reached Munich, telling me that I must visit Medjugorje and offering to make good any expenses I might incur in making the detour.

My initial reaction to any reports of apparitions of Our Lady is one of scepticism, because there have been many reports on such appearances in recent decades – in Portugal, Spain, central and south America, Egypt, Ireland, and even in England. One visionary in Nicaragua claimed that Our Lady had appeared with a message in support of the Contras. This visionary was exceptional in being so blatantly political; most ardent supporters of appearances of Our Lady, in whatever place, tend to an other-worldly spirituality, which provides simple answers to the most complex problems, namely that the salvation of the world will be effected by frequent recitation of the rosary and the practice of penance – penance being understood as the practice of self-deprivation and not, as the Gospel understands it, as a complete change of mind and heart, of inner attitudes and style of living. This, like other forms of simplistic spirituality, saves its adherents from the risk and cost of social and political involvement, and allows them to benefit materially from the unjust social and political structures in which they are living. Or, if they are victims of an unjust system, their spirituality enables them to escape from the reality of the present through the hope of a better life after death, ensured by the regular recitation of the rosary and by adding voluntary deprivations to the deprivations society already imposes upon them. Apparition piety has a special appeal to people of rigid views, usually those on the far right politically and theologically, because such a spirituality does not challenge their thinking, but confirms them in their mental idleness and their unwillingness to face change, so that among the most devoted supporters of appearances of Our Lady can be found some of the staunchest supporters of a nuclear defence policy. Among Roman Catholics, eager supporters of apparition piety also tend to be papalistic, by which I mean that they reduce every argument to a question of obedience to papal authority, although, when this attitude is examined, they are found to have a very selective obedience and are usually not too well versed in the papal social encyclicals. Another phenomenon of apparition piety is that clergy, who are noted for their devotion to Mary, are often chauvinist in their attitude to women.

As a Catholic I was brought up on devotion to Our Lady, and as a small child I had learned the 'Hail Mary' with ease but the 'Our Father' with difficulty. I spent five years at Mount St Mary's, where the school motto was 'Sine Macula' and where the feast of the Immaculate Conception was the most important feast of the school year. On that day we were free from classes, had a solemn High Mass in the morning, a large dinner and a school play in the evening. So Mary was 'a good thing' in my mind, if somewhat remote, a remoteness which remained for years, encouraged by the solemn titles given her in prayer: 'Virgin of Virgins', 'Mother most pure', 'Tower of ivory,' etc., although I did like the title 'Refuge of sinners'. While teaching at Stonyhurst I used to go annually to Lourdes around Eastertime with the sick children's pilgrimage. Seeing the effect of this pilgrimage on the children and watching their delight in praying at the grotto began to change my attitude to Mary. She ceased to be 'Tower of Ivory', and became mother of joy and laughter as well as mother of sorrows.

I had heard enthusiastic reports of Medjugorje from Christopher and Mary Campbell-Johnston whose judgement I trusted, and I knew that the message which the children claimed to be receiving was a message of peace for the whole world, so I decided to make the detour to the village on my way from Split to Dubrovnik.

On Thursday, April 2nd, I walked through the snow-covered streets to the cobbler and collected my shoes, now shod with thick vibram soles and heels. I also spent a few hours sticking some strips of webbing on the worn pram wheels in the hope of prolonging their life, but the webbing was in shreds after two days on the road.

Friday, April 3

The snow had disappeared but there was still a cold east wind blowing as I left Munich by train for Aying, 25 km to the south-east, where I began walking again. After a week of physical idleness I became very weary after the first three hours and my feet were hurting for the first time. The new vibram soles had left slight ridges on the inside sole of both feet, but the pain was rarely severe and the ridges disappeared after a few days. The weariness and discomfort were counterbalanced by a warm sun and the first welcome sight of the snow-covered Bavarian Alps which I was approaching all day, reaching their foothills on Saturday morning.

While in Munich, I spent one evening with a Pax Christi group, who gave me a great welcome, were full of questions about peace groups in Britain and full of information about their own activities in Germany. They were not only involved in political action for nuclear disarmament, including a campaign opposing proposals to manufacture and instal neutron bombs in Germany, bombs whose purpose is to preserve buildings while killing any human beings who may dwell in them, a horrifyingly clear expression of the real scale of values which underlies nuclear defence policies, namely that property is of greater value than persons, but they were also active in promoting East–West contacts, especially with Poland, and in human rights campaigns. Pax Christi in Germany, along with other peace organisations, had succeeded in its campaign to have conscientious objection acknowledged by law, allowing those who refused conscription for military service to do some form of social service instead. Pax Christi was also engaged in work with migrant workers and with other minority groups in the city. All this activity was sustained and strengthened by prayer, fasting, peace pilgrimages and the practice of non-violent direct action. The group spoke, too, of the lack of support they received from the Catholic hierarchy and the stronger encouragement received from the Protestant churches. Although I missed much of their conversation because I was unused to the Bavarian dialect, I understood enough to be impressed by the way they seemed to have integrated their work for peace and their Christian faith, which prompted them not only to oppose the neutron bomb but also to work on behalf of the migrant workers on their own doorstep. They asked me about my route south of Munich and telephoned friends to organise lodgings for my remaining two nights in Germany. The first night's accommodation was in an attic flat belonging to a Pax Christi member, Sepp Rothmayr, in a village called Vagen, where his brother, Hermann and sister-in-law, Irmgard, lived with their four children. They gave me a warm welcome and supper before taking me across the road to the flat. Next morning they invited me over for breakfast and soon I was on the road again for the next stretch to Nüssdorf, where I was to stay with another Pax Christi member, Hans Weinberger.

Saturday, April 4

At first the walking was easy in bright sunshine and a moderate wind with the welcoming mountains ahead of me, but by the afternoon the wind had strengthened and was at gale force as I crossed the Inn river, swollen and fast-flowing with melted snow. I reached Nüssdorf very exhausted and asked for directions to the Weinberger house, only to discover that it was another 7 km away and off my route. Unfortunately, I did not have their telephone number, and I was too tired and footsore after 38 km on the road, so I stayed at a gasthaus in the village for the night and had a large supper of sausage, sauerkraut and beer. Outside a hurricane was blowing, which blew the roof off the Munich sports stadium, according to reports in the next morning's papers.

Sunday, April 5

I attended Mass in the village church where I met and apologised to Frau Weinberger, who had been expecting me the night before. Her husband was away at a Pax Christi meeting all day but she invited me to come and stay at their house where I could meet him in the evening. I declined her kind offer as I had already spent longer than I intended in Munich, and set off for the Austrian border only a few miles away.

In Frankfurt I had met an Austrian Jesuit, who had large-scale maps of the country and he had shown me an excellent route through to Villach, near the Yugoslav border, following minor roads and tracks and through the one pass which would certainly be open at this time of year. The Gospel at Mass today had been from John 11, the raising of Lazarus. As I crossed the Austrian border into this magnificent country with its steep snow-covered peaks sparkling in the sunlight, its deep valleys, roaring streams, fast-flowing rivers, and its friendly pine forests, I had a glimpse of the elation of the risen Lazarus and a delight in being on this journey. Although the countryside was still snow-covered, the roads were clear and the sun so warm that I was able to walk for the first time without wearing both jacket and sweater and I sat having lunch in the open without feeling frozen. In the afternoon I had a long stretch on winding paths through forests and farmland to Walchsee.

With the warmer weather I resumed my habit of resting for ten minutes after every hour's walking. In Austria the rest period was usually spent sitting on snow, but I had a light waterproof mat which insulated against damp and provided a comfortable cushion even on craggy rocks. A few kilometres from Walchsee I was feeling so tired that I put on my cagoul and waterproof trousers, lay on the mat in the snow and fell asleep. I was woken by a large dog licking my face. The family to which it belonged then appeared and stopped to chat, my first taste of the warmth and friendliness which I was to meet throughout Austria.

At Walchsee I called at what appeared to be an unusually small presbytery next to the church, knocked at the door, and waited. As there was no answer, I walked round the house, peeped in a window and realised I was looking in at the parish morgue. When I found the presbytery the housekeeper told me the parish priest would not be back for two hours, so I sat for the two hours on a gasthaus terrace overlooking the frozen and snow-covered Walchsee.

In ordinary life I would be irritated at having to wait for two hours with nothing to do; on this walk I enjoyed the waiting, an enjoyment not only due to the beer I was drinking. I began to see more clearly another truth which this pilgrimage was teaching me.

The source of most pain is in the conflict between the reality we would like to encounter and the reality in which we find ourselves, in our inability to shape reality to our own requirements. Yet the obdurate quality of reality, its refusal to be shaped by our demands, is a blessing, because it forces us out of the prison of our own conditioning, our own narrowness, and frees us from the grooves of our habitual thinking. The raising of Lazarus is not only telling of a physical miracle performed two thousand years ago; it is describing a present reality for all of us. The God who raised Lazarus is the God now holding us in being. He is constantly saying, 'I am the resurrection and the life. Whoever believes in me will never die.' And he is constantly calling each of us by name and saying, 'Arise, come forth.' He calls us through the facts in which we find ourselves. Every situation is an invitation to arise out of our imprisoning tomb and to walk into freedom. Our problem is our love of the tomb, our preference for the familiar, our fear of freedom and terror at change. God's will is in the facts we encounter, the circumstances in which we find ourselves. Our response to God's will is in the way we react to our circumstances. In normal life, an enforced wait of two hours with nothing to do would have so irritated me that I should have wasted the two hours in internal grumbling instead of welcoming them as an opportunity to do something different from what I had intended, to step into a new freedom. The problem, of course, is to know how to react to the circumstances in which we find ourselves, but if we trust that God is in the facts, we are more likely to find the way of reacting which delivers us from the tomb and into freedom. In pain, fear, anxiety and failure, perhaps especially in these states, we need to ask, 'What is God saying to me through this?' Even in the darkness of despair, if we feel life is no longer worth living, we have to ask what the darkness is saying. God is not saying, 'Take your own life,' but he is saying, 'Your present way of life is intolerable. Change it and live.'

The threat of nuclear annihilation is a cosmic example of this truth. The danger arises because the powerful nations are trying to shape reality to their own requirements. Their requirements conflict. To promote and secure their own resources, they plunder the Third World, increase their arms, threaten all life on the planet not only through the risk of a nuclear holocaust, but by their destruction of the environment which sustains the life of us all. There may be temporary alleviations when the super-powers meet and agree to decrease their nuclear stockpile by 4 per cent, as in the I.N.F. agreement, but such agreements, although welcome, are fragile and do not touch the root of the problem, which lies in our minds and hearts. The facts are telling us that for our survival as a human race we need a radical change of mind and heart. The danger in which we live is a blessing, if only we have the eyes to recognise it, for the facts are telling us that we can never find peace, with all that peace means – fullness of life, good health of mind and body, right relations with one another, within ourselves and with creation – unless we learn that peace can never be preserved through the exercise of power. What, in fact, we are doing by our defence policy is not, as we like to think, defending ourselves against a possible threat to our Western values, democratic way of life and religious freedom; we are defending ourselves against change, against the truth of things. We are defending our tomb of death and refusing to listen to God's call to arise and step into a new way of life in freedom, refusing to throw off the bonds which bind us in the prison of our own minds. We are defending ourselves against change, and without change we are heading for disaster. King Canute had a better chance of success when he ordered the sea to turn back than we have of attaining peace through power and the amassing of nuclear arms.

The parish priest welcomed me, invited me to supper and offered me a room without, as far as I can remember, even asking to see my papers, and this was the friendly attitude of all the priests I met in Austria. Many of them, when I showed them my route, would ring a neighbouring priest who was 30–40 km further down the road and arrange my accommodation for the following night. One priest's housekeeper gave me a whole list of housekeeper friends dotted up and down the land, invitations which would have kept me zig-zagging through Austria for a month. The Irishman masquerading as a priest, who so dominated the thinking of the German clergy, had evidently not yet reached Austria.

Monday, April 6

We are dependent creatures, continuously affecting and being affected by the environment in which we are living, but unconscious of this truth most of the time. I recognise this dependency most clearly when walking in mountainous country, especially when it is snow-covered. The sight of snow-clad peaks and the sound of fast-flowing streams raises my spirits and energises me, so that I can walk long distances without tiring. The sun shone all day, although the air was cold, and after 40 km I came down into the valley of St Johann im Tal, just north of Kitzbühl, where I found another friendly presbytery.

Tuesday, April 7

The snow drifts were a metre high by the roadside as I walked another 40 km to Saalfelden. The sun was so warm that my face and the back of my hands were burning by the end of the day. There were still many skiers on the slopes of the mountains. At Saalfelden the parish priest with whom I stayed phoned his neighbour at Lend, 34 km away, who not only offered to put me up for the night, but invited me to stay till Easter.

Wednesday, April 8

It was a very strenuous 34 km, the road climbing steeply east of Saalfelden to Maria Alm. I stopped frequently to look back over Saalfelden and the valley to the west which I had walked the previous day. At Dienten I took a minor road south, 14 km downhill with a roaring stream running parallel to the road, leading into Lend, the first Austrian town I had seen which was not a ski resort. It was a depressing-looking little town, deprived of sunlight most of the day because of the steep hills on either side. The church and presbytery were built on the side of the hill and the young priest, Father Joseph, and his housekeeper gave me a great welcome and showed me to the bishop's room where I was invited to stay as long as I liked. I asked if I might stay two nights to recover my energy before starting on the stretch over the highest pass of all in my route through Austria, from Lend to Obervellach.

Thursday, April 9

My rest day in Lend became a very busy one. In the morning I was just about to go into the town to post letters when Father Joseph invited me to take his religious class in the school, a group of very lively fourteen-year-old boys, who seemed able to understand me as I explained to them who I was and what I was doing and why, but I could not understand them once they began on questions, which Joseph interpreted for me. The class were much more interested in the details of Mungo, my tent, and cooking equipment than on questions of peace, peace pilgrimages and prayer. In the afternoon I celebrated Mass for old-age pensioners in a home adjoining the church. When celebrating Mass I think most priests can sense the mood of a congregation, whether peaceful or agitated, involved in the celebration or bored. This congregation felt both peaceful and involved. They were mostly in their eighties and I would love to have been able to spend more time with them to hear the stories which had formed their features and how they had come to find peace in old age, having lived through the horrors of two world wars with six years of Nazi rule in between.

After Mass and supper, Joseph took me to spend two hours with a group from his parish, who meet regularly for Bible study and reflection. When they had finished their Bible study they began to discuss the question which featured daily in the press and on T.V. all the time I was in Austria, the appointment of a new auxiliary bishop to Vienna. The appointment of an auxiliary bishop does not normally make headline news, but this appointment had been made to a diocese already well supplied with auxiliary bishops and he had been appointed by Rome against the wishes of the Austrian Church. He was also reported to be a noted 'conservative', but the only evidence I heard in support of this label was the man's opposition to having girls as altar servers at Mass. From this group and from other conversations, I heard how hurt the Austrians were by this appointment, because they interpreted it as a mark of Rome's distrust in a local Church which had always prided itself on its loyalty to Rome. Judging from what I saw and heard in Austria, it was far from being a runaway Church; if anything, it was a Church in need of a shove into the spirit of the Second Vatican Council. The Austrians were also afraid, a fear shared by many throughout the Catholic Church, that these appointments of men noted for their loyalty to the Vatican and to Canon Law rather than to the Gospel, are contrary to the spirit of the Second Vatican Council, because they deprive national Churches of their rightful autonomy, and will do lasting damage to the Church. Years ago I would have shared their anger; now, when I hear of these appointments I experience no anger but just sadness, because I see a return to a fortress-church mentality being accepted as a return to orthodoxy, when, in fact, it is a regression to an institutional model of the Church, a model which nurtures clerical paternalism and lay infantilism, betrays the mission of the Church and 'shuts the kingdom of God in people's faces, neither going in themselves nor allowing others to go in who want to' (see Matt. 23:13).

Loyalty can be a beautiful virtue, but it can also be a most destructive vice, for loyalty may be to true religion or it may be to idolatry. We all have to examine our loyalties, but bishops of the Church must do so most of all, asking themselves whether their primary loyalty is to God, who is truth, or to their fellow bishops, whether of Rome or of their own country. To speak with one voice must never be their primary aim, for this would be to silence the Spirit of truth that is in them. It is good that they should strive for unanimity, but if they place unanimity above loyalty to their own conscience, then they are guilty of idolatry. Unanimous statements by bishops' conferences, formulated to embrace every shade of opinion, are usually so anodyne that they have no effect. When they cannot find a formula to cover their differences, the bishops tend to say nothing. In either case they give scandal to the laity, who rightly look to them for a clear lead. Laity would be much more impressed if bishops could admit that they, like other mortals, are uncertain on some questions and if they desisted from attempting the false unanimity of a political party. Underlying the desire for unanimity is a hidden paternalism, the assumption that their flock must be given clear instructions which every toddler can understand, or else be kept in ignorance. Nowhere is this desire for unanimity among bishops more damaging to the Church and to society than in their declarations on nuclear defence. The American bishops produced an excellent pastoral, but it was modified at the last minute to exclude a downright condemnation of nuclear arms. Why should not bishops' statements admit fundamental differences between them and why not make these differences public? Is God in truth? Such differences among bishops, openly expressed, would encourage the laity to think and pray more deeply on the questions in dispute, would make them more sympathetic and supportive of the bishops, besides making them more confident that the bishops do speak out of personal conviction, born of faith, and are not just transmitters of a party line.

Friday, April 10

Lend was at its gloomiest as I left it under heavy cloud and cold drizzle and began the first of the many steep hills I was to encounter that day. After the climb out of Lend, the road was level for a stretch before it began climbing again to Bad Gastein. Before starting to climb I stopped to buy something for lunch and when I came out of the shop there was a cluster of small children grouped around Mungo and full of questions as to where I had come from, whither and why. So I told them why Mungo was so called and that I was walking to Jerusalem. One of them, a beautiful child about ten years old and with lovely eyes, asked, 'Do you believe in God?' 'Yes,' I said, 'and he is all around, especially in this beautiful place and in each of you.' She smiled and said, 'Ich finde es nett, dass du an Gott glaubst' (I think it is lovely that you believe in God), and she looked delighted. When I think back on the pilgrimage, there are some scenes engraved in my memory and this child's radiant face is one of them. After the radiance came heavy rain so I took refuge where I so often took refuge on this pilgrimage, in a bus shelter, which served also as a dining room for my lunch. When I began walking again I could see the outline of the mountains ahead towering above me through the mist. After struggling to what I thought was the summit of the pass, I saw Bad Gastein ahead of me, 6 km away and about 400 metres higher.

The town, perched on rock, is a fashionable ski resort and most of the skiers were spending this wet afternoon shopping. I knew that beyond Bad Gastein I would have to take a train through the Tauern tunnel to Mallnitz on the far side of the pass, but I had no idea where the station was, or the train times, so I asked two passing youngsters. They looked very puzzled, then answered in broad Scouse, 'We're from Liverpool and can't speak German,' so I asked them in English, to which they replied, 'Haven't a clue. Did you think we wuz foreigners then?' and seemed very pleased when I told them I thought they might be. The station fortunately had a restaurant and I had time for a meal before catching the train through the tunnel. Mungo was soaking after a day in the rain and I was cold, damp and very tired, so at first I planned to find lodgings in Mallnitz, where the train stopped.

Mallnitz looked and felt like a Siberian wasteland, snow-covered, with a perishing wind blowing from the east. To the west I could see the outline of the Tauern mountains and to the east, about 1,000 metres below, the valley leading to Obervellach with the main road twisting down the mountainside. So I decided to continue and walked downhill for two hours into Obervellach, which restored my circulation and with it my spirits, which dropped again during the hour I spent in trying to find lodgings. I was so tired and damp that I did not want to inflict myself on any parish priest. When I did eventually ask for lodgings in a busy gasthaus, the waitress asked me to wait 'ein Moment'. It was an hour later before I was shown to a room without heating or hot water, but at least I was able to get a good meal to restore my energy, depleted after a 40-km walk in the rain, which included a 1,000-metre climb.

It is amazing how quickly a mood can change as a result of a meal. As I finished the last mouthful of sausage and sauerkraut, I was thinking of the ancient Celtic monks who wandered Europe without a penny, sleeping rough and eating when they could. Then I began to wonder if they really did travel as roughly as I was imagining. I would love to know how they did travel. They must have been extraordinarily tough men, but even tough men have their limits and they must have devised ways of constructing simple shelters at night so that they could sleep comfortably. Their routes probably followed rivers and streams to ensure a regular supply of fish.

A few years ago a friend, knowing my intention of a walk to Jerusalem, lent me a book written in the last century and entitled *How to Survive in Wild and Savage Countries*. It was written by a Victorian explorer, drew on his experience, mostly in Africa, and contained, besides his outrageous racial prejudice, most useful tips on survival in the wilderness. One chapter entitled, 'The Management of Savages', opens with the suggestion that the most effective way of dealing with savages is to adopt a cheerful, jocular, but confident manner! I have now forgotten most of the book with its descriptions of how to amputate a leg, extract troublesome teeth and split logs without an axe, but what I do remember is his wise advice always to ensure, on long journeys, that you eat adequately and sleep in comfort, otherwise the mind will be so full of thoughts of the end of the hardship and of the flesh-pots to come that the present will always be ignored and the journey wasted, advice which is true not only of long journeys on foot, but of the journey which all of us have to make through life.

Saturday, April 11

The next day's walking from Obervellach to Spittal was easy
and pleasant, a level stretch with a following wind and bright
sunshine. I was stopped on the road by a lone minibus driver,
a Scot who had lost his way, driving home after a holiday in
Turkey. At Spittal I introduced myself to the parish priest,
who offered me an episcopal suite of rooms, the bedroom
including an enormous bed of beautifully carved wood, raised
to a height of two feet on three sides – with a fourth side and
a top it would have made a luxurious coffin for his lordship.

Sunday, April 12

The parish priest and his curate could not have been more
kind, and they made me feel at home in their house. On Palm
Sunday morning the curate invited me to go with him to an
outlying church and to read the Gospel at the Blessing of
Palms service. The service was held outside the church
entrance, the mountains forming a background to the children
in national dress, who were holding, instead of palms, catkin
branches decorated with sweets and tiny Easter eggs. After
the last Mass of the morning in the main church, the congregation were invited into the presbytery for coffee. It seemed
to be a most friendly and open parish and I was sorry not to
be able to accept their invitation to stay on for Holy Week
and Easter, for I had already arranged to spend Easter near
Villach, about 50 km away.

I left Spittal early in the afternoon of Palm Sunday, the
weather so clear that I could soon see the mountains south
of Villach. After 20 km I had the first serious foot trouble of
the whole journey and knew from the feel of the blister on
the ball of the foot that it had become septic. The only lodging
I could find was in a motel, which produced a record number
of forms to be filled in, a very cold room with no hot water
and a defective cold tap, a meagre breakfast and a large bill
at the end of it. I tried to operate on the septic blister with
a sterilised needle, but the skin was so hard that only a scalpel
could have released the poison, so I covered it in Dr Scholl's
pads and prayed that it would not spread through my leg. It

remained painful until I reached my destination at Schloss Wernberg a few kilometres east of Villach.

Monday, April 13

Before leaving Birmingham I had written to a few Jesuit houses in Europe asking if I might have post forwarded and spend a day or two with them. I thought the house to which I had written in Austria was near to Villach, but when I reached Munich, there was a letter from the superior of the Austrian house, telling me that he was 70 km and a mountain range away from Villach, so he had arranged for me to stay at Kloster Wernberg, a convent with guest house attached. Soon after midday I stopped at a restaurant for a meal and to ask directions to the Kloster. On entering, the manager approached, looked at Mungo in wonder, shook hands, showed me to a table and told me that the Kloster was only one kilometre away. I was ravenously hungry after a 30–km walk and hardly any breakfast, so I ordered a mixed grill with vegetables and chips. The attentive manager hovered around asking me if I were enjoying it and when I came to ask for the bill, he would accept nothing. Throughout the pilgrimage, but especially in Austria and Yugoslavia, I was amazed at the spontaneous generosity of people to a stranger and they seemed to delight in it.

Kloster Wernberg is a massive ancient castle, parts of it dating from the twelfth century and now houses a community of sixty-five nuns, mostly elderly, together with a guest house which can accommodate fifty. I was welcomed and taken up stone stairs and through stone-flagged corridors, passing suits of armour on the way, to a room perched at the top of the house with a glorious view to the south, looking on to the snow-covered range of mountains separating Austria from Yugoslavia. I sat by the window for some time, delighting in the view and relishing the thought of six days rest in this beautiful place. 'God arranges all things sweetly,' is a statement I have frequently doubted, but on this pilgrimage my doubts began to vanish and I saw this room and this view as his gift to me, freely given in spite of all my doubtings. This truth made the view even more attractive, for its beauty was a token and a promise from him, source of all beauty and goodness, who is constantly giving himself through all that we see and yet beckoning us beyond what our eyes can see and our hands can touch.

At supper time I was directed to a table reserved for the elderly chaplain to the convent. Besides salt and pepper cruets there was a little bottle which I took to be vinegar. So I was surprised to see the chaplain pour some liberally into his tea and wondered if this might be some Austrian Lenten austerity. However, he invited me to do the same and told me that rum in tea was an excellent pick-me-up. It is.

Tuesday, April 14 — Saturday, April 18

I spent my days in Wernberg answering letters, writing another article for *The Tablet*, attending the Holy Week services, doing some gentle walking on my blistered foot, which healed after three days. I also read a fascinating biography of Franz Pfanner, an Austrian diocesan priest who later became a Trappist monk and founded the congregation of the Sisters of the Precious Blood, a missionary congregation working in South Africa and which, in the 1930s, had bought Kloster Wernberg.

Born in 1825, Franz Pfanner had a stormy career. On becoming a Trappist he was sent to Rome to restore a ruined monastery. I think it was while he was still in Rome that he was expelled from his Order without any reasons being given to him. He appealed to Rome against the dismissal and was reinstated. He was then sent to found a monastery in what is now Yugoslavia and was then in Turkish hands. He was such an excellent farmer and amateur doctor that the Turks accepted him and came to him for advice and healing. He was summoned on one occasion by the Grand Vizier to atttend to one of his wives in the harem and successfully rescued her from what the Vizier feared was imminent death. Franz Pfanner, when asked later to explain the cure, said that the lady was only suffering from severe indigestion, easily cured by an enforced fast. His main life's work began when he was over fifty and sent to found a monastery in South Africa. After a fearsome voyage and an attempt to found a monastery on land sold to him by some swindler and impossible to farm, he acquired land near Durban and founded Marianhill, which became the great mission centre of the Catholic church in South Africa and which still flourishes today. He had running battles with his superiors back in Europe, whose one concern seems to have been that the community should observe the Trappist rule in all its detail, a standard of observance which Franz Pfanner found to conflict with his struggle for survival and his desire to spread the mission of the Church. For a year he was suspended from all priestly functions and eventually he left the Trappist Order. While still a Trappist he made many begging tours in support of his missionary work, meeting, besides the Grand Vizier, Cecil Rhodes in South Africa; he was also in touch with Gandhi and Mark Twain. Queen Victoria appointed him a Justice of the Peace!

Easter Sunday, April 19

Easter Sunday was one of the days which stand out most clearly in my memories of the pilgrimage. At 4.00 a.m. the community and visitors assembled round a fire which lit up the castle courtyard for the first part of the Easter Vigil service, the blessing and lighting of the paschal candle, symbol of the Risen Christ, light of our darkness, the Alpha and Omega, to whom all time and all ages belong. The candle is lit from the newly blessed fire, and from this light the congregation light their candles, symbolising the truth that we communicate Christ's life to one another. The celebrant then sang the 'Exultet', an ancient and beautiful plain-chant hymn, in which the singer invites all creation to join in the joy of Christ's victory, which banishes the powers of darkness forever. The hymn includes the words, 'O happy fault, O necessary sin of Adam, which gained for us so great a redeemer'. At the end of the hymn there was a great blast of trumpets and clashing of cymbals from an Austrian brass band.

It was a wonderful moment as we walked towards the church to the band's accompaniment, the snow-covered mountains clear in the moonlight. I used to find the Easter Vigil service very complicated until I learned not to try to analyse it, but simply to look and let the symbols teach their own message. I looked at the candle in the darkness and recognised the darkness in all the bewilderment, numbness, frustration, helplessness and anxiety I had experienced on this pilgrimage for peace. The light came into the darkness and I felt the joy of it, an inner certainty in all my uncertainty, a hope when everything seemed hopeless, an assurance that all manner of things will be well and that Christ is greater than all my stupidity and sinfulness. I knew then that I was caught up in something far greater than my mind can ever grasp, and that the conviction which has grown in me that peace can never be established through power, whether in the inidividual or in the nation, was not a madness, but the wisdom of God. I thanked him for the pilgrimage so far, for the protection and the joy of it, for the people I had met and the kindness they had shown, for the protection I had experienced and the moments of joy I had felt, for the thinness of the veil and the closeness of the dead, all of which far outweighed any hardship I had endured, and I prayed that this symbolic journey to Jerusalem, city of peace, would one day bring me and all the human race to the reality.

When we left the church at the end of the Easter service, the sun had risen and the congregation gathered on the lawn within the castle quadrangle and sang and danced until breakfast was ready, an enormous meal, which kept me walking without feeling hungry until I reached Strau, 40 km away, the last town before the Yugoslav border. When I went to pay for my six days' board and lodging, the Sisters refused any payment because I had spent one and a half hours with them on Good Friday evening talking with them on peace spirituality. When I set off for Strau, the whole community and the guests came to see me off and wish me well on the road to Jerusalem.

7

Through the Mountains to the Sea – Yugoslavia

Arise, O man, work of my hands, arise, you who were fashioned in my image. Rise, let us go hence; for you in me and I in you, together we are one undivided person.

                  (From an ancient homily for Holy Saturday)

Easter Sunday, April 19 (continued)

Aileen Ireland, a Pax Christi member from Huddersfield, had kindly arranged meetings for me with peace groups in Ljubljana, where she had friends whom she was visiting. She came to Kloster Wernberg on Easter Sunday morning and offered to carry Mungo in her car to Strau where we met up again in the evening. Every day's walking through Austria had been enjoyable, but this Easter Sunday walk from Wernberg to Strau was the most delightful of all. I walked all day in bright sunshine with the mountains separating Austria and Yugoslavia on my right, rivers and a lake to my left, and road borders carpeted with wild flowers. It was as though the whole of nature was rejoicing in the Resurrection, obeying Isaiah's call,

> Let the wilderness and the dry lands exult,
> let the wasteland rejoice and bloom,
> let it bring forth flowers like the jonquil,
> let it rejoice and sing for joy.   (Isa. 35:1–2)

When walking I find it impossible to keep my mind on a consistent train of thought, so I gave up trying to think things out, but would focus my mind on a topic at the beginning of an hour's walking and then see what memory and imagination provided. In the early part of the walk on Easter Sunday I was not thinking at all, just enjoying the scenery, feeling the gladness of Easter and praying to know the reality of the Resurrection now.

There is a homily by an anonymous ancient author which imagines Christ, after his death, descending to hell, grasping Adam's hand and saying, 'Awake, O sleeper, and arise from the dead, and Christ shall give you light. . . . Arise, O man, work of my hands, arise, you who were fashioned in my image. Rise, let us go hence; for you in me and I in you, together we are one undivided person.' What an astonishing statement: 'Together we are one undivided person.' The whole of Christian spirituality is contained in that phrase. It is the heart of the matter, and the only journey worth making is the road through the matter of our lives to a realisation of this truth. Then my mind started jumping from memory to memory of past Easter Sundays, and two, in particular, stood out.

One memory was from fifteen years before. I was celebrating the Easter morning Mass in Turnbull Hall, the Catholic chaplaincy in Glasgow University, and had asked two children, a seven-year-old boy and his three-year-old sister, to bring up the offertory gifts. This was to be their moment of glory, so when the time came to bring up the gifts, they made the most of it, proceeding up the aisle like royalty on a walkabout, beaming with delight at everyone as they passed. When the three-year-old handed me the gifts, she could no longer contain her joy and whispered to me, 'I've got a new pair of shoes on.' She has become one of my favourite memories of Easter. I compare her with that other child in Hopkins' poem 'Spring and Fall', which begins

> Margaret, are you grieving
> Over Goldengrove unleaving?

and ends:

> It is the blight you were born for,
> It is Margaret you mourn for.

This child on Easter Sunday had reached a still deeper spring than Margaret's spring of sorrow. She thought that her new shoes were the cause of her joy, but I pray for her that one day, having passed from shoes to dresses, to hats and rings, through pain and loss and disappointment, she will delight and know why, for she will discover that the real source of her joy was not in her new shoes, dresses, hats or rings, nor in her health, wealth or social status, but comes from within her and beyond her, from the Risen Christ, source of her life and goal of it, her meaning and her identity.

The other memory was Easter Sunday morning in the Stonyhurst playground in 1961, and the whisper I heard, 'Is it not blasphemy to encourage these children to celebrate the feast of the Resurrection with the weapons of death?' Now, twenty-six years later, it was no longer a whisper, but it had taken years before I could hear clearly. And even now I can still hear the other voices of 'common sense', of tradition, of authority, religious as well as civil, asking, 'Do you not think it irresponsible, foolish and arrogant to think that you know better than the majority of Christians, of people much wiser, more intelligent and better informed than you, who for centuries have accepted a theory of just war? Do you not realise that opposition to the possession of nuclear arms, a possession which the highest authorities in the Catholic Church accept as a regrettable necessity, in fact makes the outbreak of war more likely and therefore endangers the lives of innocent people? These voices still trouble me. When I pray, the objections do not disappear, but I know at a level deeper than these objections, that the possession of nuclear arms is as destructive to the nation possessing them as it is to any enemy. In the light of this truth, the truth of Christ's resurrection has become much clearer, by which I mean that I catch a glimpse of the wonder of it, not that I understand it. Jesus is the image of the God we cannot see, of the love which is at the heart of all things and of every human being. 'God wanted all perfection to be found in him and all things to be reconciled through him and for him, everything in heaven and everything on earth, when he made peace by his death on the cross' (Col. 1:19–20). He made peace by giving his life, not by threatening to take the lives of others in defence of his values. His value is to give life, even his own life. 'God's foolishness is wiser than human wisdom, and God's weakness is stronger than human strength,' and he reveals himself not to the wise and the clever, but to little children.

My face and arms were burning with the heat of the sun when I reached Strau, and my feet were aching, but the septic blister had healed. While waiting for Aileen to arrive with Mungo, I found an excellent campsite and was looking forward to sleeping in my tent for the first time on the pilgrimage so far, but the campsite was not yet open for the season, so I found a gasthaus. Aileen then arrived with Mungo and we had an excellent Easter Sunday dinner in a restaurant, where it was warm enough to sit outside for a drink before dinner. Aileen, when not engaged in peace and Third World activities, lectures in English literature at Bretton Hall College, Wakefield, and was currently on an M.A. course at Lancaster University. She is so steeped in English literature that apt quotations pour out from her naturally in conversation on any topic and I wished she had been teaching English when I was at school where parsing and analysis destroyed any delight in the text itself. She is now teaching English to some lucky adults in Ecuador.

Monday, April 20

On Easter Monday Aileen took Mungo and arranged to meet me on the Yugoslav border at the summit of the Loibl pass, 18 km away and 1,000 metres above us. The ascent was mostly through forest along a twisting road, which carried little morning traffic. Forests are like cities: each has its own mood, its own feel. Some cities are dark and ponderous, others light and merry; some feel unfriendly, others are welcoming. This forest was a mixture, for it felt solemn and not at all friendly at first, but as I climbed and shafts of sunlight broke through the branches, it was as though the solemn forest was winking and the rushing streams below became a gurgle of laughter. The laughter of humans beings must correspond to something in God. He shares our sorrows: he must also share our laughter, so I prayed to recognise the wink of God and to hear his laughter in my own and other people's seriousness and solemnity. When I thought I was near the summit, which I later discovered was only half way, I heard the loud roar of a waterfall and found a path leading to it. I sat on the rocks below the fall, my feet in the water and the rest of me enjoying a gentle shower from the spray. When exhausted, rushing water has a wonderful effect, restoring energy, soothing pain, removing stiffness, so that I was still feeling alive when I met Aileen at the top of the pass, where the snow was still deep on the mountainside. We stopped for a sandwich lunch, generously supplemented by two elderly Canadian couples who joined us. They were doing a tour of Europe in a large car, the boot full of groceries which they were afraid might go off if not eaten immediately. I saved them from that worry. From the summit I could see the thin line of road twisting down the mountains to a valley below, leading towards Kranj, which I hoped to reach that evening.

I was very grateful to be free of Mungo for the descent into Yugoslavia, for the road was narrow, full of sharp bends and crumbling verges, with a constant flow of German and Austrian cars returning home from Easter holidays in Yugoslavia. Near the summit of the pass there was a stark memorial to the thousands of people from many different nations who had died in constructing the Loibl pass tunnel through the mountains, forced labour inflicted on concentration camp prisoners. The names of the nations and the numbers who had died were carved into the rocks. It was ironic that forty years later, it was the Germans and Austrians who were now prospering and able to afford cheap holidays in Yugoslavia, while the Yugoslavs were suffering severe poverty and an inflation rate of over 120 per cent.

The distance from Strau to Kranj is 48 km, so I was glad when I spotted Aileen's car waiting at a junction 8 km out of Kranj, where the roads leading into the city forked. She was driving on that evening to Ljubljana, to stay with friends and to make contact with Jasa Zlobec, who was organising my meetings with peace groups, but she first helped me to find lodgings for the night. We tried the tourist office in the centre of Kranj where we were told that the only places offering accommodation were the two hotels nearby. The two hotels were well beyond my means and more expensive than anything I had met in Europe so far, so we returned to the tourist office, where we were directed to another place about 8 km away. On the way we became hopelessly lost, so I returned to the hotel and hoped that the rest of Yugoslavia would be as cheap as I had been told. The hotel looked modern, like some of the dreadful glass and steel constructions in Birmingham. The bedroom, with bathroom en suite, looked very splendid, but the lavatory seat came away in my hands, the sink taps wobbled and the shower did not work. However, the bed was comfortable.

In the evening I took a walk through the town, which had some fine ancient buildings, but here, as in most of the other towns and cities I saw in Yugoslavia, the modern buildings were hideous; a few like the hotel were blocks of dark glass and steel, but most were soulless constructions of dull concrete, which looked permanently damp. The main roads were wide with very little traffic, the side roads thronged with people strolling in small groups. I passed a church with lights on inside. There was standing room only in the porch, for the church was filled with people, young and old, more men than women, and the Mass of Easter Monday was just ending. This was the first time I had been in a communist country since a brief visit to East Berlin in 1962. Under an atheistic government the churches were fuller on a weekday than anything I had ever seen in Britain.

After Mass I looked for somewhere cheap to eat. The only place I could find looked as modern as the prohibitively expensive hotel, but hunger drove me in. The restaurant was a large room filled with men in their shirt-sleeves and braces and a few women sitting at tables, drinking beer, playing cards, and at some tables they had a large plate of chips in the middle. At the end of the room there were a few tables set for dinner, with only two occupied by well dressed men, who were probably visiting capitalists from the West. Feeling like one of them, I sat down and with the help of a Berlitz phrase book ordered a meal which was plain, plentiful and cost less than £2.00.

Tuesday, April 21

On Tuesday I woke up to rain. Aileen had taken Mungo, with my cagoul in it, to Ljubljana the evening before. A slight drizzle persisted all morning as I walked a flat and dull 25 km from Kranj to Ljubljana, the road flanked on its outskirts by rows of dull concrete tenements, the only colour being the clothes hanging out to dry on the verandahs. I had difficulty in finding the Franciscan church, where I had arranged to meet Aileen, and arrived half an hour late, but she was there with Jasa Zlobec, who took me back to his flat and told me to have a rest as he had organised a busy evening for me, beginning with a talk to the congregation in St Francis Church after the 6.00 p.m. Mass, followed by a longer meeting with representatives from various peace groups in the church hall afterwards. Jasa works in a publishing house, speaks excellent English and has been engaged in peace work, often at great personal cost, since his student days. He did not tell me, but I learned later, that another student almost burned himself to death in a peace protest in the 1960s; Jasa offered himself anonymously to the hospital to provide skin grafts for the injured man and found himself occupying the next bed in the hospital. He introduced me to his wife Stefka and his two children Grusa and Fedja, and we had tea before I tried to prepare myself for the evening sessions.

The large Franciscan church was as full for Mass on Easter Tuesday as the Kranj church on Monday. At the end of Mass I was led up the steps to a microphone on the left side of the sanctuary, a Francisan friar stood with another microphone on the right-hand side and in between us stood an interpreter. The friar's role was to feed me questions: why was I making a peace pilgrimage? why on foot? There were lots of questions about the attitude in Britain to the peace movement, the Church's attitude to the nuclear deterrent, the place of prayer and fasting in peace work. As I knew no Slovene, I could not judge the interpreter's accuracy, but her translation of the friar's questions was clear and fluent. The congregation, as far as I could see their faces in the dimly lit church, seemed interested and smiled or laughed at the right times, but there was no time for questions or comment from them. After this half-hour session I had a much longer and more informal session with about thirty peace workers, ending with a buffet supper. The interpreter was still present, although many of the group spoke excellent English.

The first thing I learned from them was that in Yugoslavia, as elsewhere in communist countries, there are vigorous and active peace groups which are distinct from the official, state-sponsored peace groups. At international peace meetings, only the officially sponsored groups are represented, and these give the party line. Consequently, the real thinking of the country on peace is not heard in the West. The group were critical of what they knew of the peace movement in Britain, reckoning that it concentrated far too much on the abolition of nuclear weapons and ignored the root problem, the problem of human rights, without which there can be no lasting peace, and so they saw the promotion of cultural exchanges between East and West as the most important contribution to peace and to the survival of both. They then discussed among themselves whether, as Christians, they could and should co-operate with Communists in work for peace and justice. The majority insisted on the need for co-operation and claimed that in their experience such co-operation deepened their Christian commitment and helped them to see God at work in every human being. I was glad to hear this, because it has also been my own limited experience.

It was reading the atheist writer, Albert Camus, which led me to read the Old Testament prophets again. Years later, I organised a lecture on the Sermon on the Mount at Turnbull Hall, inviting both Professor William Barclay, the famous Scripture scholar, and Jimmy Reid, then a communist, who had organised and led a sit-in of Clyde shipyard workers when they were threatened with closure. Professor Barclay, as always, gave a very clear explanation of the Greek text and its meaning: Jimmy Reid had no Greek, but he had a passionate commitment to the Beatitudes, on which he spoke with such feeling that he had all the good practising Catholics sitting on the edge of their chairs in wonder and some alarm as they heard from the Communist what they were committed to as Christians. The first step in any conflict situation is to listen carefully to whatever the opposing side is saying. As the Quakers say, there is that which is of God in everyone. He is always greater than any church, doctrinal affirmation or ideology. The object of a teaching authority in the Catholic Church is to enable us to find God within, amongst and beyond us. We need such a teaching authority, to warn and guard us against our own narrowness and tendency to create a God in our own image and likeness. The teaching authority must guard the mystery in all its richness and preserve us from oversimplifying it. The object of Christian doctrine should be to keep questions open and to encourage us to inquire further, not to close questions or pretend that any doctrine gives the last word on the subject. Heresy is oversimplification or, to use another image, heresy is a signpost which leads us down a cul-de-sac. It is an abuse and a perversion of the teaching authority in the Church when it is used to discourage research and questioning.

God is a living reality, not a concept, and we meet him, not through uttering a creed, but in the way we live and relate to one another, to ourselves and to all creation. Those who hunger and thirst after justice, hunger and thirst for God, no matter what their faith or ideology may be. If they care for their neighbour as they care for themselves, then they are meeting God, even if they do not know, or even if they deny his name. Therefore, for Catholic, or for any other Christians to say, 'Before we can work together for justice and peace on earth, we must first settle our doctrinal, or ethical, or political differences, is a long-winded way of saying, 'We cannot work together for justice and peace,' or, 'We are unwilling to do so.' When we reach heaven we shall discover that many people called 'unbelievers', 'communists', 'atheists' or 'humanists' have entered the kingdom of God before those who have prided themselves on their Christian orthodoxy and who, locked in their own exclusive righteousness, have contributed nothing to justice and peace, but only fostered division.

The proposed Council of all the Christian Churches on peace, justice and the integrity of creation is of primary importance, not because the Churches, divided as they are at present, are likely to have much effect, but because such a council will focus our attention on our universal mission, divert us from preoccupation with our own maintenance, and help us to see that God is calling us to put aside our own petty claims, our prestige, influence and self-importance so that we can be living witnesses to our master. 'His state was divine, yet he did not cling to his equality with God but emptied himself to assume the condition of a slave, and became as men are; and being as all men are, he was humbler yet, even to accepting death, death on a cross' (Phil. 2:6–8).

When we returned to Jasa's flat, he showed me a large

book containing detailed maps of Yugoslavia (scale 1:50,000, whereas the only maps I could obtain in shops were 1:600,000). He told me there was a newly opened cross-country walk from Ljubljana to Rijeka on the north coast of the Adriatic. As it would be impossible with Mungo, Jasa offered to take Mungo next morning to the railway station and make inquiries about having the haversack sent by train to Rijeka.

Wednesday, April 22

On April 22nd I set off with Jasa and Mungo for the Franciscan church, where Aileen was waiting. While she and Jasa went to the station, I went to Mass and then to visit one of the Franciscans, who had left a message the evening before asking me to call in and see him. He greeted me like a long lost brother, told me how much he had enjoyed my two books and how grateful he was for my lectures at Heythrop College, London, where he had studied for a year. I have never lectured at Heythrop, but was grateful for the compliment. There are two Jesuits in Britain called Gerard Hughes, distinguished among our fellow Jesuits as Gerry Talk and Gerry Walk. Gerry Talk is Gerard J. Hughes, a philosopher, who teaches at Heythrop. The shared name causes endless confusion, but this particular confusion gave me an identity problem, for the Franciscan, having sat at Gerry J.'s feet for a year, thought that I was the same person. When I explained the confusion, the Franciscan told me that all the time at Heythrop he had assumed that his lecturer was the author of the two books I had written, so that when I appeared, it was Gerry J. he saw, which is a very cautionary tale about the nature of our perception and our tendency to see only what we are expecting to see.

Later in the morning Jasa and Aileen returned with the sad news that Mungo could not be accepted on Yugoslav railways for I had no means of padlocking the haversack, so I would have to work out my own route by side roads and tracks from Ljubljana to the coast. As we were leaving the church an old lady pushed some leaflets into my hand and talked excitedly. Jasa translated. She was exhorting me to visit Medjugorje on my way through Yugoslavia and the leaflets were giving further information.

Aileen and I did some sightseeing, climbing up to the ancient castle, set on a hill and with a splendid view across the plain to the mountains in the south – my route for the next day. We went to Aileen's hostess, Mrs Gradisnik, for a lunch of innumerable and tasty courses, preceded by schnapps and accompanied by Yugoslav wine. In the afternoon I went in search of the Jesuit house in the city, which I found with difficulty, a broken-down building behind a church, one of the earliest baroque churches, which included a beautiful altar-piece featuring two angels illustrating the truth that God is known not only with the mind, but also with the heart. There was only one Jesuit in residence at the time, the others being at a meeting. The Jesuits first came to Ljubljana in 1590. In 1948, along with most other orders and congregations, they were expelled from the city and had only returned in 1981. The Franciscans, however, were allowed to stay after the war because of their wartime services to the partisans.

In the evening, Jasa took us to a Serb restaurant. He had invited also a lawyer friend, and during the excellent meal I learned a little more about Yugoslavia, a country of such complex divisions that Northern Ireland sounds simple in comparison. This relatively small country, which only came into existence as Yugoslavia after the First World War, contains six different republics, three main ethnic groups, three main religious divisions, different languages and two different official scripts. About 40 per cent of the population are Orthodox, 30 per cent Catholic and 12 per cent Muslim. Only about 12 per cent of the population are Communist, and this includes many who are party members, not out of conviction but from economic necessity, party membership being a condition of certain jobs, including responsible academic ones. I heard no one in Yugoslavia speak in favour of the Communist government, which most considered to be intellectually and culturally, as well as economically, bankrupt, but this did not mean that they were not in favour of a socialist state. Jasa, for example, approved of the socialist ideas of his country, of a classless society, of their national health service, their educational opportunities, and of the small disparity in wages compared with the West.

When we returned to Jasa's flat it was almost midnight and I spent another two hours studying his maps. I worked out a route almost directly south from Ljubljana to the coast at Novi Vinodolski, about 80 km south of Rijeka. I made notes on the route; their painful inadequacy was revealed in the next few days.

Thursday, April 23

Aileen came to the flat early next morning and drove me to a point on the south side of the city where we parted, she for Huddersfield and I for Jerusalem. The first 10 km were on a level stretch of road, leading to a village called Ig, the last flat stretch I was to have before reaching the coast. After Ig I had my first problem with the map, which showed only one road leading to Rob, my destination, but the village had roads leading in all directions and none of them were signposted. So I relied on my compass and began a long climb into the hills. After six steep kilometres I saw a notice forbidding foreigners to proceed any further. As the only alternative to ignoring the notice was to return downhill and try another road, with no guarantee that it would not also ban foreigners, and as there was no one in sight from whom to ask directions, I asked the Lord to be my shepherd and continued. I then met a much more threatening notice, printed in white on a red background and giving a list of times. The first notice had been printed in German and English as well as Slovene. Presuming all foreigners would have obeyed, this second notice was in Slovene only, and what I could not understand was whether the times given were the safe times or the dangerous times. I presumed they were the dangerous times when the army would be practising with live ammunition, consulted my watch and reckoned I should be safe for the next two hours. It was a scenic stretch through woodland. I saw no one and heard no gunfire, but I did see many more notices giving directions to what were presumably army camps. After 10 km I found a welcome notice forbidding any foreigner to proceed in the direction from which I had come, but I wondered if this was to be the pattern of my walk through rural Yugoslavia to the coastland.

In the evening I reached the village of Rob and inquired about restaurants and lodgings. Rob had neither, just a small village shop, which was shut. I came to the end of the village and asked in German the woman who answered the door whether there was any place in the area where I could eat and pitch my tent for the night. She could speak only Slovene. I made my request in signs. She smiled and brought me a glass of water. I tried again. This time she took me into the house, through the kitchen and into a sitting room where her husband, who looked as though he were recovering from a stroke, was lying on a couch. He, having been a prisoner-of-war in Germany, could speak a little German and interpreted my request to his wife, who told me I was most welcome to camp in the garden and then produced for her husband and me coffee and schnapps, a colourless liquid which travels at the speed of light from the tip of the tongue to the toes. She then reappeared and introduced me to her grandchildren, who were on holiday from Italy, and in the kitchen she produced home-made bread and jam.

The garden was an excellent campsite with a fast-flowing stream running through it. The grandchildren helped me put up the tent. I was preparing my own supper when a small boy appeared with a large roll of rubber foam to serve as a mattress, reappearing a few minutes later with hot milk and large slices of home-made bread. Later, Grandmother appeared with two blankets for which I was very grateful, for the night was cold.

Friday, April 24

There was a thick early morning frost, so my feet were numb after standing in the stream for a quick wash and shave. When I went to pay next morning, Grandmother looked offended, gave me more bread, hot milk and, for the journey, a large medicine-bottle full of the potent schnapps, which I poured on the earth as a libation later in the day, trusting that it would do less harm to the earth's system than to mine.

Before leaving Rob I studied my map and notes carefully

for the day's route from Rob to Sodrazica, which would be less than 20 km by the short cut I planned to take. I walked fast because of the bitter early morning cold and reached what I thought was the first right-hand turn indicated on my map sooner than I had expected. The road was asphalted at first, but when it began to climb into the hills to the south, the asphalt gave way to a stony track, made worse by falling branches. There are few things more beautiful than walking along a forest road in the early morning, the suns rays shining through the rising mist.

The track was twisting so much that it was difficult to know whether it really was the road indicated on my map running south. The rough surface was playing havoc with Mungo's pram wheels, designed for sedate walks in suburban parks. After two hours of strenuous climbing I reached a summit clearing with a wayside shrine of Our Lady, where I sat to admire the view over wooded hill country, many of the summits crowned with little chapel spires. Yugoslavia, from what I had seen so far, was less and less how I expected a communist country to be. After another hour's climbing, the track disappeared at some deserted buildings. I could see where I should have been, but could not go there cross-country with Mungo on my back, so I retraced my steps for 2 km to ask directions at a farm I had passed. The farmer, before giving the directions, offered me a choice of wine or water. In the heat of midday I gratefully accepted the water and he pointed to a path which would lead me to the road I should have reached three hours earlier, had I not taken the wrong first turn.

On reaching the road I stopped by a farm building to eat my last remaining bit of bread. The farmer joined me and we spoke in German. He had been a partisan during the war, was captured in 1942 and spent most of the war in Dachau concentration camp. He talked without bitterness of his time there, then summoned his wife, who soon reappeared with coffee and the inevitable schnapps. A few kilometres further on, I found a shop open. Shops in the country districts of Yugoslavia are not easy to spot, because they do not go in for window display or advertising signs. In the grocery store there was a very limited variety of food, the fruit limited to apples and a few sad oranges, the cheese rubbery and tasteless

– but by British standards it was very cheap. I stopped by the side of the road after shopping to have a late lunch and was just preparing to start walking again when a car drew up. It was the girl from the grocer's shop offering to give me a lift into Sodrazica, a lift I gladly accepted after the strenuous frustrations of the day.

It had been a remarkable twenty-four hours, not only for the scenery, but most of all for the extraordinary friendliness I had met with from complete strangers and the lavish generosity from a people who had very little material wealth. I thought of the destructive lunacy of the phrase, 'Better dead than Red'. The roots of violence are in our minds, especially in our tendency to generalise, to build up a shadow world of abstract concepts, which we accept as reality, while the reality from which these abstract concepts arise are our own fears, especially our own fear of change. In Yugoslavia, as in most other communist countries, only a small percentage of the population are party members, and of that percentage many are members for reasons of expediency, not conviction. In the West and in the East we are both fed with propaganda, the vapourings of fearful, greedy and manipulative minds, presenting a totally false picture of communist and capitalist countries, as though communist countries are teeming with ardent party members, whose one ambition is to destroy all that is good, fine and noble in our Western democracies, while Western countries are presented as filled with ruthless capitalists, whose one desire is to devour every comrade. These lies are being accepted on both sides.

In Yugoslavia, although there were many complaints about the repressiveness of its communist government which has acted with callous ruthlessness, all were agreed that the situation was improving. Criticism could now be made of the government which, five years earlier, would have brought hefty prison sentences. In this country with an atheistic government, which bans all religious teaching from its education programme, I had already seen more obvious signs of religious observance than I have seen in Britain, Holland, Germany and Austria, and I was to see much more once I reached the Croat area. The government, I was told, is very worried by the growing interest in religion especially among the youth.

There is a spirit in the human heart which no amount of government repression can kill. The enemy in capitalist countries is not communism: the enemy in communist countries is not capitalism. We have a common enemy: whatever can stifle or kill the human spirit. In the Spiritual Exercises meditation on the Two Standards, Lucifer from his smoky throne does not tell the demons to set up police states and concentration camps, to deprive people of their human rights, oppress and torture them, because Lucifer knows from bitter experience that such measures can produce men, women and children of extraordinary spiritual strength, who can do immense damage to his regime. It is the poor, oppressed and powerless whom Lucifer most fears. He therefore instructs the demons to use different tactics, to 'ensnare human beings with a love of riches, leading to love of honour, and so to overweening pride'. The affluent society, in which the accumulation of wealth and status are accepted as the highest good, is much more effective in crushing the human spirit than death squads and torturers. Once the human spirit – the spirit of love, of compassion and tenderness – is stifled then Lucifer can take his ease because his minions will do his work for him and, to protect their wealth and their status, they will destroy not only themselves, but all life on earth. That is why I believe that we in the West are in a much more perilous spiritual state than the people living under communist regimes.

At Sodrazica I found a hotel which provided bed and breakfast for the equivalent of £5. It took me a long time to master the Yugoslav currency because they had impressive notes to the value of less than one British penny. Consequently, my wallet bulged with paper money and the equivalent of £5 took a long time to reckon and count out.

Saturday, April 25

From Sodrazica I walked 30 km on smooth-surfaced and traffic-free roads with a clear sky all day and found a drab-looking hotel at Cabar. The hotels were so cheap and the nights still so cold, that I did not attempt camping. There was a dilapidated church in the village with some vandalised shrines around it. The hotel staff may have been loyal party members because, when I asked about Mass times in the church on Sunday morning, they looked at me in amazement and shrugged their shoulders.

Sunday, April 26

I was up early and went round again to the church. It was still locked, so I set off on the road for Crni Lug, 30 km away. The route was level at first, a tree-lined road by a river, but I was soon into mountain country and climbing up on a track of unending turns and a bumping Mungo behind me. The final stretch of 18 km was more level and the surface smoother. One of the joys of walking in Yugoslavia is the absence of road traffic. Over this 30–km stretch only a few cars passed me. The scenery felt familiar, for it reminded me of the Scottish Highlands, but the frequent wayside monuments to partisans killed in the war made it clear to me that I was in Yugoslavia. At Crni Lug there was no hotel, so I went into a pub, called a '*bifé*', which was full of men playing cards in a thick haze of cigarette smoke. As in most *bifés*, the only women in sight were behind the bar, serving. The feminist movement has made no great inroads into the country parts of Yugoslavia. I asked an elderly man about lodgings. He took me outside and said in a whisper, 'Privat', and pointed to a house. 'Privat', I later discovered, meant that the householders had dispensed with the licence required for taking in lodgers and so earned some tax-free money. The people at this 'privat' house wanted to be paid in dollars, but were only charging the equivalent of five pounds, for a beautiful room with a most comfortable bed and an enormous breakfast next morning of bacon, scrambled egg, cold meat and bread. Most *pensions* in which I stayed later provided bed only, without breakfast.

Monday, April 27

On Monday I reached Fuzine, a distance of just over 20 km from Crni Lug that included some strenuous climbs on bumpy, winding tracks. At Fuzine, I had my first experience, to be repeated often, of going to a hotel and being asked, 'How many are you?' When I answered, 'I am on my own,' the next question was, 'How many nights do you intend staying?' When I answered, 'One night only,' I would be told that there was no room. It was later explained to me that it did not pay these managers of state hotels to have single guests for one night. I found a 'privat', a cold damp house with damp sheets and no breakfast provided. Already lodging there was a Dutch girl, a drama teacher, who was travelling on her own through Yugoslavia with a rucksack. She was tired and frustrated, for she had spent much of her time trying to find cheap lodgings each night. She was active in peace work, saw her profession as a drama teacher to be a contribution to peace, because it was educating people to think not only with their heads, but also with their emotions and every movement of their bodies. She was not a Christian and was scandalised at the approval and support of a nuclear defence policy which she found among some of her Catholic friends. For her, the important values in life were first to trust, then take risks and avoid trying to have everything first worked out in detail before embarking on something worth doing. I did not have time in our short conversation to ask more about the grounds for her trusting attitude, and when I left the house the next morning she had not yet appeared.

Tuesday, April 28

Of all my days of walking, the most memorable was April 28th, when I walked from Fuzine in the mountains to Novi Vinodolski on the coast, passing from the winter snow and bare trees of the mountains, through spring, as I descended, to summer weather by the sea.

For the first 4 km to a village called Lic, there was no problem apart from the cold. At Lic my map had a clearly marked yellow road leading south to a village called Kastelj.

I searched for this road without success. The first man I asked could speak Italian. When I showed him the map he shrugged his shoulders and told me the road did not exist. This I could not believe, so I tried an elderly couple. They examined the map with interest, then gave me directions, she pointing east and he to the west. They then began quarrelling with each other, so I left them to it and asked the next passerby, a smartly dressed young woman, with a confident, didactic manner. She bade me follow, which I did. She led me into the local shop. When I said, 'But where is my road?' she pointed clearly to the road to Fuzine, whence I had come. The shopkeeper, noticing my difficulty, came out from behind his counter leaving the shop unattended. He, too, assured me that the splendid road on my map existed only in the minds of the planners and he pointed to a path across wasteland leading to hills in the distance and said that I would eventually find a forest track which would bring me out on a main road.

It was a rough, stony, pot-holed track running through an extensive rubbish dump for several kilometres. When I did reach the forest track, it had all the defects of the previous one, but with fallen branches in addition. Mungo never properly recovered from this long ascent. I reached the summit, where the track joined an asphalted road leading into barren-looking country with only the occasional farm building in sight. The road turned and to my delight I saw a board hanging from a tree with 'Vagabunda restaurant' written on it. It was a beautiful place, empty save for two German couples on holiday and the manager and his wife, who spent all their time talking in German with their guests. It had been the longest winter in memory and the couple had lived like hermits, seeing nobody and shut in by snow much of the time. They had just opened for the season and told us of their delight at being able to work again after their long period of enforced idleness, which, the wife complained, had played havoc with her figure. Their wall decorations included a massive bearskin, formerly a local inhabitant, according to the proprietor.

The Germans kindly offered me a lift down to the coast, but I had recovered my energy after the meal and did not want to miss the long descent. I have walked few stretches of road which can compare with the 20 km from the Vagabunda restaurant to the sea. A short distance from the restaurant I caught my first sight of the sea and of the islands cloaked in light haze. It was a moment of great delight, arising partly from the false assumption that the most strenuous part of the pilgrimage was now over and all that was left was a downhill run to Athens and a pleasant sail to Israel. The road to Novi Vinodolski ran downhill, and I had my first sight of this part of the coastline, known as the stone desert, large grey-white boulders with beautiful salamanders darting in and out of them. The sun grew warmer as I descended from 1,000 metres to sea level, the spring blossom already fading from the trees. Novi Vinodolski looked much more prosperous than anything I had seen in Yugoslavia so far, a popular holiday resort with pleasant-looking houses, many of them with boards advertising rooms. The sun had set and darkness was falling as I began to look for lodgings, calling at the houses advertising rooms. Some were not yet open for the season, others asked, 'How many are you?' and, 'How long are you staying?', before refusing a room. There were large hotels on the sea front, which I reckoned would be too expensive, but having failed at the houses and feeling exhausted, I asked for a room for the night in a large hotel where, for the equivalent of £11, I had a large room with its own bathroom and a verandah overlooking the sea. I was so delighted with it and so tired after the walk from Ljubljana, that I went straight to the reception desk and asked if I could stay for two nights.

Wednesday, April 29

The hotel was full of men and women in tracksuits, mostly Yugoslavs, but there was also a large French party with its own notice board, advertising the holiday programme, which included many events in the 'Salle d'Animation' and an afternoon programme called 'Tennis Perfectionnement'. That evening the Salle d'Animation, which was uncomfortably near my room, had a disco. I could still hear it at 1.30 a.m. and was beginning to regret my impulsive decision to spend two nights in the hotel. Next day, with animation all around, I spent in idleness, wandering around the town, sitting on the verandah looking at the sea and writing up my diary, which

I had neglected for five days. I also washed all my clothes, hanging them out to dry on the verandah, but when I returned to my room, there was a wind blowing and few clothes left on the verandah. So I had my day's animation in trying to recover them. Fortunately, there was no disco that evening and I sat looking at the sea before going to bed, thanking God for the pilgrimage so far. I had been looking forward to this long stretch along the coast to Albania, but that evening I felt a touch of gloom and apprehension. It was partly caused by feelings of loneliness, which never afflicted me when I was on my own, but did affect me among the holiday crowds in this hotel, and partly by physical tiredness; together these started up the questions which recurred intermittently all the way to Jerusalem. 'What do you think you are doing wandering through Europe trailing Mungo? What possible contribution can this make to peace?' 'Is this walk some subtle form of escape?' I recognised these questions and the gloom that accompanied them as demoralising and destructive, yet I also knew they had to be answered. I went to sleep remembering the nightmare image I had in the snowstorm on the way to Walldürn of walking in a nuclear winter, and although this memory did not dispel the gloom, nor answer all my questions, it did drive away any thoughts of abandoning the pilgrimage.

8

Dalmatian Animation and Desolation –
Adriatic Coast

When will you ever, Peace, wild wooddove, shy wings shut,
Your round me roaming end, and under be my boughs?
When, when, Peace, will you, Peace? I'll not play hypocrite
To own my heart: I yield you do come sometimes: but
That piecemeal peace is poor peace. What pure peace allows
Alarms of wars, the daunting wars, the death of it?

O surely, reaving Peace, my Lord should leave in lieu
Some good! And so he does leave Patience exquisite,
That plumes to Peace thereafter. And when Peace here does house
He comes with work to do, he does not come to coo,
                    He comes to brood and sit.
                              (G. M. Hopkins, 'Peace')

Thursday, April 30

The sun was already warm in a pale, cloudless sky when I
left the hotel in Novi Vinodolski, to begin the long stretch
south along the Dalmatian coast. At first I felt a touch of the
elation I had experienced two days before when I first caught
sight of the sea. The elation was short-lived, for soon the road
began to climb high above the coastline and Mungo was
behaving oddly, hard to pull and frequently keeling over. The
road was narrow and twisting, with little or no verge, bound
on one side by steep rocks and by precipitous drops on the
other, leaving little room to manoeuvre as heavy lorries came
round sharp bends. The scenery, too, became increasingly
barren and I was walking through a white stone desert with
little sign of human habitation and no trace of a mountain
stream. I was told later that centuries ago this coastline had

153

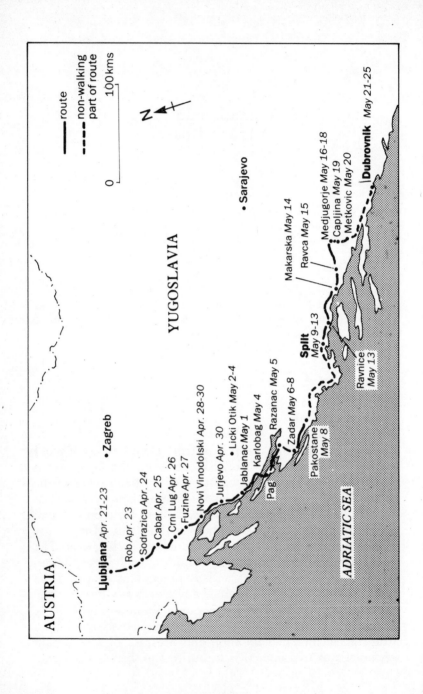

been forest land, but plunderers, mostly Venetians, had dev-astated the hillsides by cutting down all the trees. After thirty trying kilometres I stopped at Jurjevo, exhausted, examined Mungo and discovered that one of the bolts securing the haversack to the wheeled frame had sheered off, which accounted for the frequent keeling over. I put the whole machine on my back and staggered into the town where I found a church with a presbytery next to it. There was no answer to my first ring on the bell, but on the second ring a sleepy and dishevelled man appeared. I introduced myself. He told me that he was the parish priest, that he had just begun his siesta, was going up to a village in the mountains to celebrate an evening Mass in a few hours time and that I was welcome to accompany him, if I could return to the presbytery in two hours' time. I showed him the broken Mungo and he directed me to a local handyman nearby. The handyman was a morose character, who shook his head at Mungo, sighed deeply, said he could not repair the bolt, nor could anyone else in the neighbourhood, for the May 1st celebrations had already begun and no work would be done until Monday, May 4th. He did, however, offer me a length of twine, a kind gesture but a useless gift.

With two hours to wait I went to the shore, sat on a rock with my feet in the water and thought. I could not continue walking carrying Mungo on my back because it was too heavy, and even if I leaned forward with the machine on my shoulders, the axle of the wheels knocked against the back of my knees forcing me to walk with mincing gait. If Mungo was to be repaired, I would have to stay in Jurjevo until Monday, and even then I might only be presented with more twine. The alternative was to remove the haversack from its aluminium frame, leave the frame on one of the many road-side rubbish tips, present my tent and cooking equipment to a local presbytery, along with anything else I could jettison, and walk with a lightened haversack. The disadvantages were that I would then be restricted each day, having to ensure that I arrived each evening at some place where accommo-dation was available, and without cooking equipment I would be dependent on restaurants and cafés and the pilgrimage would become too expensive. I moved from the rock to a restaurant table by the shore, where I sat thinking gloomy thoughts of a premature end to the walk, when the parish priest appeared to tell me he had had a change of plan and unfortunately could not take me with him to the mountain parish. He assured me that I would easily find accommodation in the village.

The pilgrimage provided plenty of opportunity for practising faith. It is easy to say, 'I believe in God the Father almighty,' along with a few hundred other people at Mass: it is not so easy when sunk in gloom, when plans go awry and there is no place to sleep for the night. I did not really feel convinced when I reminded myself that God is in the facts, so the facts must be kind. I felt even less convinced after trying two houses for a room and being turned away from both. However, at the third I was offered not only a room for the night but also coffee and schnapps. Neither the husband nor wife could speak English, but I showed them the damaged Mungo. The husband disappeared, returning a few minutes later with an electric drill to remove the sheered bolt. Fortunately, the far-sighted Ian Tweedie had provided me with a spare, and Mungo was ready for the road next morning.

Friday, May 1

It was a national holiday, and in Yugoslavia they were celebrating not only the workers of the world uniting but, in particular, the triumph of the partisans during the Second World War and their hero, Tito.

The main road climbed again from sea level into the heights of the stone desert. Mungo was steadier after the repairs, though still not pulling easily, and I had soon emptied all but an emergency sip from my water bottle. But the facts were kind and I found a restaurant in the wilderness providing an excellent lunch of fried liver, chips and salad. Entertainment was provided by a group of raucous partisans, dressed in military uniform and roaring patriotic songs, punctuated by drunken shouts.

After 32 km walking I could see two villages on the coast below. I made for the nearest, Stirnica, but I could see nothing but factory buildings. I inquired at a house and was told the nearest lodgings were at Jablanac, 4 km away. As I approached along a tree-lined road bordering the sea, my spirits rose and I entered a most beautiful little town built round the three sides of a harbour full of pleasure boats, its streets crowded with holidaymakers. There was no camping site, nor room at the hotel, but I found a room near the harbour. I was unpacking Mungo, when I heard church bells nearby and went along, hoping there might be an evening Mass. In the small church there was a gathering of elderly women dressed in black with a jovial-looking priest facing them and reciting prayers. When I entered he looked up, greeted me in Serbo-Croat and asked where I came from. I replied in German, which he then translated for the congregation before inviting me to join them for Vespers. At the end he invited me to have supper with him at the hotel, where he seemed to know everyone. We were joined by an Austrian artist whom he had commissioned to do some painting and restoration work on his church. The supper was excellent, and the parish priest provided non-stop entertainment with his stories of life under communist rule in Yugoslavia, especially the immediate post-war years when the Church was severely persecuted. He claimed that there had been many attempts on his life by the 'comrades', as he always called them. He told, too, of a priest friend of his who had been condemned to death four times and four times was reprieved, because the minister responsible for executions was an old classmate of the priest. Throughout the meal he bubbled mirth and managed to extract humour from horrendous situations. He was a man who seemed to have unwavering confidence in himself and in his opinions, with a steam-roller mind able to flatten all difficulties and produce simple answers to the most complex problems. On Medjugorje he had no problem. The whole phenomenon was simply explained as a plot by the Franciscans to undermine the authority of the bishop, for Franciscans had never taken kindly to bishops in Yugoslavia. As for the phenomenon of a revolving sun seen by thousands at Medjugorje, this was an illusion based on an account of a whirling sun in the last century. Although he said the most outrageous things, he managed to do so without any trace of malice. Having spoken thus of the Franciscans, he then invited me to accompany him next day to visit some Franciscan friends of his at Karlobag, about 30 km further down the coast, an offer I readily accepted to avoid more walking in the stone desert.

Saturday, May 2

Before leaving for Karlobag the Austrian artist, who had hardly got a word in at supper, took me to see a fourteenth-century chapel on which he was working. The chapel was built high on a hill above the town, such sites being chosen for protection from marauding pirates. As he was showing me the features of the church, I commented on the sentimentality and ugliness of some of the modern art which I had seen in Catholic churches in Yugoslavia. The comment acted like the ignition key on a Ferrari racing car, and the artist, so silent the night before, spoke rapidly and with passion on the deplorable state not only of the 'kitsch' in Catholic churches in Yugoslavia, but of modern art in general. He believed the West had lost its soul and that the only art of which it was capable was the portrayal of ugliness, cruelty, deformity and brokenness. Most modern religious art, he claimed, was therefore necessarily artificial, sentimental, divorced from reality, portraying a dream world which served only to anaesthetise against the horror of the reality in which we were living without attempting to come to grips with it or enabling us to work with hope to overcome it.

This conversation with the artist came back to me often throughout the rest of the pilgrimage and it is still with me. It is not only art which expresses the loss of our Western soul. The loss is also expressed in our divinisation of reason and contempt for feeling and emotions, as though they were some kind of weakness which rational man should overcome, while tolerating the 'defect' in women! The fractured nature of our spirituality is most clearly and perilously expressed in our ideas about national defence and security. It is generally accepted in the West, by Christians as well as by atheists, that our security can only be assured by threatening our enemies with such destruction that even our own survival may be threatened by so doing. Losing our souls means, among other things, losing sight of the truth of the unity of all creation and of all human beings, so that whatever damage we inflict on another is always damage inflicted on ourselves. Because we are fractured in spirit, therefore we create division around us and call it the preservation of peace.

In Karlobag the priest and I had lunch with an elderly community of Capuchin friars, living in an ancient and crumbling building, which they could neither afford to repair nor obtain government permission to do so, even if they had the money. One of the community, a very gentle and friendly old man, had spent five years in prison after the war, a sentence which could be imposed for any criticism of the government. During and after lunch the parish priest continued to talk, mostly about the iniquities of the 'comrades' and enough to earn him a life sentence in the bad old days. The artist, who had accompanied us, fell asleep shortly before I did, and I woke to find the parish priest was addressing me, telling me that he had planned to send me up to a mountain parish for the weekend. He had been appointed by the bishop to promote ecumenism in the diocese, an activity which, he told me, was not popular among the Catholic clergy and little progress had been made so far. He was sending me up the mountain to give me experience of a Yugoslavian country parish, but also to make contact with the Orthodox priest there, for whom he gave me an introductory note. I was not asked whether I would like to go and, before I had time to think, he was driving me to the bus stop.

The bus climbed slowly from the coast to the mountain villages about 1,000 metres above, and an hour later I had reached the town where I was to be met. I had no difficulty in recognising the parish priest at the bus stop, for he was dressed in a soutane and had a biretta with a little pom-pom on his head. He led me to a tiny car which bounced as soon as we entered and proceeded in kangaroo hops along the broken roads. I then saw the wisdom of Father's biretta with its pom-pom on top, for it acted as a kind of safety helmet as his head hit the roof of the bouncing car. The presbytery stood in its own grounds, and included a small orchard, chicken run and vegetable patch, cared for by two nuns, neither of whom could speak anything but Serbo-Croat. The parish priest had only a little German, so our conversation was very limited. What they did communicate very clearly was their warm welcome, friendliness and generous sharing of their very simple lifestyle. The hens and the vegetable patch were not an eccentricity of the parish priest, but were needed for survival. Supper was an enormous meal of sausage, hard-boiled eggs, a kind of horse-radish, bread and tea. This was also the breakfast for the next two mornings, supplemented with some very tough and salty ham, which removed a filling from my tooth.

Sunday, May 3

Over the weekend I attended three public Masses and I doubt if there were more than ten men at all three of them, the congregations being predominantly elderly women dressed in black and a few little children. The congregation was passive during the Masses, all the readings being done by the parish priest, who also preached for about thirty minutes at each Mass. I could not understand a word, but to judge from the rather worried look on the faces of the congregation and the frequent deep sighs with which the parish priest punctuated his sentences, the Easter message was communicating woe rather than joy. The hymn singing was dominated by the piercing voice of one of the sisters, and there was a very sad quality in the singing – even the Easter Alleluia sounded like a lament. As I learned more of Yugoslavia's history, I understood better the sadness I had detected in this congregation. At Holy Communion very few came forward to receive. The pictures and statues in the church were the worst I had seen anywhere, the favourite colours being pink, lilac and a sickly purple. When I asked the parish priest later about the small numbers of men he said that if they were seen to attend Mass they were likely to lose their jobs. Even if they had secure jobs, they would be devoted men who would endure those woeful celebrations every Sunday.

I asked the parish priest about visiting the Orthodox priest to whom I had an introduction, but he declined to take me. He gave me his own extraordinary views on ecumenism, claiming New Testament authority for his belief that Catholics should look after Catholics and that co-operation with the Orthodox should be limited to prayers for their conversion. He then went on to sing the praises of Pope John Paul II, whom he saw as the champion of Catholicism against the ravages of all Communists, Orthodox Christians and Serbs!

I felt very sad as I listened to this parish priest, who was obviously a man of great natural kindness and warmth, but whose conditioning had left him closed, rigid and resistant to any suggestions of change. Violence, whatever form it takes, breeds violence, for the violence of the aggressor infects its victim. In a country where the Church is treated violently by the state, the danger is that the Church reacts by using the very methods it so deplores in its persecutor, refuses to listen and becomes so insistent on resisting the state that it has no energy left to think, reflect, or initiate change within itself; it clings to forms, traditions and customs without trying to understand them, or asking whether they are still communicating the mystery of God to people and expressing the peoples' response to God. Just as an individual, when constantly unfairly treated, can retreat into eccentricity or illness, so the Church can be damaged by persecution. In face of violence from the state the Church can only escape the infection in so far as, like her master, she remains vulnerable, which means open to criticism and to change, if necessary. Refusing to change simply through fear that the enemy might consider such change a sign of capitulation, is to allow the enemy to dominate.

After my experience of walking by the stone desert route along the coast, I thought of continuing my journey by an inland route, but the parish priest was horrified at the suggestion, told me that the country was wild, with long stretches without any human habitation, full of danger from wolves and also from human violence. I had no means of knowing whether these views were based on truth or on prejudice, but decided to return to Karlobag on the coast in the morning. Having studied the map I saw that I could avoid the stone desert coast road by taking a ferry from Karlobag to the Pag peninusla, a narrow strip of land leading to the ancient city of Zadar.

Monday, May 4

A storm was raging when I left the mountain village by bus, and it was still raging when I reached Karlobag, delaying the ferry across the narrow strip of water to Pag. The storm worsened, and after a five-hour wait it was announced that there would be no further sailings until Tuesday. I made for the Capuchin monastery to beg a room for the night and arrived with a sodden Mungo, for the rain was bucketing down and I had difficulty in negotiating the steps leading up to the monastery which had become a mini-waterfall, submerging my feet above the ankles. The Franciscans took pity and I was glad of a further opportunity to chat with them, for on the previous Saturday, the parish priest's non-stop chatter had reduced them to silence. I told them about my own weekend experience and they confirmed that at parish level there was little or no contact between Catholics and Orthodox, but said there was more contact at episcopal level and that in the University of Zagreb Catholics and Orthodox were studying together. On Medjugorje the Capuchins were non-committal, but said they were very impressed by the inner change effected in many people who had gone there on pilgrimage.

Tuesday, May 5

By the next day the storm had abated and I caught a morning ferry to Pag. The walking was easy compared with the stone desert, but it was a dull, flat and uninteresting 30-km stretch that day, the most striking feature of the landscape being the heaps of rubbish piled at the side of the road. In contrast with the other countries I had passed through, the Yugoslav countryside, although strikingly beautiful, had an uncared-for look, acres of wasteland with little cultivated plots here and there being worked by hand, usually by women. The few farm tractors were tiny machines.

In the evening I reached Razanac where the map indicated two campsites. Both were closed. I went to the village shop to buy food for an evening meal and for next morning's breakfast and inquired about lodgings. The girl at the cash desk told me there was plenty of room in a hotel nearby. When I asked at the hotel I knew I would not get a room, for the first question was, 'How many are you?' and the second, 'How many nights are you staying?' When I asked where in the village I might find a bed, the manager shrugged his shoulders and could suggest nothing. There was a great contrast in Yugoslavia between the friendliness of ordinary people and the inhumanity of petty officials.

As I came out of the hotel I heard church bells and arrived just as the large congregation was coming out from Mass. I approached a nun who was with an elderly woman and asked if they could tell me where I might find a room for the night. Neither could speak English or German, but I gathered from the nun's tone of voice and gestures that there was no hope of finding anything in Razanac. The nun then moved away, but the woman beckoned me on and introduced me to her husband. They conferred together, then asked me to follow. We went through the village and the man pointed to one of the few large houses, told me to ring the bell and try there. The couple stayed at the garden gate while I went to the door, which was answered by the nun I had met a few minutes before, but her startled look, jabbered reply and vigorous hand-gesture pointing into the far distance was clear enough. The old couple conferred again before leading me further. We entered a junk yard with a small concrete building in the middle of it. They invited me into the hallway which had a sofa by the wall. The kitchen was on one side of the hall, their bedroom on the other. They told me I was welcome to the hall sofa for the night and then took me into the kitchen, gave me coffee and schnapps, which the old man told me was home-made and cost him the equivalent of £1.00 a litre. We then shared supper. The woman boiled cabbage with a bit of bacon in it, while I produced my mixture of bread, cheese, pâté and apples. They were desperately poor and both in bad health, but their house felt peaceful and they seemed a serene couple, interested in life and ready to laugh as we tried to communicate in signs. Washing facilities consisted of a basin in the middle of the junk yard, connected to the house water supply with a piece of rubber hosing. The toilet was at the end of the garden, doorless and waterless. Next morning they insisted that I stay for a breakfast of eggs fried in oil with coffee and schnapps, but I declined the fiery schnapps.

Wednesday, May 6

After Monday's storm the weather remained cloudy and cold. When I set out, there was light drizzle which persisted all day until it turned into heavy rain near Zadar. It was another dull stretch of walking, with many derelict, unfinished houses of dull, damp, concrete punctuating the rubbish heaps by the side of the road. Occasionally ancient two-engined planes would pass noisily overhead, flying so slowly that they looked as though they might drop out of the sky at any moment, but their sound was soothing compared to the screaming jets of Holland and Germany.

My spirits were at their lowest at this stage of the walk and I could not identify the feeling of sadness which hovered around me. I could think of many contributory causes, the wet weather, the lack of hot water and drying facilities in the places where I had stayed, Mungo's growing tendency to list and capsize, physical tiredness and so on. Reminding myself that pilgrims of old did not have hot water and drying facilities, or even a roof over their heads, did not help, but I knew these difficulties were not the cause of the sadness. It was as though the sadness was like some noxious gas seeping up through the earth and spreading everywhere. During my time in Yugoslavia I learned more of the sad and bloody history of this part of the world, which had been ravaged by foreign invaders – Italians, Venetians, Turks, Austrians, Hungarians and Germans – and torn apart for centuries by fierce internal strife between Serbs and Croats, Catholics, Orthodox and Muslims, internal strife which was at its fiercest during and after the Second World War. It was not surprising that its bloodied earth communicated a sense of sadness.

I reached Zadar by early afternoon on Wednesday, May 6th, called at a Franciscan friary, was made most welcome and invited to stay for as long as I liked. The friary was one of the earliest Franciscan foundations on this coast and dates back to the thirteenth century. It included a small museum whose greatest treasure was a twelfth-century painting of the crucifixion 12 feet high.

Thursday, May 7

I stayed for two nights in Zadar and had Thursday to explore the ancient and the modern city. One of the Franciscans took me on a guided tour. Although the holiday season had not yet begun, the cafés and restaurants were thronged with people mid-morning. I asked my companion if it was some public holiday. He laughed and said that had it been a public holiday, the cafés and restaurants in the city would be empty, because all the workers would be at home. The café crowds were enjoying prolonged elevenses. There were also many off-duty, but uniformed, military on the streets. Yugoslavia is not a member of the Warsaw Pact; it is a non-aligned country, and its armed forces are planned and trained only for defence of their own land, not for aggression. Even so, national defence, which includes two years' military conscription, is a heavy burden on a very poor country, which also tries to provide a comprehensive health service for all its people – an admirable intention, but only possible for a relatively wealthy nation, which Yugoslavia is not.

There is a beautiful Benedictine museum in Zadar with a collection of early and late medieval paintings, sculptures, carvings and reliquaries. I remembered the Austrian artist's words, as I looked at this art celebrating the wonder of God in the tears and joys, pain and delight of human life and compared it with some of the modern art I had seen in Yugoslav churches, celebrating a kind of heavenly Disney-land.

The friary in Zadar was in much better repair than the one at Karlobag, but the friars at Zadar told me that they had had to wait twenty-five years for building permission for repairs and extensions even although they had the money to pay for them. Almost everyone I spoke to in Yugoslavia complained about the stupidity and inefficiency of local and national communist bureaucracy, and of the spiritual and moral, as well as the economic bankruptcy of the communist party, but I did not meet anyone who did not approve of socialist ideals. What they complained about was its implementation, leaving the majority without any say in determining how they were to live.

Before leaving Zadar, I checked Mungo's bolts and springs. While tightening one of the nuts securing the haversack to the frame, the outer edge of the bolt sheered off, so that only a part of it was now holding the haversack in place. It was unlikely to hold for long, but I hoped it would hold until Split, where I could probably get it repaired.

Friday, May 8

As I left Zadar the weather cleared, the scenery improved, and once I was clear of the city and on the road running by the edge of the sea my spirits began to rise again from slavonic gloom. After 32 km I reached Pakostane and began the hunt for a room. After three refusals I found an excellent room with a verandah, hot water and a restaurant nearby for supper. When I returned to my lodgings, the family invited me to join them, the eighteen-year-old daughter, who spoke excellent English, acting as interpreter. She told me that her school contemporaries were not much interested in social, political or religious questions, as their immediate interest was in passing the necessary examinations to get a university place. Of her class of thirty-five, twenty-five were Christian, but there was no problem in relations between believers and non-believers. She hoped to study medicine and did not think that her being a Catholic would be a disadvantage in finding a place in medical school, although it might affect her promotion chances later.

Saturday, May 9

The weather had improved for walking, with a cool wind and warm sun, and the tree-lined road ran by the side of the shore. I was enjoying every minute of it and looking forward to many more such days when Mungo keeled over. When I tried to right the machine I saw that one of the main struts supporting the machine on its pram wheels had buckled and torn, the result of rough treatment on bumpy mountain tracks. I was far from any town, still about 90 km away from Split, and it was Saturday afternoon with everything closed down until Monday.

The walk had begun to teach me patience, a virtue I find difficult, so I sat on the roadside and decided to enjoy this beautiful spot by the sea until a bus arrived for Split. An elderly couple working on a boat at the water's edge had told me a bus would arrive in half an hour. Two hours later I was still sitting in the same spot. Three buses had already passed, but did not stop for all my waving at them, nor did any of the few cars which passed. Eventually a battered little car, with two occupants and luggage piled on the roof, did stop, added Mungo to the roof luggage with a piece of rope, and took me to a village further on where buses were bound to stop. Among the group waiting for the Split bus there was a German-speaking engineer who examined Mungo, assured me the strut could easily be mended in Split, and wrote out for me a sentence in Serbo-Croat for use at a metal workshop.

As I sat in the bus and saw the coastal scenery flying past, I regretted missing this stretch of walking and decided that once Mungo was mended I would walk from Split to Medjugorje instead of taking public transport for this detour, as I had at first intended.

Split is a very ancient, large and beautiful city, and the Emperor Diocletian, whatever his other faults, showed good taste in having his imperial palace there. Like the other Roman emperors, he gave himself the title 'Divine Emperor' and was the fiercest persecutor of the Christians. His mausoleum, which is still standing and in daily use, has served for centuries as the Catholic cathedral of Split. A new and much more spacious cathedral had recently been built and was due to open in a few months' time, a remarkable achievement in communist Yugoslavia, where the government is reluctant to give permission even for church repairs.

There would have been no problem in finding a room in Split because as soon as the bus arrived we were besieged by people offering to provide rooms, to carry luggage and find taxis. I had the address of a Jesuit house and had already arranged to stay there for a few days. Arriving several days earlier than expected was no problem, as the house, a noviceship, had a few spare rooms. There were nine novices in the house and another four had had to interrupt their noviceship to do their military training; it was a very healthy number in a communist country, which had only 200 Jesuits in its Croatian province. All but one of the novices had entered the Jesuits by way of minor seminaries, institutions which have been abandoned in most Western countries, because painful experience has taught the unwisdom of educating boys from about the age of twelve in boarding schools with a view to becoming priests. Later I stayed in a minor seminary in Dubrovnik, where the Rector defended such institutions in Yugoslavia because there was no other way of providing a Catholic education for youngsters, Catholic schools being forbidden. The novices gave Mungo a thorough examination and assured me that there would be no difficulty in having it repaired.

Sunday, May 10

I stayed at the noviceship house in Split until Wednesday, May 13. There was a pile of letters waiting for me, and besides answering them, I hoped to write another article for *The Tablet* during my stay and to see something of this ancient city. One of the novices took me on a tour to Diocletian's mausoleum and then on to the hills above the city to see the magnificent bay. Later he took me to a Jesuit parish in the city. The Franciscans in Zadar had waited twenty-five years for building permission. The Jesuits in Split were more crafty. They built a very large house. If any building, even a private house, is to be used for religious purposes, permission must first be obtained from the local authority. If there is no reply within two weeks, it may be assumed that permission has been granted. Permission was requested and no refusal received within two weeks, so the Jesuits now had both a church and a presbytery, for they had the house so constructed that the ground floor could serve as lecture and meeting rooms, the first floor was one large room, the church, and the top floor was a residence! When I met with the two Jesuits in charge of this parish, they said they had contact with about half of the 20,000 Catholics who, they reckoned, were within the parish area. A thousand children came through the house every week for religious instruction.

Monday, May 11

In the morning, one of the community took me to visit the 'vulcaniser' to see about the repair of Mungo. He looked at the machine in wonder and promised to have it repaired that evening. I spent the morning writing and in the afternoon walked to the Croatian archaeological museum, which included most beautiful stone tracery work on baptism fonts dating from the seventh century. There is a striking similarity between early Croatian and Celtic art. In the evening I returned to the vulcaniser, who proudly brought out the repaired Mungo, newly equipped with an identical aluminium strut. I gave the machine a cursory shove and the wheels revolved, so I declared myself satisfied and paid the very modest bill.

Tuesday, May 12

The novice master asked me to give a talk to the novices about Jesuit life in Britain on Tuesday morning and I also wanted to complete *The Tablet* article, so I delayed my departure from Split until Wednesday. I spoke to the novices in German and the novice master translated into Serbo-Croat. The novices, a sturdy-looking group of young men, listened politely, but they had few questions and I think they would have been more interested in the state of British football than in the spirituality of justice and peace. I spent the rest of Tuesday writing, happy to be inside, because the weather had changed from bright sunshine to heavy clouds and rain.

Wednesday, May 13

When I wrote up my diary for May 13th, the opening sentence was, 'This has been by far the worst day so far,' a personal worst which was surpassed two days later. It was wet and blustery as I set off. Foolishly, I had not tested Mungo fully packed, and within yards of the novice house I realised there was something seriously wrong, because the wheels revolved only occasionally under the weight of the packed haversack and most of the time I had to drag it skidding behind me. I stopped to repair the new nuts which had been put on the wheels, but had no spanner which would fit them, nor was such a tool to be found in any of the shops I tried. So I dragged on. Then one of the supporting springs broke and I spent half-an-hour sitting by the side of the road in the rain trying to repair it, adjusting the diminished spring to match the three other springs so it would not cause imbalance. I then dragged the wretched machine to the nearest garage. The garage lent, but could not sell me a spanner, so I adjusted the wheels as best I could and continued in the rain until the evening, when I began to hunt for a room for the night. Two hours later and after six attempts to find rooms in houses advertising vacancies, I found a seventh, which took me in my soaking state. The room was cold and had neither hot water nor drying facilities, but at least it provided a shelter for the night and I was too exhausted to search further. Fortunately, there was a café nearby where I had my first meal since breakfast, and as I ate I was regretting my folly in ever having thought of walking to Jerusalem.

Thursday, May 14

I awoke to thunder and heavy rain, made coffee and had some bread in my room, for this house did not provide break-fast, and set off on the next stretch of coast road to Makarska. The rain continued until 2.00 p.m. when the sun began to break through and I was warm, dry and in much better spirits when I reached Makarska, where I found a room at my first attempt. The son and daughter of the house showed me up to a room and began to make the bed as I unpacked. A large, many-legged insect moved quickly across the mattress as they put on the first sheet, but I slept undisturbed through the night and suffered no insect bites then or throughout the journey, until I reached Israel.

Friday, May 15

From Makarska I would begin the detour up the mountains to Medjugorje and I reckoned that if all went well I should make the journey in two days, with another two days from Medjugorje to get back on to the coast road leading to Dubrovnik. I had not only slept well in Makarska, but a good supper and a colourful sunset also helped to revive my drooping spirits, so I was looking forward to this next stretch of the road, which, I had been told, was breathtakingly beautiful.

On Friday I woke again to thunder and heavy rain. As the weather had looked so settled the evening before, I had left some clothes out to dry on the verandah of the room. I packed them in their sodden state in two plastic bags and set off in the downpour for the mountain road. As I stepped off the pavement outside my lodgings, the swirling water on the road was ankle deep, so I began the walk with squelching shoes. The road twisted and turned up a gradient for 15 km, the mist becoming thicker as I climbed and obscuring the breathtaking scenery. As I passed steep black rocks to my left and saw the right-hand side of the road disappear in a vertical drop to the mist below, it brought back memories of mountain climbs on wet days in Scotland. But on the Scottish hills I was not encumbered by Mungo, which, although the wheels no longer skidded, was still hard to pull and lopsided because of the defective spring. I passed through an occasional village, but there were no cafés, no shops, not even a bus shelter, so I sat on the wet rocks for lunch and ate sodden bread and cheese. Although my cagoul was waterproof, the wind had freshened and the rain was getting in around the hood and seeping through me. Suddenly, out of the mist came a lone figure with springy step and bright yellow cagoul. It was an elderly lady from East Germany, who spoke, like the rain, in torrents. Having exchanged 'Guten Tag' and without any further introduction, she said she could not understand the people of Yugoslavia, who did not climb their own beautiful mountains, nor provide clearly marked paths and signposts for those who did appreciate their beauty, for she herself had been looking for such paths since early morning and had failed to find any, but now she must hurry back to rejoin her party, for she was already late for lunch. In the brief pause which followed this outburst I asked her whether she had seen any shops or restaurants further back on the road. 'Nichts,' she replied, 'Gar nichts,' and with this cheering news she went bouncing out of sight down the hill. I crawled on upwards, the haversack growing heavier as it absorbed more rain and my body now soaked to the skin.

Around 4.00 p.m., drenched and frozen, I reached a village with a pub, inquired about rooms, and was directed to a house across the way, where I was led to a beautifully furnished room with a large duvet on the bed. I asked if I could dry some clothes and was taken to the kitchen, which had a little wood stove in the corner. I sat in my soaking clothes and waited for my spare clothes to dry out, for the plastic in which they were wrapped had saved them from soaking, leaving them only damp. The grandmother of the house and her grandson sat with me, the grandson practising his English, which did not stretch much beyond the names of a few football teams. When the clothes were dry I returned to the bedroom, changed into dry clothes and crept beneath the duvet, but an hour later I was still shivering and got up to try and get a meal at the pub. The evening fare was dry bread, tasteless cheese and raw salty bacon. When I returned to my room, I was still too cold to write up my diary and it took two hours beneath the duvet before I was warm enough to fall asleep.

Saturday, May 16

Next morning the rain was still falling from a leaden sky. From the wet haversack pocket I took out my diary, which was sodden, its pages stuck together, and many of them illegible. The worst casualty was my sleeping bag. It was wet through and consequently very heavy. The Mass readings for the day included the words from St John's Gospel, 'I tell you most solemnly, whoever believes in me will perform the same works as I do myself, he will perform even greater works, because I am going to the Father. Whatever you ask for in my name I will do, so that the Father may be glorified in the Son.' My soul was in keeping with the weather, dull and grey, my mind asking yet again whether there was any point in this pilgrimage, whether there was any point in continuing work on justice and peace spirituality about which I felt I knew so little. I recognised the dark mood and the uselessness of trying to argue against it while the mood was on me, and tried to attend to Jesus' words, 'Whatever you ask for in my name I will do.' So I prayed to know that I am in God's hands, that he is always greater, that his goodness is greater and more important than my low spirits, his wisdom more important than my nagging doubts and that he can work through my weakness if only I have faith. As I saw the truth of this, my mood began to change and although the weather showed no sign of improvement, I set off in the rain for Medjugorje.

Just as I was leaving the house a car drew up and offered me a lift to Vrgorac, 8 km along the road, an offer I gladly accepted. On arrival at Vrgorac the sky had begun to clear and the sun broke through. From this moment on I never felt cold, and had hardly any rain for the rest of the pilgrimage. A few miles along the road a motor-cyclist stopped, asked if I was on my way to Medjugorje, and invited me to stop at his house 2 km further on, to have some food and wine. I was touched by this kindness, but failed to find his house, and did not feel inclined to go round knocking at doors and asking, 'Excuse me but is this where I am invited for some food and wine?' So I walked on and eventually stopped for a beer. The barman, having served me, came out and joined me on a seat outside, asked where I was going and why, then talked on the stupidity of the arms race when so many millions did not have enough food to eat nor a roof to shelter them, and of the danger that there might not be any human beings needing food and housing. He ended the conversation with the question, 'But what can we little people do?', a question which had been on my mind ever since I had first engaged on justice and peace work, and which had sent me on this walk.

'What can we little people do?' is a most important question, if we can stay with it, and not dismiss it as too depressing to ponder. If we try to dismiss it, the question, like any other awkward question, will not disappear, because it will continue to undermine our confidence in what we are doing until we give up. The answer to the question, 'What can we little people do?' is, 'Even less than you think'. It is a very useful exercise to ponder our own powerlessness to effect any real change for the good in ourselves or in anyone else. 'Can any of you, for all your worrying, add a single cubit to your span of life? If the smallest things, therefore, are outside your control, why worry about the rest?' (Luke 12:26). All the anxiety which arises in us when we ask 'What can I do?', comes from the atheist part of ourselves. We are assuming that the real 'I' is bounded by my own narrow and distorted vision of who I am. The real 'I' is a unique manifestation of God in whom all things have their being. It is only when we can let go this narrow vision of 'I' that we can begin to glimpse who we are, and it can only be a glimpse this side of death. 'Unless you lose your life (the false sense of 'I'), you cannot find it' (the true self, the Christ-self). We live in God. Faith is living in the awareness of this truth, recognising God in the facts in which we live, letting him be God in our lives. I long for peace. This is a God-given longing. I must attend to this longing, express it not only in prayer but in all my relationships with people and with creation around me. I am very limited, live my life in relative obscurity in a tiny corner of the world for a life span which is momentary, but I am in God, who is eternal and in whom all peoples and all things of all ages have their being, so there is an eternal quality in everything I think, feel, do and say. God created me with a part to play in the story of creation and no one else can perform my role. He created me unique, with unique finger-prints, marking my identity in each of the billions of cells which make up my body. There is a unity in all creation. My inner thoughts, my thoughts of peace or of violence, have repercussions throughout the universe. I can let God be God in my being, or I can refuse to let him be God. If I refuse to let him be God, my life damages not only myself and those around me; the damage extends far beyond my consciousness. If I 'let his glory through', my life brings life and will affect people, the animals, the plants and all creation. 'Whoever believes in me will perform the same work as I do myself, he will perform even greater works.' 'What can we little people do?' Jesus' answer is, 'You can do the same work as I do myself, and even greater works.'

I thought about the barman's questions as I walked towards Ljubuski, where I arrived around 2.30 and had an excellent meal which cost less than the bread, cheese and salty bacon of the night before. Medjugorje was still 15 km away along quiet, tree-lined roads, and although I was feeling very tired after the exertions of the previous day and Mungo was hard to pull, I felt an excitement as I approached, especially when I saw the Krizevac hill in the distance. This hill stands above the village of Medjugorje, and I recognised it from having seen a BBC Everyman programme on Medjugorje a few months before.

9

Medjugorje – the Water Becomes Wine

> She, wild web, wondrous robe,
> Mantles the guilty globe,
> Since God has let dispense
> Her prayers his providence.
> (G. M. Hopkins, 'The Blessed Virgin
> Compared to the Air We Breathe')

The traffic increased as I approached Medjugorje. About a mile before the village, I took a right turn, and joined a slow procession of cars, taxis and large tourist buses. The road was narrow, the asphalt edges a few centimetres higher than the glutinous mud which bordered them. I was in a state of near exhaustion as I tried to haul Mungo through the muddy verges, its pretty red wheels almost totally submerged. There was constant hooting as car and bus drivers expressed their frustration on their horns. A massive German double-decker tourist bus was blocking the oncoming traffic. Its side panels announced its purpose, 'Luxus Reisen', and its rear window gave the details of the luxury provided, showers, a bar, hot meals and T.V.

The mind is multi-faceted. Part of mine wanted to be in a shower and have a hot meal and a drink, while watching T.V. The pharisaical part of my mind was disapproving of all pilgrims travelling by Luxus Reisen, hidden envy fuelling my disapproval. Another part was immersed in physical tired-ness and dislike of the mud, while another part was struggling to raise itself out of the mud and prepare for the evening Mass, which was the reason for the traffic jam. I remembered a hymn which we used to sing at Mount St Mary's every Saturday after night prayers and which began, 'O Mother, I

could weep for mirth,' and ended with, 'Long may the transport last'. It never was my favourite hymn, but this evening
'O Mother I could weep' expressed my feelings exactly. On
my way to the church I tried a few houses for a room, but
they were all fully booked. Decisions become more difficult
when physically tired and I dithered as to whether I should
first find lodging for the night, or whether I should put my
faith in God, go straight to the church and trust that I would
find lodgings later. Having failed at two houses and being
within a hundred yards of the church, I opted for faith.

There were already several hundred people sitting at
benches and tables under the trees with a few hundred others
standing or milling around outside the doors of the packed
church. I leaned a sagging Mungo against a tree, asking St
Mungo to look after it, found a seat on the benches and
waited for Mass to begin. Darkness was beginning to fall
along with a light drizzle dampening me and my faith. Loud-
speakers in the trees relayed the service to those outside. The
Scripture readings were given in English and German as well
as Serbo-Croat. The Sunday Gospel included the comforting
words, 'Do not let your hearts be troubled. Trust in God still,
and trust in me. There are many rooms in my Father's house'
(John 14:1–2), and I prayed that some of the rooms might
be in Medjugorje. The sermon began in Serbo-Croat and the
preacher, with a piercing, vehement voice, showed no sign of
relenting after ten minutes. I asked a neighbour how long the
service usually lasted and was told 'over two hours'.

I decided to go and look for one of the many rooms, left
the congregation and went to the tourist office, where the girl
told me that there were no rooms for miles around, adding
that camping was forbidden. As my sleeping bag was still
sodden, the camping prohibition did not disturb me. I prayed
to Mary as I began to go from door to door. The first house
I tried had no room, but the owner pointed to a bunker-like
building nearby, of the same design as the house in the junk-
yard of a few days earlier, and told me to try there. The
owners, husband and wife, were most welcoming, showed me
a room with two beds in it and said I was welcome to one of
the beds, for a Hungarian pilgrim had already booked the
other. They then offered me coffee and schnapps before showing me the other house facilities. Washing was in a cellar-like

room whose only furnishings were a tap in the wall and a plastic basin bearing the grime of earlier pilgrims. The toilet was at the far end of the garden, approached by a narrow plank spanning a deep hole in the ground and leading onto the garden wall, to be negotiated with care because of its uneven surface. At the end of the wall stood the toilet, a wooden shed with neither water nor chemical disinfectant. As the alternative was a night spent in the open, I accepted the room.

I returned to the church where the evening serivce was just finishing more than two hours after it had begun. Luxus Reisen and the other buses and taxis were returning pilgrims to their lodgings and hotels. In the church I met Father Ivan, a Franciscan, who spoke fluent German, introduced myself and arranged to meet with him next day after the 10.00 a.m. Mass, which would be in English as there were large numbers of American and Irish pilgrims. There would also be a German and a French Mass on Sunday morning, but the main Mass of each day was in the evening at 7.00.

Sunday, May 17

There was no sign of the Hungarian when I returned to my lodgings, and when I awoke next morning the bed was still empty, so the Hungarian had either spent the night in prayerful vigil or had fled after one look at his lodgings. I left the house early and walked through the village to the foot of the hill, Krizevac, which means Hill of the Cross. The huge concrete cross, 14 metres high, was erected in 1933, a Holy Year, as a protection against the fierce hailstorms which had been ruining the vines and tobacco crop for many years. The village was very still and quiet, the road deserted, a contrast to the previous evening. Outside the church there were a few people sitting, heavily clad in overcoats, finishing their all-night vigil. Further on I passed an elderly woman dressed in black and carrying a pile of brushwood in a sack on her shoulder. The sun was already bright and warming at 6.30 in the morning. Whatever the truth about the apparitions of Our Lady, Medjugorje felt a very peaceful place, and although there were many houses under construction, it was still a peasant village, with no obvious signs of commercialism at this time of the morning.

The hill is steep, the rock path not yet worn smooth by pilgrims. Progress to the top is easily measured by the thirteen stations of the cross leading to the fourteenth, the cross on the summit. The stations were simple wooden crosses, festooned with strips of cloth, sometimes with scarves and coloured T-shirts, the number of decorations increasing at each station and at the summit the strips and clothing were hung on all the surrounding bushes. There was something poignantly beautiful in these rags, as though pilgrims longed to stay in the beauty and peace of this place, could not, and so they left some of their clothing behind, a symbol of their longing for peace and immortality.

The apparitions at Medjugorje began on 24 July 1981 and have continued daily ever since to some of the children. When the children asked the apparition her name, she answered, 'Queen of Peace,' and the constant message which runs through all the children's accounts of their conversations with 'The Gospa', as they call her, is peace and reconciliation, gifts for the human race, for which we are to dispose ourselves by prayer and fasting. As I climbed past the stations of the cross I listened to Jesus' words when he appeared to the disciples in an upper room after his death. ' "Peace be to you," he said, and showed them his hands and his side' (John 20:20). He brings the peace which reconciles all that is on earth and all that is in heaven, a peace effected by his death on a cross, a peace that is costly, risky and which demands vulnerability. He had absorbed the violence of his enemies in his own body and answered it with love and forgiveness. I had prayed on this scene every day of the pilgrimage, begging to know the mystery of his peace, a peace which the world cannot give, a peace which comes not from self-protection and self-security, but from vulnerability, yet a peace which has nothing to do with passivity, but which flows from an active, passionate love which is never deflected, no matter what violence is threatened or inflicted.

The stillness of the morning was suddenly shattered by an Irish voice higher on the hill, 'Now she must be related to the Mullinses of Ballymoney.' When I came down the hill later I overtook the same party still sorting out family trees.

I went early to the church to be sure of a place for the English Mass, but the church was already filled with German pilgrims finishing their Mass. When it was over, there was a scrimmage for places as the Germans tried to leave and the English-speaking pilgrims tried to enter. In the history of Christian pilgrimage there are many accounts of pilgrims being crushed to death in the devotional rush, but there were no fatalities on this occasion, only a slight fraying at the edges of the spirit of international peace and reconciliation.

During the Mass I experienced conflicting emotions, a sense of wonder at the phenomenon of Medjugorje and of delight in being here, but also a feeling of uneasiness when I heard the sermon, which was full of pious praise of Mary, Queen of Peace, a frothy *ferverino*, totally unrelated to anything happening on earth. I also felt uneasy at the large number of priests who were concelebrating the Mass, filling the sanctuary and obscuring a view of the altar for the laity. The priest, like Christ, is to be the one who serves, and I cannot see that a large number of concelebrants serves any useful purpose: on the contrary their presence in the sanctuary can seem to those in the pew like an exercise of privilege. My uneasiness was to increase next day.

After Mass I made my way to the presbytery to have a recorded interview with Father Ivan for the Medjugorje weekly newspaper. Most of our time was spent in my answering his questions to me, and so I asked if I might have another interview on Monday in which I could put questions to him, to which he kindly agreed. I was very impressed with his quiet, calm manner and the simplicity of the presbytery. I was particularly impressed when at the end of the visit he showed me the room where the visionaries met every evening and experienced the apparitions. The room was the office of one of the friars, with books and papers all over the place, the kind of room I like to think Our Lady would be thoroughly at home in. When I left Father Ivan, groups were still meeting outside the church and I joined a Northern Ireland group, which was being addressed by Anita Curtis, a native of Northern Ireland but resident in Medjugorje since September 1984. She had come on a visit in June 1984 with no intention of staying, but was so impressed with what she experienced that she decided to live there permanently, learn Serbo-Croat, and act as interpreter for English-speaking pilgrim groups. She made no mention of whirling suns or visions in the sky. What had impressed her was the effect Medjugorje had on herself and on so many people she had met, men and women, who had arrived broken in spirit, but had recovered hope and life. She mentioned in particular a young Canadian, a world-class drummer, who arrived broken and depressed. After a few weeks at Medjugorje he felt he wanted to become a priest, but reckoned that because of his past life and present state, a call to the priesthood must be an illusion. The visionaries heard about him and the youngest, Jakov, asked Our Lady about him during one of the apparitions, reporting later that Our Lady had said that certainly he could become a priest. The young man joined the Franciscans, but finding the life too noisy, went to the Trappists instead where he was still, two years later. I told Anita about the uneasiness I had felt during Mass and of my fear that the message of peace of Medjugorje should be lost through the enthusiasm of the rosary brigade, flocking to the place for spiritual kicks and a sight of the dancing sun, seeking a false peace which would protect them from the need to change. She acknowledged the danger, mentioned a particular American group who call themselves 'the Blue Army', but said that there had been real conversions among them, too. When I commented on the large number of concelebrants at Mass, Anita told me that most priests came to Medjugorje because they were so impressed at the effect of a visit on their parishioners. The laity had taken the initiative and they were mostly responsible for organising the pilgrimages. Bishops are not allowed to organise or lead pilgrimages until Rome has officially approved of the place as a pilgrimage centre. I was to hear more about this from Father Ivan next day.

As I passed the benches outside the church on my way back to the bunker, I spotted an American lady busy on a leg of chicken, but every few seconds she would remove the chicken leg and her dark spectacles to check that the sun was still in its accustomed place.

I had just settled on my bed for a siesta when I heard a very English voice doing its best with elementary German in a conversation with the proprietor. It was Father Alan Grisewood, a diocesan priest, who has been working in

Taiwan ever since his ordination. He had been home on short leave visiting his sister in the West Highlands of Scotland. His sister, a devotee of Medjugorje, had persuaded him to leave the peace of the West Highlands and make this pilgrimage. He was excellent company, a bit sceptical about the Medjugorje phenomenon, but was very knowledgeable on its history.

That day, as on every other evening, there was Mass at 7.00 p.m. preceded for an hour by a full recitation of the rosary, the mysteries interspersed with hymns. Some people were in the church for this, others were crowding outside the presbytery, where the visionaries were also praying the rosary in the office, and it was in the course of this hour that the apparitions occurred. Apart from the children, and on this occasion there were only two of them, Jakov and Maria, the only other people allowed in with them are priests. The Mass, in Serbo-Croat, was followed by more prayer and a healing service, and it was after 9.30 before the whole service was over and I went in search of something to eat. The village supermarket was closed on Sunday and I had eaten one sausage-roll since lunchtime on Saturday, an involuntary fast.

Monday, May 18

I climbed the hill again on Monday morning, undisturbed this time by Irish or any other voices, and spent longer on the summit, which gives a magnificent view of the countryside in all directions. It looked and felt so peaceful that it was difficult to realise that this beautiful landscape had been soaked in blood only forty years earlier, Serbs and Croats torturing and murdering each other.

Yugoslavia came into existence as a nation, made up of Slovenes, Serbs and Croats, after the First World War. The new kingdom had a Serbian king and the Croats were so oppressed that they demanded independence. The Serbian king, tired of Croat restlessness, suspended the constitution, declared a dictatorship and tried to enforce unity. The Croats suffered worse oppression at the hands of the Serbs and there was a memorandum submitted to the League of Nations in

1931 giving the names of large numbers of Croats held
without trial, and complaining of the use of torture, police
brutality and other forms of oppression. Unemployment and
persecution drove many Croats to emigrate. A few Croat
extremists, led by Ante Pavelic, took refuge in Italy, where
Mussolini welcomed them as a useful tool to be used against
Yugoslavia. In 1934 Pavelic agents assassinated the Serbian
king, Alexander, but even after the murder, Pavelic and his
gang, known as the Ustase, were not taken seriously as a
political force. When the Nazis invaded in 1941, Yugoslavia
was carved up and apportioned between the Axis powers,
and Croatia became a puppet state, controlled by Germany
and Italy, but with immediate power given to Pavelic and his
Ustase. The Croats were at first delighted with their new
state and freedom from Serbian domination, but they soon
discovered that they had exchanged one form of tyranny for
an even more brutal one. Croatia was to become a two-
religion state, Catholic and Muslim, and all Orthodox
Christians, mostly Serbs, were to be deported, killed, or forced
to become Catholic.

A hundred and twenty thousand Serbs were deported, and
bands of Ustase thugs travelled through the area burning
Orthodox villages and cutting the throats of the inhabitants.
On several occasions all the males of a village were forced
into their church, which was then burnt down, while the
Ustase waited outside, ready to shoot any who tried to escape.
Estimates of the number of Serbs killed range from 60,000 to
750,000, with 200,000 forcibly converted to Catholicism. Near
Medjugorje is the Orthodox monastery of Zitomislic. On the
wall leading to its chapel is a plaque which commemorates
21 June 1941, when the entire community of monks was
taken outside by the Ustase and buried alive. There were few
dissident voices, because any opposition to the Ustase was
punished with death. Archbishop Stepinac, who had at first
welcomed the regime, became its opponent when he discovered what was happening, and although he managed to
save 7,000 Serb children from the internment camps, he could
not stem the slaughter and was attacked in the press for
meddling in politics when he tried to do so.

One effect of the persecution was that it drove the Croatian
Serbs into the mountains to join Tito, himself a Croat, and his

partisans to form a resistance movement. There was another resistance group of Serbs under Colonel Mihailovic, called 'Cetniks'. The Allies backed Tito rather than Mihailovic and the two groups spent more of their energy in trying to destroy each other and the Ustase than in fighting the Germans. The villages around Medjugorje were terrorised by the three warring factions. By 1945 the partisans were in control. In Hercegovina some of the Ustase fled to a Franciscan friary. The partisans surrounded it and killed everyone within it.

When the Ustase government was forced out in May 1945, about 200,000 Croat soldiers and some Cetniks fled to the Austrian border and tried to surrender to the British forces. The British turned them back to Yugoslavia and to death. It is reckoned that 16,000 Croats were put to death in one day. The post-war Communist rule was as ruthless as the Ustase had been and a determined effort was made to break the power of the Church, whether Catholic or Orthodox, but through all the persecution the majority of the population remained Christian.

There was some improvement in relations between the Communist government and the Vatican after the Second Vatican Council and an attempt at dialogue with the Orthodox, but when one Catholic bishop admitted in a pastoral letter that Catholics had committed crimes against the Serbian Orthodox, some priests in his diocese refused to read his letter from their pulpits.

After 1963 the Communist government made some attempt to liberalise its regime and there were renewed demands from the Croats to have an independent state. In 1971 students in Zagreb took to the streets, troops were brought in and there were 400 arrests with long prison sentences for the offenders. The Zagreb diocesan newspaper was banned for using the paper for 'nationalist propaganda'. Tito feared the Croatian threat to national unity and blamed the Croats for the unrest. The Church was attracting the young in Yugoslavia, and the arrival of John Paul II as Pope and his influence in Poland made the Yugoslav Communist government even more fearful of a Croatian rising. In February 1981, 7,000 Croats marked the twenty-first anniversary of Archbishop Stepinac's death with a demonstration around his tomb, and this made the government even more nervous. It was therefore not surprising that the Communist government's first reaction to the reports of apparitions of Our Lady at Medjugorje, beginning in July 1981, was to suspect that it was all part of a Croatian independence plot.

I returned to the village, bought some food in the supermarket and then returned to the church for the 10.00 a.m. Mass in English. It was just as crowded as on Sunday, the sanctuary again filled with concelebrating priests. The singing was good, but the sermon was as frothy as on Sunday, pious gyrations of an unreflective mind, which seemed to be detached from this world into which Christ came and in which, with all its horror, darkness, cruelty and conflict, he now lives. I felt anger that this message of peace, which the children claimed was the message they were given daily in the apparitions, (a peace which is costly, risky, and demands individual and corporate vulnerability,) a peace which will always be restless and disturbing as long as any human being is the victim of oppression, exploitation and fear, was being turned into a bland spirituality, bringing false comfort to the pious, anaesthetising them to the pain of the world and so shielding them from the need to change and concern themselves with the sufferings of their sisters and brothers throughout the world. I found myself praying to be with fringe Christians who are disillusioned with the Church as they experience it, with unbelievers and with those who feel rejected by the Church and by society.

After Mass I went to the presbytery for my second interview with Father Ivan. He gave me a potted history of the apparitions at Medjugorje, how the first apparition was on 24 June 1981 to two young girls, Ivanka and Mirjana on their way down the hill behind the house where they were staying in the village of Bijakovici, which adjoins Medjugorje. They had gone up the hill not to pray but to have a furtive smoke. Ivanka, looking up, saw in the distance the shadowy figure of a young woman, apparently hovering above ground level. She cried to Mirjana, 'Look there, it's the Madonna.' Mirjana replied, 'Don't be idiotic,' but was frightened by the look on Ivanka's face. They both ran back to the village, where they met a friend, Milka, who asked them to help her round up some sheep, an operation which brought them back to the spot where Ivanka had seen the mysterious figure. Again Ivanka saw the apparition in the distance, but not distinctly, and this time Mirjana and Milka also saw the woman. Later, Mirjana said of this appearance, 'We couldn't see her face, but something inside us insisted that it was the Madonna.' Meanwhile, a friend of the three, Vicka, came looking for them and when she joined them and they pointed and said, 'Look, it's the Madonna,' Vicka fled down the hill in terror. On the road below she met Ivan Ivankovic and Ivan Dragicevic, who was carrying apples in a plastic bag. Vicka asked them to come up the hill with her for, as she reported later 'something was drawing me back there'. When they reached the spot where the others were gathered, Ivan Dragicevic took to his heels and ran, dropping the apples. The other Ivan and Vicka both saw the figure and Vicka later described it,

> All of a sudden, I looked up and saw her standing there, just as clearly as I can see you now. She wore a grey dress with a white veil, a crown of stars, blue eyes, dark hair and rosy cheeks. And she was floating about this high on a grey cloud, not touching the ground. She had something in her left hand that she kept covering and uncovering, but you couldn't see what it was. She called us to go nearer, but none of us dared to. (From a BBC interview transcript for 'Everyman')

When they returned home and told their families, they were not believed. Next day Vicka, Ivanka, Mirjana, together with Ivan Dragicevic, who had decided to overcome his fears, went up the hill again. Milka had to mind the sheep, but her older sister, Marija, said to Vicka, 'If you see the Madonna today, let me know.' On the hill, it was Ivanka who first stopped and said, 'Look, the Madonna,' and this time they could see her face clearly. Vicka, remembering her promise to Marija, rushed down the hill and found her with ten-year-old Jakov Colo, who both dropped what they were doing and ran after Vicka. They all saw the lady and it was Ivanka who first had the courage to speak to her, asking her about her mother, who had died alone in hospital a few weeks before, and whether her mother had any messages for the children. The lady smiled and said, 'Take special care of your grandmother now that she is old and unable to work.' Then Mirjana said 'Dear Madonna, they won't believe us, you know. They'll say we're mad.' In reply, the Madonna just smiled again. It is to this group of six children that the apparitions appeared daily ever since. Mirjana has not seen them since December 1982 and they have also now ceased for Ivanka. When I visited, Ivan had been called up for national service and was no longer seeing the apparitions.

Every evening the 'visionaries' as the children are called, meet in the presbytery for prayer at 6.00. The apparitions occur around 6.40 p.m. each evening and may last anything from five to thirty minutes, beginning and ending simultaneously for each visionary. During this time their eyes are focused on the same point, the appearances invisible to the onlooker. Tests have been done on the children during the apparitions which have ruled out the possibility that they are in a state of coma, or hallucination. Their bodies are relaxed and functioning normally, and tests on their brain activity indicate that they are in a state of deep contemplation. They are so absorbed in what they are experiencing that when someone stuck a needle into Vicka, she did not notice, nor did she bleed. On one occasion, a portly doctor placed himself in front of Vicka and the point on which she was focusing. When the apparition was over, the doctor asked, 'Did you notice I was in the way?' 'No,' said Vicka, 'but there was a slight mist between me and the Madonna.'

The Medjugorje apparitions are different from other alleged apparitions in their frequency, daily over a period of six years, and in their simultaneous occurrence to as many of the children as are present. During the apparitions the children sometimes move their lips, smile and show all the expressions of people engaged in conversation, but onlookers see and hear nothing. I asked Father Ivan whether anyone skilled in lip-reading had ever been present, but surprisingly no one had. The children claim that their conversations with the Madonna are about matters personal to them, about the Church and about the world, and that Our Lady appears as three-dimensional and as real to them as any other person. The children have been asked to keep a written record of their conversations, which now forms a mass of material.

The essential and repeated message communicated by the

children is scriptural and simple in content. In one of the earliest apparitions, Marija saw a vision of the cross without a figure on it, but shining with a whole spectrum of colours. In front of the cross and weeping stood the Madonna, who said, 'Peace, you must seek peace. There must be peace on earth, you must be reconciled with God and with each other. Peace, peace, peace.' Marija said it was an overwhelming experience, which drove her to commit herself totally to search for peace, peace in her own heart, peace within families, peace in the world.

Father Ivan told me that on one occasion the children had asked the Madonna whether all religions were good and received the answer, 'Before God they are all the same.' This is a surprising answer to come from peasant children brought up in a strongly Catholic environment where relations with the Orthodox and Muslims have been so bitter. It is also an answer to keep the theologians usefully occupied for many centuries! If I remember rightly, the context of this question was another question about some local Catholic girl, who was engaged to a Muslim, and the children were asking whether this marriage was right before God. The answer was that before God the marriage was good, but that there would be human difficulties.

There were also human difficulties for the visionaries, who were disbelieved, cross-questioned, subjected to rigorous examination by doctors, psychiatrists, theologians and the police. At one police interrogation a revolver was held at Vicka's head. She showed no sign of fear but told the policeman to put the gun away and not upset the economy further by wasting bullets. At first, the clergy were even more opposed to the visionaries than the state authorities, and suspected a case of demonic possession. The local bishop, Zanic of Mostar, interrogated the children about a month after the first reports of the apparitions, and after the interview he declared, 'These children are not telling lies.' Later, he preached in the Medjugorje church stating his belief that the children were not lying, that no one could be manipulating them. He could not say whether the apparitions were purely subjective or something supernatural, but the messages given to the children so far were in accordance with the Gospel and they were bringing about reconciliations among enemies and a spirit of prayer and penance in the area.

In Yugoslavia there is a long history of difficult relations between the Franciscan friars, who for centuries had been the only priests allowed to operate in the country, and the diocesan clergy, who entered the country only in 1881. In 1982 Bishop Zanic expelled two young Franciscan friars from his diocese. The friars visited Medjugorje. The children, aware of the friars' problem, had asked the Madonna about their case and claimed that the Madonna had answered that the bishop had acted too hastily and that the two friars were innocent. The children claimed that they had received this answer on thirteen separate occasions and that on the fourteenth the Madonna complained to Vicka, 'You think of nothing else but those two friars.' Since then the Bishop Zanic of Mostar seems to have thought of little else but this reply, has denounced the apparitions as a Franciscan plot and has been a more implacable enemy of Medjugorje than the communist authorities. Bishop Zanic formed a commission, chosen by himself, to investigate the phenomenon, and sent the condemnatory results to Rome. Rome did not accept his conclusions and has set up another commission in which, I believe, all the bishops of Yugoslavia are involved.

I was impressed with the objective way in which Father Ivan recounted this story, so painful to him and to all the other Franciscans, without any sign of bitterness; he was also able to laugh. Whatever the conclusions of this new commission will be, it will have to explain how it is that six children, very different in character, background and intellectual ability, with no obvious leader among them, can claim to have seen apparitions daily over a period of six years and to have heard answers to their questions which reveal such insight, wisdom and theological assuredness. Where do they get their knowledge and how is it that they show such a remarkable consistency in their accounts of the apparitions, which vary, as is to be expected, according to their different temperaments, but do not conflict?

On Monday afternoon I joined the Northern Ireland group for a visit to Vicka outside her house. She arrived late for the meeting because she had been held up by an earlier group and then had to prepare lunch for some workmen. She is a beautiful girl, whose normal expression is a very natural smile, but there is also suffering in her face. For the last few years she has been suffering from an inoperable cyst on the brain, which causes her much pain and often prevents her from joining the others at the presbytery each evening. But, I was told, she sees the apparitions at the same time in her own room. Father Ivan told me that she was confident the cyst would disappear in time. She spoke very simply on her experience of the apparitions and on Our Lady's message of peace and reconciliation, gifts for which we were to prepare ourselves by the practice of prayer and fasting. Her answers to questions were also simple and she was not afraid to say, 'I don't know.' The questions tended to be on the more extravagant manifestations at Medjugorje, the dancing sun, light above the cross on the hill, etc. In her answers Vicka made little of these happenings and kept returning to the essence of the message. While she was speaking, standing against the wall of a house, a young lad came past on a bicycle with earphones on his head, rang his bell, waved to Vicka, and proceeded on his way. This was Jakov, now 16 years old, who does not like talking to pilgrims and prefers to give his time to football and music.

Father Ivan, when I saw him in the morning, had told me to call at the presbytery after the service that evening to collect some sandwiches for my journey next day. When I rang the presbytery bell, it was answered by Marija, whom I recognised from photographs as one of the visionaries. I told her my business, but also added that I was delighted to meet her and would appreciate her prayers for the rest of my pilgrimage to Jerusalem. This she promised to do, but her main concern was to find my sandwiches, so she led me to the kitchen and saw to it that I got them.

Vicka preparing lunch for the workmen, Marija caring about my sandwiches and Jakov riding past with his head-phones impressed me more than all I had heard and read about Medjugorje. In spite of all the publicity and harass-ment, the children appear to have remained unspoiled, natural and poor. There has been a great renewal of faith in the village and beyond, and reconciliations effected between individuals and communities, which previously had been deadly enemies. And many claim to have been miraculously healed: 'The blind see, the lame walk, the poor have the Gospel preached to them.'

Since visiting Medjugorje I have often been asked what I thought of it and I want to answer, 'What I think about it is not important. It is the facts which are important. These children have stuck to their story of daily apparitions over a period of six years in spite of interrogations by state police, church authorities, experts in theology and spirituality. They have undergone many medical and psychological tests which have all declared them to be thoroughly normal. Their story has brought them publicity, slander and harassment, yet they show no signs of bitterness, nor any sign of trying to use the publicity to their own advantage. Their message has brought millions of pilgrims from all over the world to this peasant village in the mountains of a communist country. Thousands claim to have been spiritually healed by their visit, hundreds physically, and in the immediate area there has been a religious revival, filling the churches, and bringing reconciliation between lifelong enemies. The essential message which the children give is true to Scripture, and its emphasis on prayer and fasting for peace and reconciliation is vital for our day if we are to survive as a human race on earth.

These are the facts which are important: their interpretation is secondary. The peace of Christ demands faith, prayer and fasting. It is an expensive peace, which costs little less than everything and to which every human being has to contribute. It demands a faith which recognises the Spirit of God in every human being, and this the Medjugorje messages make clear, a faith which can remove mountains of unbelief within ourselves as well as in others, a faith which hopes when everything seems hopeless and acts accordingly. It demands prayer so that the mind and heart of Christ can take possession of every part of our being, and fasting to eradicate the violence of greed and fear in all its forms within us. The peace of Christ overcomes our fears, making us vulnerable, not safe, and it reacts to violence with love and forgiveness. 'Fear not, I have overcome the world.' A sword pierced the heart of the Queen of Peace, a lance the heart of her Son.

My uneasiness with Medjugorje is not with the place or the facts. I found the place inspiring, peaceful and homely,

191

and the facts awe-inspiring. My uneasiness comes from the fear that the message may be distorted, offering not Christ's peace, but a cheap and private peace to individuals. This I see as a false peace, because it absolves us from any need to examine our own lives and so allows us to continue complacently supporting, either actively or by our silence, government policies which oppress the poor and enrich the rich in our own country and in the Third World, and the murderous intentions of our nations, which hide under the name 'national security'. We are absolved from involving ourselves in these questions provided we substitute a particular prayer formula, a pilgrimage to Medjugorje, or even to Jerusalem.

Among some charismatics and devotees of Medjugorje I have found a chilling divide between their religious profession of dedication to peace and their firm belief in the value of the nuclear deterrent in preserving peace in Europe for over forty years, an inconsistency which often scandalises atheists and agnostics, as well as many Christians. Our attitude to nuclear arms is one of the reality checks on our spirituality. Does our spirituality allow God to be God of all creation, or only of that section of creation to which I happen to belong? When we talk of peace, do we mean peace through power, as the Romans understood it, 'To preserve peace, prepare for war', the power to inflict death on any who threaten our way of life, even if that way of life can only be maintained at the expense of other people's oppression, exploitation, or even annihilation? Or do we understand by peace, the peace of Christ, a peace which is the fruit of justice, respect and love for every human being, a peace which is risky, costly and demands vulnerability? ' "Peace," he said, and showed them his hands and his side' (John 20:20).

Now to the unimportant question, what do I believe about Medjugorje? I believe from all that I have seen and read so far that the children are telling the truth of their own experience and that the essence of their message emphasises a central truth of the Gospel, which every individual, every Church and every nation needs to hear, namely that God loves all his creation and wills the salvation of every human being. But do I believe that Our Lady is actually appearing to them? This question I cannot answer with a simple 'Yes', because the question contains too many other questions and

needs to be rephrased. I do not believe that every evening at
about 6.40, Jesus reminds Mary that it is time to keep her
Medjugorje appointment. I believe that our conscious minds
grasp only a tiny fraction of the reality in which we all live.
In God we live and move and have our being, and he is
nearer to us than we are to ourselves. He is in everyone and
in everything. Ultimately, our true identity is in him. The
whole universe is in each one of us, and each one is in unity
with all creation, although we are only very dimly aware of
this. Those whom we consider to be dead, still live in God
and are therefore in union with each of us. Some mystics have
written of their awareness of this truth. Some minds do break
through at times to this awareness, but they find it impossible
to describe their insights adequately in words. Father Ivan
told me that he found one of the visionaries in tears one day.
She was trying to obey the order, given her by the Franciscans, to record their meeting with the Madonna, and the girl
said there was no way she could express in words what she
had experienced. The only way they can express, or even
have an awareness of what is happening to them when they
make this breakthrough to an awareness of the reality in
which we are all living, is through the words, images and
concepts which are familiar to them. That is why Vicka, when
describing Our Lady, said 'She wore a grey dress with a
white veil, a crown of stars, blue eyes, dark hair and rosy
cheeks. And she was floating about this high in the air on a
grey cloud, not touching the ground,' I believe she broke
through to an awareness of the reality of Mary, mother of
Jesus, who is always close to her and to every other human
being. But this awareness could only come to Vicka through
her own way of perceiving, her own memory and store of
mental images. In other words, I believe the apparition can
be genuine, but it does not follow that Our Lady has blue
eyes, red cheeks and is dressed in grey. Similarly, in reporting
their conversations with the Madonna, they report through
the medium of the ideas and concepts which are familiar to
them. So it does not follow that what they report is literally
the message they have been given, but the words they use
contain the gist of the message. Generally, in assessing the
revelations of mystics and visionaries, the Church has always
recognised the need to sift the essence of the message from

the words, ideas and images in which it may be expressed, and also to distinguish the immediate revelation from any later interpretation which the visionaries may put on it. That is why I think that the reported conversations with Our Lady on the subject of the Bishop of Mostar's treatment of the Franciscan friars could be rejected, without therefore concluding the Medjugorje phenomenon to be false.

In the Gospels Jesus is represented as condemning those who look for signs and wonders. And in the desert he rejected the temptation to give a startling sign which would impress people, to leap off the temple pinnacle. When he did perform miracles, they were given as signs pointing to the miracle of life, that the kingdom of God had broken through and is now within and amongst us. It is faith in the presence of God in all things which heals and saves. It is the rising and setting of the sun each day which is the miracle, not that it whirls occasionally for some. The experience of a whirling sun – there is the record of an old woman in the Outer Hebrides who claimed that all who believed saw the sun dance every Easter day – is only of value in so far as it enables those who witness such a phenomenon to marvel at the sun every day. Medjugorje is of value in so far as it makes us more aware of the mystery and miracle of life now, and helps us to live in the constant awareness that we live enfolded in the goodness and the love of God. Such awareness would bring us to repentance, individual and national, for our violence in the past, and to a renunciation of the threat of mass violence by nuclear deterrence for the future. A public act of repentance by the Yugoslav Catholic hierarchy for the crimes committed against the Orthodox Christians would be a much more convincing sign of the genuineness of the apparitions than any number of reports of whirling suns.

Tuesday, May 19

I arose early and worked on Mungo's nuts, bolts and springs to try and cure its persistent lopsidedness, an operation hampered by my inability to find open spanners which would fit the small nuts. I attended the English Mass, at which an American priest preached an excellent sermon relating the

Medjugorje message of peace to his own country and its international relations. At Mass I thanked God for bringing me so far and prayed to reach Jerusalem. After saying good-bye to some of the Northern Ireland pilgrims, I set off with Mungo, who had not been cured at Medjugorje.

My plan was to take the shortest route back to the coast, follow it to near the Albanian border, take public transport inland to Pec, and walk from there to Athens. My immediate destination was Capljina, just over 20 km away. My small-scale map showed one road only, but there was a network of little unsignposted roads between the villages in the area, so I relied for direction on compass bearings and would set off on a road which seemed to be running south but either changed direction or ended in a farmyard. By midday the sun's rays were burning, Mungo was listing as badly as ever and I was parched with thirst. The Medjugorje peace with which I had begun the day was evaporating in the burning sun. I called at a house to ask directions for Capljina. A young boy, speaking fluent German, told me that some workmen nearby would be driving there in about an hour's time. He invited me into the house to rest meantime and asked if I would prefer to drink wine or water. Parched with thirst, I asked for water first. He brought a large water jug with what I presumed to be some kind of lemon essence in it and I drank two tumblersful straightaway. I then pulled out my diary, which I had not written up for three days and began to write while sipping a third tumblerful. Then I remembered the opening lines of 'The Dream of Gerontius':

> Jesu, Maria, I am near to death and thou art calling me. I know it now, not by the token of this faltering breath, this chill at heart, this dampness on my brow. It is this feeling never felt before, this strange and uttermost collapse of all that makes me man.

The 'lemon' drink was, in fact, wine and the alcohol had a clear run to my head, for I had eaten nothing but a piece of bread for breakfast. I ate the Franciscan sandwiches as a kind of first aid and then tried to concentrate my mind on the diary. The wine cannot have been very strong, for I still have the diary pages, coherent and grammatical but with the odd spelling error, and a vivid memory of the house and of the drive to Capljina. I had asked Marija to pray for me to Our Lady for the rest of my pilgrimage. The visionaries said the Madonna had a sense of humour, so I wondered if the wine I had received when I asked for water was an answer to Marija's prayers.

As it was still early afternoon when the workmen dropped me in Capljina, I began to walk towards Metkovic, but I had gone only a few yards when Mungo collapsed behind me. The second bolt holding the haversack to the aluminium frame had sheered, so I put the whole contraption on my shoulders and began the hunt for lodgings. I failed at the first two attempts and was trying a third house, when I saw a Franciscan church nearby. They gave me lodgings for the night and also summoned a mechanic friend, who lent me his tool bag for Mungo's repair.

Wednesday, May 20

I left Capljina in a confident mood. I had visited a bank to draw money for the next two weeks in Yugoslavia and then a tool shop to find open spanners for Mungo's wheels. They had a variety of spanners suitable for heavy tractors but nothing for pram wheels. After two hours walking in the heat of the sun with a still listing Mungo, I stopped by a river bank, adjusted Mungo's springs and tightened all the bolts I could tighten. Then I started on lunch. Suddenly the thought came to me, 'I've walked far enough. Why not do the rest of the pilgrimage by public transport?' There was no internal struggle; it was as though I was being presented with a decision which had already been made. My only slight hesitation was the fact that I was being sponsored on behalf of Pax Christi for a 1,700-mile walk. I had no idea at this stage how much the sponsorship money was worth, but I reckoned that if I added to the distance I had already covered the 270 miles from Ayrshire to Hull which I had walked as part of the pilgrimage in summer 1983, together with another 130 miles walking in Israel, then my total would exceed 1,700 miles. Although I felt this was the right decision and it had not been made in a fit of gloom, I decided to postpone a definite decision until next day and heaved Mungo the rest of the way to Metkovic, where I found lodgings.

In the evening I settled down to pray over the decision and opened the Bible at random. It was Ezekiel chapter 1, and as I read I began to laugh, for the chapter described Ezekiel's vision of the chariot of the Lord, drawn by four animals in human form, who had wheels beneath their feet. 'Where the spirit urged them, there the wheels went, since the spirit of the animal was in the wheels.' As Mungo's wheels were now beginning to grate and grind and were resisting all efforts by me and by vulcanisers to improve their performance, I took this passage as a confirmation of my decision to give up walking and trusted the spirit would carry me on other wheels. I was sure that this method of using and interpreting the Scriptures would not be approved at the Biblical Institute in Jerusalem, where I had arranged to stay, but it was good enough for me and I felt happy with the decision. Two years later, I still think it was the right decision, although I am sorry not to have been able to walk the whole distance.

10

The Spirit Changes Wheels –
Dubrovnik to Haifa

Je sens en moi quatre identités: je suis vraiment chrétien et
prêtre, je suis vraiment juif, je suis vraiment israelien et je me
sens, sinon vraiment égyptien, du moins très proche des Arabes
que je connais et que j'aime. Il n'est pas confortable, surtout
dans les circonstances actuelles, de maintenir en moi-meme ces
quatres identités qui s'opposent souvent les unes aux autres –
et la tentation est grande de n'en garder qu'une et delaisser
les trois autre de côté.

(I am conscious of four self-identities. In reality I am a
Christian and a priest, I am also a Jew, an Israeli, and although
I am not really an Egyptian, I feel kinship with the Arabs,
whom I know and love. It is not easy, especially in the actual
circumstances, to hold together these four identities which are
often in conflict – and I am strongly tempted to keep only one
and cast the other three aside.)

(Fr Bruno Hussar o.p., in an address to the United
Nations Extraordinary General Assembly in 1967, after
the Six Day War)

Thursday, May 21

It was raining heavily when I left Metkovic by bus and it
was still pouring when I arrived in Dubrovnik's bus station
around midday. There was a queue waiting to board the
bus returning to Metkovic. As I approached, pulling Mungo
behind me, someone in the queue said, 'Hello, Father
Hughes.' The voice came from a small group from Mold,
near St Beuno's, who recognised me from a lecture I had
given a few years before. One of the group said, 'We've been
following your walk in *The Tablet*,' but they were polite enough

not to show surprise that they had caught the walker getting off a bus. They were on their way to Medjugorje.

I had the address of a Jesuit house in Dubrovnik and called in at a tourist office to consult a city map. There are two Dubrovniks, the modern city and, about two miles away, the medieval walled city where the Jesuits have had a house for almost four hundred years. I walked on in the rain and soon saw the red roofs and the ramparts of the old city below. It is like a deep, unshapely saucer dipped into the edge of the sea, the ramparts forming the outer rim and the main street crossing the diameter. There is only one approach by road, which is closed to all traffic except delivery vans. All the other approaches are by steep stone steps trod by generations, flanked by shops and restaurants, and leading to the broad, paved main road which forms the city centre. The summer migrations had begun and the centre was already thronged with elderly visitors, mostly American. I was climbing my way out of the saucer in search of the Jesuit house, which I knew was on the seaward side, my attention concentrated on getting myself with Mungo on my back safely to the top, when I heard, 'Say, honey, have you ever seen such a beautiful set of stairways?' So I stood with the American couple who were passing and admired the stairways.

The Jesuit church and house stood at the top of the stairway, its rear windows within a few feet of the city ramparts. The Jesuits probably chose Dubrovnik because in the sixteenth century it was a meeting point for East and West and an excellent base from which to conduct an apostolate among the Turks, a project dear to Ignatius who, before founding the Jesuit Order, had dreamed of living in Palestine to convert what was called in those days 'the infidel'.

The Jesuit community was very welcoming and gave me a room overlooking the ramparts and the sea. The house was also a junior seminary for youths between the ages of 14–18 years. While at Medjugorje I had read that one of the visionaries, Ivan of the apples, was a Curé of Ars type of character, slow in mind and without academic ability. He wanted to become a priest, but could not cope with the seminary studies. It was the Dubrovnik seminary which he had attended. When I mentioned this fact to one of the seminary staff, he laughed and said he did not think Ivan was at all slow of mind or

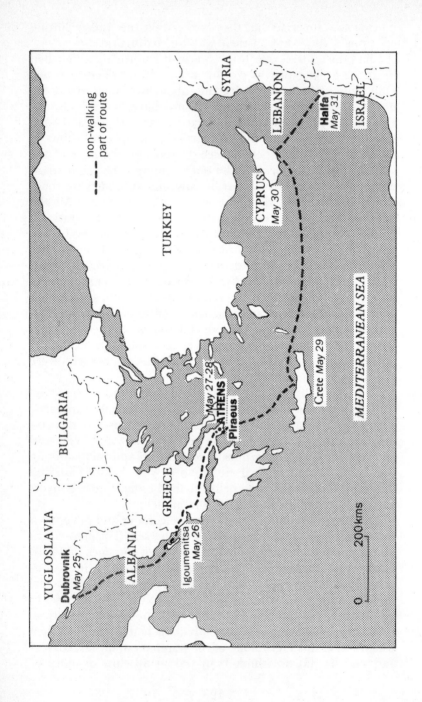

unacademic, but just idle, and so this staff member could not accept the genuineness of his claims to have seen the Madonna. From what I have read and the little I saw of the visionaries, they have never claimed to be models of virtue nor suggested that the Madonna so considered them. Perhaps God and Our Lady are less fussy about idleness than we are. The idle may be free to give more attention to hidden things, which the more virtuous and hard-working are too busy to notice.

Few of the community could speak English or German and I had only mastered a few polite phrases in Serbo-Croat, so I suggested we speak in Latin saying, 'Loquimur Latine?' denoting the question mark by the inflection of my voice. An elderly priest, who, I later discovered was the seminary's professor of Latin, corrected me, saying, 'Loquamur Latine' ('Let us speak in Latin'), so I took great care in future conversations to be as classical as I could remember. The old man continued to correct me, but showed great pleasure whenever I got a sentence right. The content of what I was trying to say seemed of very minor interest to him.

Friday, May 22 – Saturday, May 23

There was one Jesuit scholastic, the name Jesuits give to those in training, in the house and he spoke excellent English, so he became my guide and interpreter, taking me to the tourist office to book a passage from Dubrovnik to Igoumenitsa in western Greece, and to a tool shop where, for the first time in Yugoslavia, I was able to buy open spanners which fitted all the nuts holding Mungo together. He also gave me conducted tours and supplied me with literature on Dubrovnik.

At the travel agent, I booked a place on the next ferry for Greece, due to sail on Monday, May 26th, so I had a leisurely weekend in Dubrovnik, walking the city's ramparts and the hills above it. The most enjoyable time was at late evening, strolling with hundreds of others along the broad, traffic-free, main street. The crowds walked in little groups, natives and visitors, a gathering of the nations, talking together, laughing, gesticulating, singing, with never a sound of brawling. On the broad stairways parties were dining at candle-lit tables,

set in tiers. The scene was a glimpse of peace, of the tranquillity of order, of which St Augustine wrote, of men, women
and children enjoying one another's company, giving one
another life and laughter, walking without fear, and I thought
of the sad state of our own inner cities where so many now
fear to walk at night.

Dubrovnik, like the rest of Yugoslavia, has a bloody history
of invasion and conquest, mostly by Venetians and Turks,
but also by France under Napoleon, by Italy and Germany.
The city has also suffered fire, famine and plague and has
learned not only the art of survival, but the greater art of
retaining its independence even while under foreign rule.
Many of its inhabitants have become diplomats, learning
their skill through generations of oppression.

The official tourist guidebooks describe the present communist age as the fulfilment of Dubrovnik's struggle for freedom
through the ages, but no one believes the official propaganda.
Dubrovnik, true to its history, still retains a measure of independence and individuality in spite of the present government.

Each morning I went to Mass in the Jesuit church. The
congregation was not encouraged to participate, all the readings being performed by the celebrant, and very few among
the congregation received Holy Communion, even on Sundays. Nor was there any sign of ecumenism at parish level,
confirming the impression I had received elsewhere in Yugoslavia that the Church, when battling against a rigid, repress-
ive and unco-operative regime, herself becomes infected with
the same rigidity and clings to old ways, not because they
are appropriate or helpful to the people, but because they are
seen as signs of opposition to the oppressor, and therefore to
be continued.

Sunday, May 24

In the afternoon, I walked up the hill behind the city. I left
the main path and wandering through the woods I found
myself, camera in hand, in a clearing where the military were
encamped. They must have been a detachment of Yugoslavia's home guard because they did not even ask to see my

passport, but directed me back to the main path. Twenty years earlier, a friend of mine, holidaying in Yugoslavia, was arrested and imprisoned for passing near a military camp with a camera in his hand.

The encounter with the military brought my thoughts back to peace. The human mind can be compared to a moonscape, pockmarked with deep craters. Our consciousness is a tiny figure scurrying from one point to another and constantly falling into one of the craters, where it usually remains, because the crater is familiar and provides no clear exit. In discussing the nuclear deterrence question, the first crater, from which few emerge, is the objection, 'Then how are we to defend ourselves against an unjust aggressor?' and British audiences usually add, as they descend deeper into the crater, 'and what would have happened if we had not defended ourselves against Hitler in 1939?' The answer, 'The Germans would probably have assassinated him,' is considered flippant and unconvincing.

The intuition that nuclear deterrence is both evil and ineffective can be a true insight, but it does not follow that those who know this truth with inner certainty must themselves be able to present an instant and comprehensive defence policy. Yet this assumption, like another crater within the crater, prevents most people from considering the possibilities of non-nuclear defence, or of effective defence by non-violent means.

These mental craters not only restrict our thinking about nuclear defence, they also affect all our thinking, knowing and relating to God and to one another. Faith is a way of seeing the reality in which we live. Literally, faith does not remove mountains, but through faith we see the mountain, and every other created thing, in a new way, so that what was previously seen as an insuperable obstacle is now perceived as a challenge, or as an invitation to change. 'Every mountain will be brought low, every valley filled.' Faith is a seeing, but not all who have faith can give a coherent answer to every objection brought against it. St Anselm wrote of faith as 'quaerens intellectum', seeking understanding, an understanding of faith which energised and inspired a Kepler, a Galileo, a Newton. They believed that creation bore the imprint of the

Creator, that creation was therefore intelligent, so they spent their lives on the track of their Creator.

Monday, May 25

I left Dubrovnik by evening ferry for Igoumenitsa. The ship was full of bronzed, backpacking youth preparing to swarm over Greece and I felt dinosaur-like as I embarked, stooped beneath the weight of Mungo, now in better shape after more repairs in Dubrovnik, but still listing slightly and difficult to manoeuvre.

The Yugoslav ferry had class distinctions, an expensive cabin class, a much cheaper second class, which provided reclining seats, and cheapest of all was the open deck. I had a reclining seat which I could not sleep on, but as the neighbouring two seats were empty, I was able to stretch out and sleep. The class division applied only to the sleeping accommodation, the lounges, restaurant and bar being available to all passengers.

In the evening light I stood on the upper deck and watched the Albanian coastline slip by. This mysterious and isolated country, suspicious of the lone walker, seemed to keep its secrets hidden even from ships passing in the night, for the land looked uninhabited, beautiful but barren.

Tuesday, May 26

We put in at Corfu during the morning and reached Igoumenitsa by 1.00 p.m. There I had a five-hour wait before catching the overnight bus to Athens.

Having studied Latin and Greek, I have probably spent more imagination time in ancient Greece and Rome than in any other part of the world apart from Palestine. In imagination Greece was a sunlit land, each day beginning with a rosy-fingered dawn. Stately ships skimmed over wine-dark seas and put in at enchanting islands. In beautiful cities wise men walked with measured stride, flanked by eager youths listening to them discourse on the perennial questions of the One and the Many and the nature of truth and justice, or the whole city was gathered all day in a vast amphitheatre, watching and discussing the latest productions by Aeschylus, Sophocles, Euripides and Aristophanes. Even in wartime they seemed to spend a disproportionate amount of their time listening to endless speeches by Pericles, never easy to understand but always impressive.

Twentieth-century Greece, as represented by Igoumenitsa, came as a severe culture shock. It was a messy, busy little town totally dedicated to trading. I saw no noble figures with measured stride and flanked by eager youth, but lots of shifty-looking characters flitting in and out of shops no longer selling the beautiful pottery of Mycenae, but coke cans and plastic goods, creations of the new American colonisers. However, I was grateful for the trading Greeks and had an excellent and very tasty fried chicken, enjoyed not only because it was the first meal of the day, but because it had more taste than most of the meals I had eaten in six weeks in Yugoslavia.

The overnight bus set off with a roar at 6.00 p.m., groaned its way up hillsides and hurtled down them. The driver had a mini-shrine above his dashboard, including a large icon of the Virgin Mary, several medals and a little vase of flowers. I have often noticed that the more religiously devotional a driver, the more perilous his driving, his faith in the unseen obscuring his vision of the oncoming traffic and precipices of this present life.

At 8.30 p.m. the bus stopped at a restaurant by the water's edge and the driver told us to return in an hour's time. Four and a half hours later we were still at the water's edge, waiting for a relief bus as the radiator was damaged beyond repair.

One of the great delights of the Jerusalem pilgrimage was freedom from any imposed timetable. So I could enjoy this four-hour delay, the evening still and warm, the air heavy with the scent of trees and flowers, a cloudless, star-filled sky and the water lapping gently on the shore. They were precious hours, for I saw more clearly than before how much of my life is a self-imposed imprisonment within the narrow confines of my own plans, my own timetable, so that I am not present to the present and remain unaware of what is going on around me except in a most superficial way. Among the passengers was an archaeologist returning from Corfu to Athens University, where he was due to lecture at 8.30 a.m. Had I been in his place I should have been wasting energy in irritation at the delay, but he seemed to be not at all worried.

As I walked up and down, or sat by the water's edge, I thought on Isaiah's phrase, 'See, I hold you in the hollow of my hand.' The phrase did not change the scenery, nor mend the radiator, but it changed my perception of the scenery and of the delay. The lapping waves became the pulse of God's hand, the cool air of the evening his breath, the stars the beauty of his eyes. There was no other place I wanted to be, and I could glimpse the wealth in the phrase, 'Thy will be done'. At that moment, free from preoccupation with my own plans and thoughts, I was letting God be God to me and it filled me with delight. Holiness is that glimpse become a permanent state, when the mind and heart are so rooted in God that even when the external circumstances of life are grim, threatening or painful, they cannot upset, obscure or extinguish the inner knowledge of God's protecting hand under the appearance of things.

Wednesday, May 27

Athens bus station at 6.00 a.m. bore as much resemblance to the Athens of my imagination as hell to heaven. I took a taxi to the Jesuit house where I was welcomed, given a room and a pile of letters. After two nights on boat and bus, I looked longingly at the bed, but knew I would sleep more easily if I had a passage booked from Piraeus to Haifa. At the tourist office they told me that ferries sailed only once a week and that the next ferry would sail on Thursday afternoon, leaving me twenty-four hours for sightseeing in Athens.

Instead of sleeping in the afternoon I scampered over the Parthenon with several thousand other visitors and walked among the ruins of the Acropolis. The first book I ever read in Greek was Plato's *Apologia*, which is Socrates' last conversation before his death sentence. Of all that I ever read in Greek, this book made the most lasting impression, so I walked back to the Jesuit house pondering Socrates' wisdom.

The Delphic oracle had declared Socrates to be the wisest of men. Socrates spent the rest of his life trying to disprove the oracle. He consulted all the people whom he considered more wise, more learned and more gifted than he, but while they were more knowledgeable in their own particular branch of knowledge, they all made the same mistake of thinking that their expertise in one field, qualified them in every other. Socrates discovered that the oracle was right, because he knew how little he knew, while the experts remained ignorant of their own ignorance. Poor Socrates had a communication problem in his own lifetime and so the authorities put him to death. He is still having a communication problem, because we still think ignorance is failure and therefore to be denied, if possible, and that expertise in one subject, however narrow, qualifies us to speak with authority on all.

If any of us were invited to make a list of the topics which interest us most and another list of those topics on which we consider ourselves most ignorant, it is very unlikely that anyone would have the same topic at the head of each list, so that we should confess the greatest ignorance on the topic which interests us most. Yet for everyone the first topic on both lists should be 'me', for it is the topic which interests us most, yet it is also the topic on which we know least. We may know certain facts about ourselves, our dreams and inner feelings, which are private to us, but we remain ignorant of our identity, who we really are, how we relate to other people and to the rest of creation. Yet this is a constant source of interest to us, so we examine ourselves in a mirror, look for ourselves first in a group photograph, are surprised when we hear our own voice recorded and listen intently if we overhear a conversation in which our name is mentioned. If we really knew ourselves, there would be no need to react in this way, we should be far less preoccupied with ourselves, less dependent on the opinion of others, remaining undisturbed by their criticism and unaffected by their praise. Flattery could not touch us. It is because we do not know ourselves that we do such violence to ourselves to others and to nature, assuming that when things go wrong, they must therefore be changed, destroyed or got rid of, not realising that the fault may not lie in those things, but in our perception and reaction to them. The most widespread and dangerous example of this failure to know ourselves is our national belief that peace can be secured and sustained by military power, a belief based on ignorance of our essential inter-relatedness so that we do not see that what we do, or threaten to do to another, we are also doing to ourselves and to God. 'As you do to one of these least, you are doing also to me.'

Thursday, May 28 – Saturday, May 30

May 28th was the Feast of the Ascension and I celebrated Mass in the Jesuit house before setting off for Piraeus. There was a very thorough security check before boarding. We were asked whether we were bearing any gifts to be delivered in Israel and warned against accepting any to be brought out of Israel. The security check was supervised by the most sinister-looking policemen, large gentlemen, heavily armed and dressed in black with matching revolvers, leather belts and spectacles.

The ship, which was Cypriot, also had three classes of passenger, but while the Yugoslav ferry offered freedom of access to all parts of the ship, the Cypriot boat was more unashamedly capitalist, reserving most of its space for the cabin class, who enjoyed spacious lounges, a restaurant, swimming pool and plenty of deck space, while the second and third class were confined by locked doors and metal grilles to a small section aft with very limited deck space, a lounge filled with aeroplane seats which faced towards a bar selling expensive drinks, but with nothing more solid to eat than biscuits and cold pizza. The aeroplane seats provided for second-class passengers had an impressive array of buttons for adjusting the angle and contour of the seat, but the buttons no longer worked and I spent the three nights on board sleeping on the floor. The only thing we shared with the first-class passengers was the ship's loudspeaker system, most frequently used in the evening for repeated summonses for the ship's doctor, an elusive practitioner, especially after 8.00 p.m., when the first-class passengers had most need of his attention. Fortunately, the ship was not crowded and there were three-hour stops at Crete on Friday and Cyprus on Saturday, when I was able to stretch my legs and buy food and drink for the journey.

For the first twenty-four hours I enjoyed the sail, spending much of the time standing on deck and watching the restless blue sea, the gulls flying low in the ship's wake, the sky at dawn and dusk, and chatting with passengers. There was also plenty of time to write up the articles I had promised *The Tablet*, which made them the more difficult to write because the time I spent on them expanded with the time available. I also enjoyed the effortless travel over this stretch of the pilgrimage.

The passengers included a young engaged couple, Richard from England and Sarah from Israel. They were returning to Israel to be married and Sarah, after a year's absence from home, could not wait to see her country again. As far as I remember, we did not discuss religion or politics, but it was as though her whole being was echoing the longings of generations of her people to return to their homeland. 'When God brought Zion's captives home, at first it seemed like a dream; then our mouths filled with laughter and our lips with song' (Psalm 126:1–2).

When I reached Israel and saw something of the plight of the Palestinian Arabs, the Israeli military presence everywhere, especially in the West Bank, the refugee camps, where some men and women in their forties had never known life beyond the camp, I often thought again of Sarah's longing to see her country, for it seemed such a beautiful, right and good longing. Yet this longing of the Jews has caused such suffering to both Jews and Arabs, but especially to the Arabs.

Later, in Jerusalem, I met Father Bruno Hussar o.p., a Jew born of non-practising parents and brought up and educated with Arabs in Cairo. While studying engineering in France in the 1930s, a mountain-guide friend of his was killed and Bruno attended his funeral, a requiem Mass in a Catholic Church. The ceremony had a profound effect on him. After much thought and struggle he was received into the Catholic Church and wanted to become a Carthusian monk. His relatives told him that his first duty was to support his mother and family. Like Topo in *Fiddler on the Roof*, Bruno discussed his worries with God, telling him that when his mother told him explicitly that he had done enough and must now give his life to God, then he would join the Carthusians. Nine years later this was exactly what his mother did say to him, by which time he had decided to become a Dominican. His conversion to Catholicism and especially his experience in wartime France, far from drawing him away from his Jewish roots, had strengthened them and bound him closer to his Jewish people.

Ordained as a Dominican priest in 1948, his Provincial invited him to found in Jerusalem a Dominican centre for the study of Judaism. Before setting out he was warned by a priest friend, 'If you want to be accepted in the country, never say a word about your Jewish origins, even to your closest friends.' He ignored the advice, never denied his Jewish origins and had to bear the pain of being unacceptable to Jews for being a Christian, suspected by his Christian brothers and sisters for being a Jew, and although he loved the Arabs, his companions in his youth, yet in Israel he was a Jew and an Israeli.

While in Israel he had a dream of setting up a village community in which Jews, Christians and Muslims would live together in community and in peace, each member true to their own faith and traditions while respecting those of others and finding enrichment through their differences. He dreamed that the village would become 'a school for peace', a centre to which groups of Jews and Arabs could come from all over Israel and beyond, to live together and break down the barriers of fear, contempt, ignorance and prejudice which separate them, building instead bridges of confidence, mutual respect and understanding through seminars, group meetings, manual work and recreation together. When he mentioned this dream, many told him that he was being unrealistic and utopian, but Israel is a land where utopia has often become reality. The dream, too, had a solid scriptural basis,

> In the days to come the mountain of the Temple of God will be put on top of the mountains . . . The peoples will stream to it, nations without number will come to it; and they will say, 'Come, let us go up to the mountain of God so . . . that he may teach us his ways and we may walk in his paths; since from Zion the Law will go out, and the oracle of God from Jerusalem.' He will wield authority over many peoples and arbitrate for mighty nations; they will hammer their swords into ploughshares, their spears into

sickles. Nation will not lift sword against nation, and there
will be no more training for war. (Micah 4:1–3)

Bruno found a hilltop at Latrun, scene of fierce fighting in
the Six-Day War. The land belonged to a Carthusian monastery and he was at first given it for a nominal rent. With a few
companions he took up residence on the bare mountainside
without running water or electricity, living in a makeshift
shelter. People came to visit and a few wandering hippies
would stay for a while, but no Jewish or Arab families would
settle there. After three years on the desert hillside, Bruno
again discussed the matter with God, telling him that he
would give him a year to send Jewish and Arab families and
also funds to finance the project, otherwise Bruno would
abandon the project. Within a few months the first Jewish
family arrived and funds began to come in, initially from Pax
Christi in Germany, and this enabled them to buy an electricity generator, instal solar heating on the roofs of their
houses and build an approach road.

By 1982, the village, called 'Neve Shalom', Oasis of Peace,
consisted of seven families: four Jewish, two Muslim, one
mixed Jewish and Catholic, together with several single
people who were both Jewish and Christian, one of the
Christians being an Arab. Today, many thousands of Jewish
and Arab youngsters come to Neve Shalom to listen to one
another, understand and enjoy one another's company. The
reputation of Neve Shalom has spread abroad and groups
from other trouble spots, including Northern Ireland, come
to learn.

When the Israelites were in the wilderness on their way to
the Promised Land, a cloud used to settle over the tabernacle,
the Tent of Testimony. 'Whenever the Cloud lifted above the
Tent, the sons of Israel broke camp; whenever the Cloud
halted, there the sons of Israel pitched camp. The sons of
Israel set out at the command of God, and at his command
they pitched camp' (Numbers 9:17–18). Having initiated
Neve Shalom, Bruno has now retired from it and is in Jerusalem, where he is waiting for the Cloud to rise and then he
will pitch his camp elsewhere.

The roots of peace lie in mutual understanding, but to
understand we have to meet and listen. There are innumer-

able stories of the transformation which has occurred in both Jews and Arabs as they meet and listen to each other in Neve Shalom. This should not be surprising. After all, for centuries the Jews were welcome and lived amicably with the Muslims, and many Jews fled from persecution in Christian Europe to find refuge among the Moors, Islam being much more tolerant of other religions than Christianity at that time.

There is no surer recipe for violence than to keep people in close physical proximity while ensuring that they have little or no communication with each other. When this separation is supported by political, social and religious structures, and reinforced either by discriminatory legislation, or by discrimination in its application, then violence is inevitable. For the dominating group, 'Peace' then comes to mean the successful continuation of the oppression by force of arms, whether by the police or the military, the operation being presented in high-flown rhetoric about the preservation of freedom, democracy, sovereignty, loyalty and orthodoxy.

If a fraction of the money spent on arms were to be spent in setting up centres like Neve Shalom, schools of peace, theology faculties of peace, in setting up cultural exchanges between nations and the factions within nations, what a transformation there could be, removing fear and hate and replacing it with trust and mutual respect, and what an effective, enjoyable and relatively cheap way it would be of ensuring our national security!

Neve Shalom was originally intended to be characterised by its religious element, for Arabs, Jews and Christians all believe in the one God, Father of Abraham, Isaac and Jacob. In fact it has become a non-religious community, and although many of its members are practising Christians, Jews and Muslims, each group worshipping in its own way, some members are non-believers. This non-religious character of Neve Shalom has scandalised some visiting Christians, who attacked Bruno. 'How can you, a Catholic priest, live with Jews, Muslims and atheists without trying to convince them of the truth of the Christian faith? In reply, Bruno quotes to them Matthew, chapter 25, in which Jesus describes the final judgement when all the world will be assembled and divided into the sheep, who are to enter the kingdom of God, and the goats, who are to be excluded from it. One would expect

212

Jesus, of all people, to make religious belief and practice, as we understand it, a criterion for selection for the Kingdom. His criterion, is, of course religious, but it is not religion as we understand it, for he says, 'I was hungry and you gave me to eat, I was thirsty and you gave me to drink, I was naked and you clothed me, a stranger and you took me in, sick and you visited me.' The chosen ask God in astonishment, 'But when did we see you like this?' and he answers, 'As you did this to one of the least of these my brothers, you did it to me.'

So Bruno answers his critics, 'These men and women and their families, living in this village, have left the comfort and security of their kibbutz, village and home to come here, where life is hard, primitive and offers no security for the future. They have done so because they cannot bear to live in this land, where two peoples do violence to each other, without doing anything to effect reconciliation in peace. Do you not believe that one day, after their death, Jesus will come to them and say, "I hungered for peace and reconciliation and you fed me?" How can you say that these people of goodwill, these peacemakers, are not children of God?'

I believe Neve Shalom is prophetic for the Church and for society, because it is revealing a pattern for the future mission of the Church and offering a new way of understanding evangelisation. Someone once said, 'Whenever you meet with people of another religion, or of no religion, tread warily, because God has been there before you.' Soon after I returned from Jerusalem, I stumbled across a remarkable confirmation of this truth, but that belongs to the epilogue.

At the end of my visit to Bruno, he made a final remark, which has remained with me ever since. 'There are situations where it is impossible to do justice immediately to both sides, and Israel today is one. There are times when we have to learn to live in peace in injustice.' I know this statement will make many hackles rise and that it can be misinterpreted to mean that the victims of injustice must accept the injustice meekly and passively. We must hunger and thirst after justice; passive acceptance of injustice has no place in Christian life, but Bruno's comment is a corrective to that other statement, which is also true, but can be misinterpreted, 'There can be no peace without justice.' The statement is frequently misused to justify violence until such time as justice can be enforced. It was through his death on a cross that Jesus reconciled all things. He opposed injustice, but non-violently. When he became the victim of violence from the unjust civil and religious powers of his day, he accepted death on a cross and prayed for the forgiveness of his enemies. When he arose from the dead, he said to his disciples, 'Peace be to you,' wishing them peace now, not at some future date when all injustice would have been removed from the earth. Trying to live in peace in an unjust situation, we are more likely to reach eventually a more just solution. Trying to bring justice in an unjust situation without trying to live peacefully in the meantime, brings neither peace nor justice.

On the Friday afternoon I was standing on the deck, feeling like 'Pooh' who said somewhere, 'There's nothing I like better than doing nothing.' There is much to be said in favour of doing nothing, withdrawing from all activity for a time and keeping silence, including a silence of the mind, for then we can become aware of deeper levels of our mind and heart. These deeper levels may bring peace, happiness and delight, but they can also be very disturbing and frightening.

I was hanging over the ship's rails thinking of nothing in particular, when suddenly a feeling of despondency hit me like a large wave and submerged me for the next twenty-four hours. I do not know whether the despondency brought to mind the images, or the images the despondency, but whatever the order, the images released thoughts which, as I soon recognised, had been lurking below the surface for a long time.

The first image was of the child whom St Augustine once met on the shore. The child was scooping a hole in the sand at the water's edge with a shell, then filling the shell with water and pouring it into the hole, hoping in this way to empty the ocean. The other image was from a sentence in Wittgenstein in which he compares the philosopher to a fly caught in an empty bottle, expending all its energy in a vain attempt to escape, but circling endlessly round in the same confined space.

The two images expressed thoughts and feelings not only

about this pilgrimage, but about my whole spiritual journey until now, especially in the last three years, when I had focused my attention on nuclear defence as a faith question.

The conviction that nuclear deterrence is a faith question, that our attitude to nuclear deterrence reflects our image of what God is like and therefore enters into every aspect of our faith and life, that trusting in the security provided by nuclear weapons is an expression of atheism incompatible with faith in God, who has revealed himself in Jesus, had gradually become so clear to me over the last twenty-five years that I could no longer doubt it. Yet the opposing conviction, that peace can only be preserved within and between nations by the use of armed force, and that our national security lies in our possession, accumulation and constant modernisation of nuclear weapons, is as widespread and deep in Christian consciousness as the ocean, and any attempt to change that conviction is as useless as the child's efforts with the shell.

The image of the buzzing fly caught in the bottle represented the feeling within my own mind when I thought about what I was trying to do and how totally ineffective it all seemed to be, as though I were caught within the prison of my own mind from which there was no escape, not even in religion, because very religious people were among the most ardent supporters of nuclear deterrence. They also prayed 'Our Father' and celebrated the Eucharist together, yet they believed it was not against the Father's will that we should spend billions of pounds on weaponry which could destroy all life on earth in order to preserve 'peace', while a fraction of the money spent on weaponry could be used to provide food, clean water and shelter for the millions who are homeless and malnourished. The depth of the despondency was the thought that life is absurd, a sick cosmic joke, that ultimately everything is meaningless and all our religious yearnings are useless velleities, attempts to escape the inevitable cruelty, brutishness and emptiness of human life.

Late that night as I was returning to the lounge and had to step over the bodies of sleeping Greeks and Jews, Americans, Australians, and an assortment of Europeans from East and West, the despondency ebbed a little as I reflected, 'Yes, trundling through Europe with a wobbling Mungo is a useless exercise from many points of view, but it has meaning, for it was undertaken for the peace of Christ, for you and me, for your nations and for mine, not for my security at the cost of your lives. This pilgrimage and plodding away on work for justice and peace may be ineffective, but at least it is harmless, whereas the prevalent assumption that peace can be preserved by threatening the enemy with 'unacceptable losses', which means the murder of their civilian populations, if our national interest, or what our leaders claim to be our national interest, is threatened, is not only ineffective as a means of defence, but it is a monstrous arrogance and demonic deceit leading to the absurd belief that all that is most precious in life can only be preserved by preparing for its destruction.

Once I had reached Israel and when the pilgrimage was over, I began to see the value of this and similar attacks of despondency, which can be so overwhelming while they occur. It was the same image of the fly buzzing around in the bottle which helped, because in the mood of despondency I was buzzing around within the prison of that part of my mind which was not letting God be God in it. The despondency had taken me down into the roots of my pride. Seeing this did not cause the problems of nuclear deterrence to disappear, so that they need not concern me any more, but it did deliver me from the confines of the bottle, for I knew that God is much more concerned about life on earth and about my life than I can ever be and that he can bring good out of every situation, no matter how frightening and hopeless it appears to us. One answer to the Yugoslav barman's question 'What can we little people do?' is, 'Trust in God and stop taking yourself so seriously.'

When I went up on deck early on Sunday morning, Sarah was already there, waiting for her first sighting of Israel. As we approached the coast she took great delight in pointing out every building she could recognise on Mount Carmel. Her enthusiasm was infectious and dispelled my gloom as the morning sun dispelled the mist on Mount Carmel. But my elation was tempered by the sight of twelve destroyers anchored in the harbour and of the armed military standing on the pier.

11

The Promised Land – Haifa to Jerusalem

With the drawing of this Love and the voice of this Calling
We shall not cease from exploration,
And the end of all our exploring
Will be to arrive where we started
And know the place for the first time.
                    (T. S. Eliot, 'Little Gidding')

Sunday, May 31

For three months I had been looking forward to the moment when I would set foot in Israel, planning to walk through it slowly, expecting the Gospel to become more alive with every step. In my first two minutes on land two gentlemen approached me, not begging, but offering me money for anything I might have to sell and promising very good prices. Haifa's streets were already crowded at 9.00 a.m., most of the pavement space filled with goods for sale, distracting my attention from the Gospel while I manoeuvred Mungo through the crowds and pavement wares.

As I left Haifa along the foot of Mount Carmel on the Nazareth road, the sun was already at burning heat and I was parched after three days with little exercise or sleep. I was beginning to wish I had accepted the offer to sell Mungo. Any attempt I made to picture the land in Jesus' time was interrupted by thundering military trucks full of armed Israelis.

I remembered occasions when I have stood in large crowds, at Lourdes, for example, or in St Peter's in Rome, singing the creed at Mass, professing belief in Christ, 'God from God, Light from Light, true God from true God, begotten, not

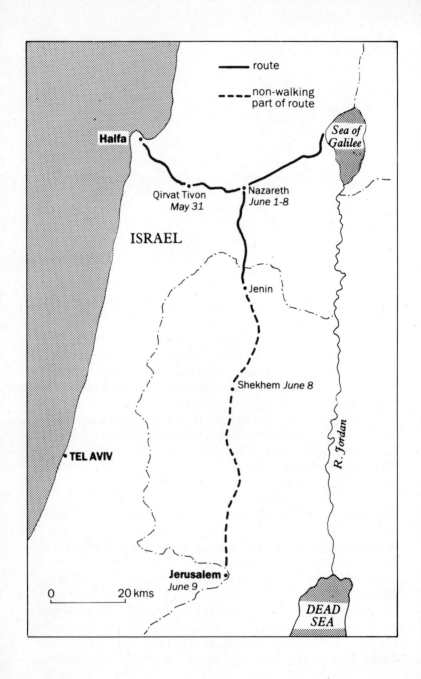

made, of one being with the Father. For us and for our salvation he came down from heaven: by the power of the Holy Spirit he became incarnate from the Virgin Mary and was made man,' and the wonderful feeling it gives of being part of a body which is universal and to which every human being is called. Now I was walking in Jesus' own land and to his own town 2,000 years later, a land in which only 2 per cent of the population was Christian – a tiny minority split into innumerable and often opposing sects – while his own people were now heavily armed in their attempt to hold down two million Palestinians. The Jews, as in Jesus' time, were still bitterly divided among themselves, the orthodox with their ringlets, stove hats and forbidding black suits, stoning their unorthodox brothers and sisters, who form the majority, if they attempt to drive their cars on the sabbath.

By mid-afternoon, weak with heat, thirst and sleeplessness, I reached Qirvat Tivon, drank two litres of lemonade and decided to abandon my plan to reach Nazareth that evening. Qirvat Tivon had a campsite, but the manager kindly warned me that a hundred children were expected later in the evening and directed me to a *pension* nearby. As I entered the garden I could hear a piano, so beautifully played that I thought it must be a recording. When I rang the bell, the piano stopped and a chubby and cheerful looking twelve-year-old, speaking perfect English, answered the door. He led me round to the back of the house, opened a door to a small room with whitewashed walls, a bed and a chair, and off it a small kitchen and bathroom. I took to it at once and asked him the price. '100 dollars a night' he replied. When I showed surprise and said I would have to go elsewhere, he thought he could be mistaken about the price, that it might be 10 dollars, but his father would be returning soon to let me know the official price.

The father did soon arrive, introduced himself as 'Eliahu', and apologised that he could speak no English, but only what he described as 'Yiddish Deutsch'. The price of the room, he told me, was either 15 dollars or 18 shekels, the discrepancy because of the present fluctuating value of the shekel. He then showed me his little garden, which included orange, grapefuit and plum trees as well as red and black currant bushes, inviting me to help myself to as much as I wanted. He told me of his four sons, one of whom was attending a Rudolph Steiner school in England, where his piano-playing youngest son would soon be following, and he invited me to join his family and guests later in the evening.

The guests included a young married couple, the husband a Jewish biologist, with his Indian wife. They had spent several years together wandering in Europe and taking casual work, including in a circus in Norway, roof-mending in North Wales, a long stay in Aberdeen in a vain attempt to find work on an oil-rig, and a spell with the Findhorn community in the north of Scotland. The conversation ranged over many topics, from the exceptional size and flavour of Findhorn's vegetables, attributed to the love and care with which they were planted and tended on unpromising sandy soil, to Tolkien's *Lord of the Rings*. The husband seemed very knowledgeable on many subjects, until the conversation turned on my walk to Jerusalem. When I told him that I was a Jesuit priest on a peace pilgrimage to Jerusalem, I discovered that his previous knowledge of Catholic priests was wholly derived from a recent film he had seen, Umberto Eco's *The Name of the Rose*, a medieval whodunnit, from which he concluded that Catholic priests were mostly murderous perverts. I do not think the company were impressed by my attempts to explain that the Catholic priesthood could not be known, still less understood and judged, by a twentieth-century fiction of life in a medieval monastery.

I was amazed at this ignorance in such a cultivated, charming and friendly group. Later, I reflected on the far more shameful, widespread and destructive Christian ignorance of Judaism, an ignorance destructive not only to the Jews, but to Christianity itself, which is rooted in Judaism. In the basilica of St Sabina in Rome there is a fifth-century mosaic which shows two women each holding an open book in their hands. Beneath one of them is an inscription, 'Ecclesia ex Circumcisione' the Church which stems from the Jews, and beneath the other, 'Ecclesia ex Gentibus' the Church coming from the pagan nations. In the fifth century the Church understood herself to consist of two essential parts, the Jews and the pagans. It is with the Jewish race that God made his everlasting covenant.

I am most grateful for the hospitality of Eliahu and his

family, because it has made me a little more aware of the importance of Jewish–Christian relations. The conversation also took me later on a visit to the Findhorn community, where the most important work is not in growing prize pumpkins, but in its nurture of the human spirit.

Monday, June 1

I left Qirvat Tivon at 8.30 a.m., when the sun was already uncomfortably hot, to complete the remaining 18 km to Nazareth. I felt a thrill when first I caught sight of the hill on which Nazareth is built, but as I approached I could better understand the Gospel comment, 'Can anything good come out of Nazareth?' because it was a dirty, untidy and unattractive town. I had no idea where to stay, but remembering the frequent phrase in the Gospel, 'He went up the hill to pray', I made for the highest point I could see. There I found a college called 'Jesus the Adolescent', formerly an orphanage, and now a technical school for Arab boys run by Salesian priests, most of them Italian. The Superior, Father Angelino, who spoke English, welcomed me and gave me a room which overlooked the town to the plains and the ancient city of Megiddo, scene of many battles.

I spent a long time at the window trying to realise that I really was in Nazareth, gazing at the landscape on which Jesus must have gazed daily for most of his life. Angelino had invited me to stay as long as I liked in Nazareth, and I stayed for a week. It was the countryside, the towns and villages which made the Gospel live for me more than the shrines and churches. It was this countryside which had nurtured Jesus and he drew on it for his later teaching. Whatever he saw and experienced, clouds in the sky, sheep grazing, wild flowers, weeds, birds of the air, seed being sown, crops growing and being harvested, vineyards, funerals, wedding feasts, children playing, men fishing, how people dressed, how they addressed each other, their protocol and observances, women sweeping the house or kneading dough or salting meat, he saw everything in relationship to God, whom he called 'Abba', a child's name for father.

Tuesday, June 2

After an early-morning Mass in Italian and breakfast, I set off to walk to the Lake of Galilee, about 32 km away. Below the college I could see the dome of the Church of the Annunciation a few hundred feet below and I made a bee-line for it, but I was soon lost in a maze of steep and narrow cobbled streets, lined with Arab shops and workshops, with a groove running down the middle of the street to drain away the refuse. The streets were already busy and the air heavy with the sweetly-sick smell of spices. The Church of the Annunciation was in complete contrast, being spacious, clean and silent. It was this contrast between the beautiful church and its sordid surroundings which struck me in almost all the sacred places I visited, not just the physical contrast, but the contrast between the Good News which these buildings proclaimed and the torn world in which they stand. Nazareth was one of the clearest examples of this contrast. The Nazareth in which Jesus lived for thirty years was probably just as messy and the country as bitterly divided then as now. Near Nazareth, in Jesus' own lifetime, the Romans crucified two thousand Jews because of an attempted insurrection.

We need shrines, temples and churches, and they should be as beautiful as we can make them, but the danger is that we then confine God to the temple and keep him off the streets, so nurturing a spirituality which encourages temple attendance and temple construction and adornment, but diverts attention from the living temple, which is the body of every human being everywhere. We worship God, in whom all things have their being, the God of unity, in our separate churches and temples, so giving divine sanction to our dividedness and accusing those who try to break down the barriers which separate us of disloyalty, infidelity and unorthodoxy.

When Jesus preached in the synagogue at Nazareth after his forty days in the desert, he unrolled the scroll of the prophet Isaiah and read the verses, 'The spirit of the Lord has been given to me . . . He has sent me to bring the good news to the poor, to proclaim liberty to captives and to the blind new sight, to set the downtrodden free, to proclaim the

Lord's year of favour.' Having read it, he said, 'This text is being fulfilled today even as you listen.' The congregation were very pleased with him. But when he went on to say that no prophet is ever accepted in his own country and gave the example of two pagans, a widow of Zarephath to whom Elijah was sent, and Naaman the Syrian, whom Elisha cured of leprosy, then the faithful turned nasty and tried to throw him over the cliff on which the city was built (Luke 4).

How would we receive him today? An imaginative exercise can help us to answer the question.

Imagine that one evening there is a ring at your front door bell. On answering you find that Jesus himself is standing on the doorstep. The exercise is in your imagining what happens then, which will be different in detail for each individual, but presumably you will experience a flood of emotions, wonder, disbelief, delight, invite Jesus in and find yourself saying ridiculous things like 'Jesus, do make yourself at home', and summoning all the family to meet him. Having imagined this first encounter, you then imagine the scene two weeks later, Jesus having taken you at your word and made himself at home. In the Gospel he said, 'I have come not to bring peace, but the sword, to set daughter against mother, son against father, daughter-in-law against mother-in-law,' so there have probably been some tense moments in those two weeks, with some members of the family retiring early from table, banging the door as they leave the room, or perhaps the front door as they leave the house never to return.

Jesus, having made himself at home, invites whom he will. While on earth, the scribes and pharisees complained, 'This man welcomes sinners and eats with them,' so there will be many undesirable characters coming to visit and the neighbours will be complaining about the noise and the rapid drop in property values in the area.

We will not, of course, feel it right to keep Jesus all to ourselves and will introduce him to the local parish, where he might give an address to, let us say, a combined gathering of the Knights of St Columba and the Union of Catholic Mothers. In the course of the address he assures the audience that 'the prostitutes and sinners will enter the kingdom of heaven before you', which causes uproar and the parish loses most of its principal benefactors.

We now have a major problem on our hands. We cannot throw Jesus out of the house, yet the present state of affairs is intolerable. So we look around the house, clear a large cupboard, do it up tastefully, sparing no expense, put a strong lock on it, and place Jesus there, putting flowers and a lamp in front of the door, bowing whenever we pass by. We now have Jesus where we want him and he no longer interferes!

The child who lived in Nazareth was born in a stable, and his first visitors were shepherds, men who were considered outcasts by the orthodox Jews because they did not keep the rules and observances. Jesus' favourite title for himself was 'Son of Man', which, according to some exegetes, was a slang term meaning 'an ordinary bloke', or, as they say in Glasgow 'an ordnery punter'. The religiously devout, the professionally holy, the shepherds of the Church, have an uncanny knack of driving the Lamb of God off the streets and penning him within their shrines and temples, admitting only those who assent to the ideas and concepts which the learned have formulated. The shepherds then dedicate their lives to nurturing those who enter the shrines, encouraging them to stay within and strengthen their assent to the traditional propositions. It is not surprising that nuclear deterrence, which threatens all human life, should not be high on their agenda.

Jesus had a very different concept of God, whom he saw as primarily concerned with the outsiders, the poor and the outcast, a shepherd who leaves the ninety-nine sheep, who are safe, and searches for the one which is lost. His earthly shepherds tend to a different policy, nurturing the one which is safe, and leaving the ninety-nine who are lost.

If this seems outrageous imagery and an unfair caricature of the Church and its shepherds, then consider the following questions: what percentage of our time, energy, attention and finances do we spend on those who never enter shrines and churches and who do not understand the language and outlook of those who do enter? As Christians, how much attention do we give to the truth that the Jews are the people of the covenant and, therefore, it is only with them that we can find salvation? Among ourselves, how far do we recognise in practice that the God whom we worship is the God of unity, and that we must therefore never act separately in any pastoral work which can be done together? And when we do act together, to what extent are we conscious that whatever we do must be for the good of the whole human race? These are enormous questions, but if we took them seriously and examined our daily timetable in light of them, we should then be taking the first steps towards a Christian *perestroika*. Is it not strange that in trying to find a word to describe the Gospel's call to *metanoia*, a complete change of mind and heart, I point to a process initiated by an atheistic communist!

From the Church of the Annunciation I climbed out of the town to the main road for Tiberias on the Lake of Galilee. The road was long and dusty, but with a wide view of the plain and distant hills which Jesus must have known so well. I stopped to have a look at Cana, a few kilometres from Nazareth, where Mary and Jesus were invited to the wedding feast and Jesus performed his first miracle, turning large pots of water into wine when the wine ran out. The church at Cana, like almost all the Christian shrines in Palestine, is built on third-century foundations. Ten centuries later, the Crusaders rebuilt on these foundations, and today most of the Christian shrines are rebuilt on these spots. In the little Cana church they had replicas of the six stone waterpots, which could provide enough for a year of village wedding feasts. The miracle is commemorated every day at Mass in a beautiful offertory prayer, said as the priest places a drop of water into the wine. 'Grant that by the mixing of this water and wine, we may share in Christ's divinity, who humbled himself to share our humanity.'

In spite of the heat and dust, I enjoyed the walk to Galilee, unencumbered by Mungo. Apart from military vehicles, there was little traffic on the road, only the occasional Arab passing on an overloaded donkey. By 2.00 p.m. I was on the outskirts of Tiberias, but it took another hour to reach the water's edge, several hundred feet below sea-level, where the heat was both heavy and intense. Tiberias itself was a disappointment, a modern Israeli city from which the Arabs have been driven out. As the last bus back to Nazareth left at 4.15 p.m. I had little time to walk along the lakeside, but I knew I would be returning.

I left the bus at the top of the hill before it descended to Nazareth's town centre, presuming I could easily walk along

225

the ridge of the hill to the Salesian college. Like most short cuts, it became a difficult journey as I tried to thread my way through a maze of hillside houses, the roads ending in cul-de-sacs. By climbing a few fences and walking through a rubbish dump, I did find a road leading to the college. On the previous evening, Angelino had told me that it was uncertain where the cliff was from which the crowd had tried to throw Jesus, but in my short cut I reckoned I had seen several possibilities.

When I returned to the college an Italian priest visitor had arrived with his mother for a holiday and Angelino invited me to join them next day when he would be taking them sightseeing by the Lake of Galilee, returning by way of Mount Tabor, generally believed to be the mountain of the Transfiguration.

Wednesday, June 3

This was a sightseeing day and we began with the beautiful modern Church of the Beatitudes, built on ancient foundations and set in a garden overlooking the Sea of Galilee. From there we went down to the lakeside to Tabgha, the church commemorating the multiplication of the loaves and fishes, built on a fourth-century foundation with some of its original mosaics still preserved in the twentieth-century church. Nearby, within easy walking distance, is a tiny church built at the water's edge, commemorating Jesus' resurrection appearance to the fishing disciples, which is described in John, chapter 21. Of all the shrines I saw, this one, called 'The Supremacy of Love', was the most attractive and moving, for it was very simple and swallows flew in and out of their nest above the altar.

Further along the coast we visited the site of ancient Capernaum, built at the water's edge. Excavations there revealed the foundations of a third-century synagogue, remains of houses from the Roman era and, most interesting of all, the remains of a fifth-century octagonal church with, beneath it, remains of an earlier church, its sanctuary corresponding to a first-century house of the Roman era. According to one guide book, graffiti were found there with the names of Jesus and Peter, so it may have been the site of Peter's house.

We approached Mount Tabor by a long, rough and twisting road. The Church of the Transfiguration on the summit provides a marvellous view of the surrounding countryside. In the Gospel account, Jesus was transfigured on the mountain top,

> . . . his face shone like the sun and his clothes became as white as the light. Suddenly Moses and Elijah appeared to them; they were talking with him. Then Peter spoke to Jesus. 'Lord', he said, 'it is wonderful for us to be here: if you wish, I will make three tents here, one for you, one for Moses and one for Elijah.' (Matt. 17:1–4).

There is a long tradition of the shepherds of the Church wanting to enclose Jesus in a shrine! Jesus, on the way down the mountain, foretells his coming Passion and death. The temple is his own body, his own humanity, which will be broken, but he will rise again and be with all future generations, his temple the human heart. There are side altars in the Church of the Transfiguration dedicated to Moses and Elijah, so they got their 'tents' after all.

On our way home we called in at the little village of Nain, where Jesus raised the widow's only son as he was being carried to burial. The curator of the church is a Muslim and Mass is celebrated there only once a year.

Thursday, June 4

I was still trying to believe that I really was in Galilee. The previous day had been interesting, but I had seen too much, too quickly. On Thursday, I caught an early morning bus from Nazareth to Tiberias to spend the day on the shore of the Lake of Galilee. The bus, I was told, would continue through Tiberias and along the shore road. It did, but instead of stopping by the lakeside, it took a left turn into the hills and did not stop until it reached the village of Chorazain, high above the lake.

Jesus mentions Chorazain in the Gospel, 'Woe to you,

Chorazain'. It still looks a woeful, desolate place, the only traffic being military vehicles. I walked down the hill to the lakeside and while still 600 feet above it, a notice indicated sea-level. On my left was the Hill of the Beatitudes.

'Blessed are the poor, theirs is the kingdom of heaven.' I was thinking about the beatitudes as I came down the hill. The catechism, which I first learned at the age of seven, included the eight beatitudes, and I had to learn these by heart. One of the punishments for failing the by-heart test was having to write out these same beatitudes several times. For me they had nothing to do with happiness and not much to do with religion, which was about going to Mass, saying prayers, going to Confession and so getting to heaven. The beatitudes, apart from satisfying teachers, were an irrelevance. It took me years before I began to glimmer their explosive power.

The Greek work for 'blessed' is 'makarios' and it means a state of happiness which nothing can mar. So to be blessed is about being blissfully, unshakably happy, free from all anxiety, fear and uncertainty. It is the longing of everyone, as the advertising industry well knows, for it is constantly manipulating this desire and transferring it to cars, insurance policies, houses, clothing, health foods and sports equipment. Religion can also manipulate this longing for peace, assuring us that if we say these prayers, attend this church, follow these prescriptions and give generously to the support of our pastors, bliss will be ours both here and hereafter.

Jesus says that if we want to find bliss we must become poor. The Greeks had many different words for everything, and the word used in the Gospel for 'poor' is 'ptochoi', which means the poorest of the poor. It is the *ptochoi* who, Jesus says, are the blissfully happy, and theirs is the kingdom of God.

This teaching seems to be contradicted by the facts. Neediness does not bring bliss, but wretchedness, misery, despair and depravity. Destitution is an evil. To divinise destitution and to assure the destitute that their situation is, in fact, bliss, is to practise the oppression and exploitation denounced by all the prophets and by Jesus himself. What then does it mean, 'Blessed are the poor'.

In South Africa I once gave a retreat to an Anglican nun,

228

Sister Josephine. In the course of it she told me what had led her into a convent. She was educated at a private girls' school in England during the war. One day, the school chaplain took the sixth form on a cultural outing to London, finishing up with a symphony concert. While waiting for the train home, the air-raid sirens sounded. The only shelter available was one reserved for tramps and alcoholics. Josephine spent the night next to a gentleman of the road, who spent his walking months going from John O'Groats to Lands End and back. He struck her as a thoroughly contented and happy man and the night's conversation was the beginning of her decision to become a nun. She now lives and works in Lesotho.

The poverty of which Jesus speaks is an inner attitude which enables us to recognise our complete and total reliance upon God, shifting the basis of our confidence and trust, happiness and hope, from its false foundations – in our wealth, status, achievements, health, popularity, moral rectitude, religious orthodoxy, or whatever we consider to be our spiritual progress – and placing it instead in the only solid foundation, in God, in whom we live, move and have our being. If we were really poor in this sense, then we would see everything as gift, not as possession. We would enjoy what we receive without being anxious about losing it. We would happily share what we had received and see no point in clinging to what we did not need. If criticised, overlooked and despised, we should not be unduly upset, because regard and respect from others would not constitute our happiness. We should have a strong confidence in ourselves, not because of any track record, but because we know that our whole being is a unique manifestation of God.

The journey to this bliss is a journey away from self-preoccupation and towards a growing awareness that my neighbour is also myself. The mind which was in Christ Jesus begins to take over our minds and hearts, so that we hunger and thirst after justice, not just for me and for my family, group, church, nation or class, but for every human being and every group, including our enemies. That is why I cannot believe that it can ever be right for Christians, whose manifesto is contained in the beatitudes, to accept nuclear deterrence as a legitimate means of defence, because it necessarily includes the intention to annihilate the innocent, and that intention is not nullified no matter how piously nuclear deterrence supporters may wish that the threat need never be put into effect. Jesus did not say, 'Blessed are those who defend their own interests by threatening mass murder and endangering all human life on earth.'

When I reached the lakeside I returned to the little chapel called 'The Supremacy of Love', then walked along the shore, where I spent the rest of the day sitting on the rocks and gazing at the water.

In St Matthew's Gospel, after feeding the five thousand, Jesus sent his disciples by boat across the lake while he went up the hill to pray. In the early morning the boat was caught in a storm. Jesus walked on the water towards them. The sight terrified the disciples, so he called out to them, 'Courage, it is I, don't be afraid'. Peter said, 'If it is you, Lord, tell me to come to you across the water.'

'Come,' said Jesus. Then Peter got out of the boat and started walking towards Jesus across the water, but as soon as he felt the force of the wind, he took fright and began to sink. 'Lord! Save me,' he cried. Jesus put out his hand at once and held him. 'Man of little faith,' he said, 'why did you doubt?' (Matt. 14:27–31)

I thought on this scene as I sat on the rocks, for this scene is also saying, 'Blessed are the poor'.

When we read of Jesus walking on the water, our minds first ask, 'Did this really happen?' We then either assert that it could not possibly have happened and so dismiss the story, or else bury our doubts in the interests of orthodoxy and declare its literal truth against all comers. In either case we fail to ask the important question, the first question a Hebrew would ask, 'What does it mean?'

For the Hebrews, a stormy sea was not just a symbol of the powers of destructiveness: it was the manifestation of destructiveness itself, so that a stormy sea was not only a physical threat, but also a spiritual threat. So the disciples were terrified. In their terror they heard the voice, 'Courage, it is I, don't be afraid.' This means that Jesus has entered into destructiveness and overcome it. There is no depth of human desperation or terror where he is not. The Gospel story is not just describing a past event, but a present reality. The voice saying, 'Courage, it is I, don't be afraid,' is as present and as real now as it was on the night of the storm. 'Don't be afraid,' is the most common phrase in the Scriptures and appears, I am told, 365 times. The next most common phrase is, 'I am with you.'

Peter has reservations about trusting the voice, so he says, 'Lord, if it is you, tell me to come,' and Jesus says, 'Come.' He is still saying it, 'Come across your fears, anxieties, guilt, feelings of helplessness and hopelessness, your weakness, your inabilities.' Peter responds and lets go the one security he has to hold on to, the boat, and begins to walk towards Jesus.

Matthew then has a sentence which can keep us reflecting for a lifetime: 'As soon as Peter felt the force of the wind, he took fright and began to sink.' When we take our eyes off Christ and concentrate instead on the dangers which beset us, the damage we have done, the damage done to us, or likely to be done to us, then we begin to sink. This is what had happened to me on the boat to Haifa when I was over-whelmed with despondency when I looked at questions of peace and justice and my inability to effect anything.

The greater our fear, the more firmly we clutch at any security at hand and we fight to retain that security as though it were our very life. Fear, while it is a very necessary emotion, because it warns us of danger, is also the most destructive of emotions. National fear can lead us into the blind destructive-ness of nuclear defence.

Fear is not evil: it is benevolent, if only we can see what it is saying to us, namely that there is no ultimate safety in any created thing. For all of us there is only one rock, refuge and source of strength, which is both beyond us, yet within us. When we can face our fears, then we can begin to find our rock and refuge. Blissfully happy are those who can find their confidence in God. I prayed for a faith which is ready to risk, confident that even if I fail, Christ will grab me, as he grabbed Peter and brought him to safety.

As I returned to Nazareth by the evening bus, I thought about the final stage of the pilgrimage, from Nazareth to

Jerusalem by way of the West Bank. I doubted whether I could make the distance on foot in this scorching weather and with an unstable Mungo, so I decided to take Mungo to Jerusalem by bus, return to Nazareth the same day, then set off next day for the last four days of walking.

Friday, June 5 – Saturday, June 6

In my original schedule I hoped to arrive in Jerusalem at the end of June. When I phoned the Biblical Institute from Nazareth, they told me that the house was officially closed for two weeks, but that I was welcome to a room, if I were prepared to fend for myself. After four months on the road, this was no great hardship. I arranged to drop in with Mungo on Sunday, June 7 and to return to stay on Thursday, June 11.

I spent Friday and Saturday in Nazareth, wandering through the town, chatting with Father Angelino about the plight of the Palestinians in the last forty years, and preparing myself for the last stretch of the pilgrimage.

Sunday, June 7

I caught an early bus to Jerusalem, and it was already almost full, mostly with young Israeli military, boys and girls, picking up more of them as we entered the West Bank, when there was standing room only. The land looked barren, the grass scorched brown, the heat inside the bus oppressive.

It was a strange journey, because I did not want to think too much about where I was going in case it took the edge off Thursday's arrival on foot, but some of the pilgrim psalms were going around in my head, 'When God brought Zion's captives home, at first it seemed like a dream' (Ps. 126:1). I had no difficulty in remaining in a dream state, for the only view I could see of Jerusalem as we approached was of rows of newly built houses in the northern suburbs, until my feet were standing within the walls of the bus station, filled with military and with Jewish and Christian pilgrims from many countries.

I took a taxi to the Biblical Institute as I had only a few hours to spare before catching the last afternoon bus back to Nazareth. When I arrived, the Rector, Father Tom Hughson, an American Jesuit, welcomed me and invited me to join him in celebrating the Mass of Pentecost in the house chapel.

It was a strange and wonderful experience to celebrate Mass in a room in Jerusalem on the feast of Pentecost. 'They had all met in one room, when suddenly they heard what sounded like a powerful wind from heaven, the noise of which filled the entire house in which they were sitting; and something appeared to them that seemed like tongues of fire; these separated and came to rest on the head of each of them. They were all filled with the Holy Spirit, and began to speak foreign languages as the Spirit gave them the gift of speech.' And the people asked, 'Surely, all these men speaking are Galileans? How does it happen that each of us hears them in his own native language? Parthians, Medes and Elamites, people from Mesopotamia, Judaea and Cappadocia, Pontus and Asia, Phrygia and Pamphylia, Egypt and the parts of Libya round Cyrene; as well as visitors from Rome – Jews and proselytes alike – Cretans and Arabs' (Acts 2:1–11).

Although my mind was a jumble of thoughts and memories during the Mass, I felt a peace and a hope which did not come from the thoughts and memories, which were neither hopeful nor peaceful. I was still thinking of the bus and the bus station filled with armed soldiers, of Jesus' own torn land, of the oppression of the Palestinian Arabs by his people, of the fact that in his country only a tiny proportion of the population are Christians, divided into many different churches and sects.

An old Jesuit once told me that in his noviceship everyone was provided with a little card containing questions which they were instructed to ask themselves at the end of each day. One of the questions was, 'How is your inner eye of faith?' Some novice must have dropped his card on the street because later a workman, seeing a group of novices passing, shouted 'How's your bloody eye of faith today, mate?' I think often of that question. We say faith is a believing, but it is also a knowing, an inner perceiving and an inner certainty, which is quite compatible with, at another level, ignorance, uncertainty, bewilderment and confusion. Faith does not provide answers to our divisions within and between nations, but it does give us hope and inner assurance that there are answers other than violence, which inevitably breeds more violence. Faith assures us that no person, no group, no nation, no state of affairs is ever hopeless, that there is a real unity between all human beings and in all creation, and that we can find ourselves only in so far as we discover this unity within and amongst us. During the Pentecost Mass I knew by faith that his Spirit is still being poured out on all human beings, and this inner assurance was with me as I returned to Nazareth with a small haversack containing the bare essentials for the walk from Nazareth to Jerusalem, which I would begin next day.

Monday, June 8

It was still dark at 5.00 a.m., when I left the Salesian college. The sky above me was clear, but as I walked down the hill I was soon enveloped in a thick and chilly mist. I walked quickly, unencumbered by Mungo, wanting to cover as much distance as possible before the sun broke through. By 9.00 the mist had evaporated and the sun was already burning. I entered the West Bank area with notices warning motorists not to drive through at night except in convoy. The roads were quiet except for occasional army trucks. On one long stretch of road a few Arabs had set out a fruit stall. I bought a melon, grapefruit and some oranges, but when I went to pay, the man serving me, who could speak no English, refused to accept any payment. I kept insisting: he kept refusing, and I could not tell from his sad face why he was refusing.

As it became hotter, I wished I could be more detached from hunger, thirst and West Bank apprehension to give full attention to this road over barren hills and scorched valleys, a route which the holy family must have taken on their annual pilgrimage to Jerusalem.

Around midday I was in Jenin, where I planned to spend the night, but before searching for lodgings, I sat for a long time at a crossroads café, drinking lemonade and watching life go by. Traffic was heavy, army trucks, Arab lorries, battered cars which looked as though they were returning from

234

stock-car races, men wheeling barrows, others leading heavily laden donkeys. Nearby a tanker was pumping water into a flat above the café, giving us a cooling shower from its defective hosing. Opposite was a mosque, its loud-speakers drowning every other noise, first with a wailing chant, then with a ferocious address, delivered mostly at screaming pitch. It must have been a funeral oration, for soon hundreds of men appeared, bearing the coffin. Near me a small group of elderly Arabs were squatting on the pavement, fingering their prayer beads and apparently oblivious of all the noise and confusion around them.

To all my inquiries about lodgings I received the same answer, that there was nothing to be found in Jenin and that the nearest place was at Shekhem, 35 km away. As I had already walked about 32 km, I had not the energy to do another 35 in this heat, so I took a bus to Shekhem, a much larger town than Jenin, with an even heavier military presence. There had been shootings by the Israelis a few days before and one of the casualties was a Palestinian student, who was sitting in his room studying when he was shot. I was directed to a 'Bension'. On my way I saw a notice overhead, hanging from a first-floor window. It was in Arabic, but ended with the information, 'Ph.D. Surgery (Edinburgh)'.

The 'Bension' was on the first floor and access was through a workshop where two men were repairing radios. One of them, in answer to my inquiry, said in fluent English, 'You'll get much better accommodation as cheaply at the hotel,' and he offered to take me there. On the way he told me that he was hoping to return to England, where he had already gained a first degree, to do a doctorate in electronics. He longed to return to a country where he could walk the streets freely and feel treated as a human being. He then gave a horrifying picture of life in the West Bank, of the brutality to which the Arabs were subjected, of the daily and hourly danger of living in an occupied land. He added that he was not interested in politics and simply wanted to live in safety and freedom. He also told me of his girl friend in England and asked if I would be prepared to take a small gift back for her. I had been solemnly warned at Piraeus against accepting any gifts from third parties to be taken abroad, so I told him I would have to declare the gift, which would certainly be confiscated. He accepted this statement without argument and continued as friendly as before. If he was a 'terrorist', which I doubt, he was a most charming, courteous and kindly one.

The hotel to which my Arab friend directed me was swarming with Israeli troops, who were using its roof as a watch tower. There appeared to be no other guests, which did not surprise me once I saw the filthy room and the toilet facilities. Before going to sleep I had decided to abandon my plan to walk the rest of the way through the West Bank and to take a bus next day to Jerusalem.

Tuesday, June 9

I left the hotel early and climbed Mount Gerazim. Shekhem is an ancient town lying between two mountains, Gerazim to the south and Mount Ebal to the north. When Abram was told, 'Leave your country and your father's house for the land I will show you,' he 'passed through the land as far as Shekhem's holy place', where Yahweh appeared to him and said, 'It is to your descendants that I will give this land.' So Abram built an altar there for Yahweh (Gen. 12). Later, Jacob bought land in Shekhem and built an altar to the God of Israel (Gen. 33).

As I climbed the hill and passed some fine houses on its slopes, I thought of Amos, the earliest of the written prophets, who, in the eighth century B.C. was called by God from his shepherding on the edge of the Judean desert and told to go and preach to the affluent and expanding northern kingdom of Israel. What Amos lacked in tact, he made up for in vehemence, addressing the sophisticated ladies of Samaria as 'ye cows of Bashan'. Because the people of Samaria were oppressing the poor, trampling on the poor man, and extorting levies on his wheat, he told them, 'Those houses you have built of dressed stone, you will never live in them' (Amos 5:11). 'I mean to pull down both your winter houses and your summer houses, the houses of ivory will be destroyed, the houses of ebony will vanish. It is the Lord Yahweh who speaks' (Amos 3:15). Nor does God, through Amos, approve of Samaria's elaborate religious services, 'I hate and I despise your feasts, I take no pleasure in your solemn festivals. . . .

Let me have no more of the din of your chanting, no more of your strumming on harps. But let justice flow like water, and integrity like an unfailing stream' (Amos 5:21–4).

I stood alone on the summit of Mount Gerazim amidst the ruins of ancient temples, a strange, desolate and lonely place, which felt as though God had abandoned it. As I reached the road to return to Shekhem, a car drew up and the cheerful driver offered me a lift, which I gladly accepted. 'You have heard of the good Samaritan,' he began, 'I am one of them.' He then gave me a pamphlet to read, describing the Samaritan beliefs and way of life, which, unfortunately, I had to return when I left the car. There are only about five hundred Samaritans in the world, the majority living in a close-knit community to the west of Shekhem. They have their own language, their own script, accept only the first five books of the Bible, and consider themselves the one and only true Israel. There was one horrific sentence in the pamphlet ordering the circumcision of every child within eight days of birth, otherwise the child must be put to death. As we parted, the Samaritan looked pleased that he had been able to tell the stranger about the true Israel.

I then visited Jacob's well, where Jesus had sat with the Samaritan woman, telling her that he could give her living water. 'Whoever drinks this water will get thirsty again; but anyone who drinks the water that I shall give will never be thirsty again: the water that I shall give will turn into a spring inside, welling up to eternal life.' When the woman told Jesus that her fathers worshipped on Mount Gerazim, while the Jews said Jerusalem was the place where one ought to worship, Jesus answered, 'Believe me, woman, the hour is coming when you will worship the Father neither on this mountain, nor in Jerusalem. . . . The hour will come – in fact it is here already – when true worshippers will worship the Father in spirit and in truth' (John 4).

'It is here already.' One of the consolations of working with people active in justice and peace, who belong to different Christian denominations or a different religion, is the sense of unity experienced, especially when they pray together.

At midday I caught a bus from Shekhem to Jerusalem. I

did not go immediately to the Biblical Institute because I wanted to find some quiet spot in the Old City where I could end the pilgrimage formally. I had not studied a map, had no idea where the churches were, but trusted I would find some suitable place.

The Old City was more like an outdoor shopping market than a place of pilgrimage for Jews, Christians and Muslims. Its narrow, cobbled streets were lined with shops attracting swarms of pilgrims. At one point, where hanging T-shirts left a gap, I saw a notice, 'The Sixth Station', and, a little further on, 'The Seventh Station'. I was on the Via Dolorosa, the street which Jesus walked carrying the cross of his death. The first church I found was the Church of the Holy Sepulchre, the most ancient shrine of Christendom, built, it is claimed, over the site of Jesus' death and burial. It must also be the noisiest shrine in Christendom with tourist guides trying to make themselves heard above the chatter of their own and other groups to guide them through this dark and massive church. It is shared by six different Christian denominations, several of them conducting noisy services simultaneously in a spirit of mutual aversion. Someone later described to me the scene on Good Friday at this church, when there was a fierce argument between the denominations as to who should carry the cross!

I wandered through the shrine, found a relatively quiet spot free from tourist groups, and sat facing a sculpture of the Risen Christ appearing to Mary Magdalene. I was disturbed only once, by an Orthodox priest who came clattering by with incense billowing from the thurible he swung vigorously, clanking the smoking bowl against the chain with which he held it. I tried to settle to a prayer of thanksgiving to God for having prompted me to make this pilgrimage and bringing me safely to the end of it, but there was so much noise around me, and inside me such a jumble of thoughts, memories, emotions and reflections, that I gave up all attempt to finish the pilgrimage in the calm, orderly and peaceful way I had hoped. Instead, I just sat in the noisy shrine and listened to the noise. The words came to me, 'The time will come when we will worship God neither on this mountain, nor in Jerusalem' (John 4:21), and I felt the reassurance which had come to me so often on the road. God is beyond

238

words, deeper than any thoughts. He is: and in him all things exist.

> Through him all things came to be, not one thing had its being but through him. All that came to be had life in him, and that life was the light of all, a light that shines in the dark, a light that darkness could not overpower. . . . The Word was made flesh, he lived among us and we saw his glory. (John 1:3–5, 14)

I had been disappointed at first at this noisy ending to the pilgrimage, but as I sat, I became glad that it was this way. We need temples, churches and shrines, we need solitude and silence, but we need all these things to make us more aware of the mystery in which we are all living all the time. We want to find him in light places of our own making, in temples and churches, in systems of thought and belief which cocoon us from the pain of the world and make us feel secure and assured of our eternal salvation. Any such security is false, because the God whom we worship is in the chaos and the darkness, 'He became sin for us.' He is in the darkness of the nuclear threat, appealing to us to recognise the light, that we are all one, that what we do or threaten to another, we do also to God and to ourselves.

Lord, deliver us from our blindness which leads us to think that we can ensure our security by threatening mass annihilation. Deliver us from every form of religion which locks you up in temples, shrines and churches and does not recognise you in the mystery of every human being.

We are all called to that inner knowing which recognises God at work in all things, heart of the universe, the life-giving power, which bonds our tiny fragmented selves to the heart of God in whom all things exist. Anything, no matter how ridiculous and meaningless it seems, which can deepen that inner knowing, whether it is a walk to Jerusalem on foot, or a visit to a church, or just a moment's silence to worship him in spirit and in truth, is more precious and life-giving than anything else we can do. I had walked to Jerusalem to find Christ's peace. I left Jerusalem knowing that his peace is offered to us in every place and at every time. For its dwelling place is in our hearts.

Lord, what is the point of your presence
if our lives do not alter?
Change our lives; shatter
our complacency.
Make your word
flesh of our flesh,
blood of our blood,
and our life's purpose.
Take away that self-regard
which makes our consciences feel clear.
Press us uncomfortably.
For only thus
that other peace is made.
Your peace.

(Bishop Helder Camara)

Epilogue

Two of the questions put to me on the walk were with me before I started out and they have remained with me since, especially in writing this book: 'Aus welchem Grund? Out of what Ground?' asked by the drunken philosopher in Germany, and 'What can we little people do?' asked by the Yugoslav barman.

In 1987, my answer to both questions was 'Walk to Jerusalem', because the more I thought on questions of justice and peace, the more I suffered a kind of mental and spiritual vertigo, yet I could not dismiss the questions and live at peace. I knew from past experience that for me long-distance walking is a cure for mental and spiritual vertigo and I was lucky enough to have the health, strength, money and blessing of the Jesuit Provincial to undertake the walk.

The walk was important to me because it helped me to understand better the answer to 'What can we little people do?' The answer is not 'Walk to Jerusalem', but one that is possible for every human being and is most easily available to those who feel they are the littlest, most apparently helpless, obscure, useless, confused and incompetent.

We live in mystery, the mystery of God. What our eyes see and our hands touch, all that our minds apprehend, is only a tiny fraction, and usually a very distorted one, of the reality in which we live. This statement may sound very fanciful and verging on lunacy, but it has modern scientific backing. Not only does every physical movement in our world have repercussions throughout the whole world and universe, but every thought and movement of our hearts affects everything else. The Buddhists have been saying this for centuries, teaching those who meditate to send healing waves of compassion outwards. According to St John of the Cross one act of pure love is worth more than all external activity. Modern nuclear scientists no longer dismiss such statements as unscientific nonsense. They have undergone a revolution in their thinking, from a mechanistic view of the universe to quantum physics, and their language often sounds more akin to that of the mystics than to the language of pre-nuclear physicists.

History, as we know it, recounts the deeds, successes and failures of famous, wealthy and powerful individuals and nations, and we still believe that wealth and power are the means by which we shape history. Like the physicists, we need to undergo a revolution in our thinking and listen again to the Old Testament prophets, who kept reminding their people that salvation is not to be found in chariots and horses, in alliances with the powerful nations, or in wealth acquired through the exploitation and oppression of the poor, but only through trust in God, so that they mirror in their lives God's justice, integrity and compassion. 'He has shown the power of his arm, he has routed the proud of heart. He has pulled down the mighty from their thrones and exalted the lowly' (Luke 1:51–2).

If we could understand history more clearly, we should discover that the most important influences shaping it were not the emperors and kings, presidents and popes, generals and prime ministers, but the poor, the oppressed, the exploited and ignored, the criminals and the prostitutes who, in their affliction have found hope and trust in God, have let his love take hold on them and, through the secret longings and prayers of their hearts, have sent waves of goodness and healing through creation.

A few weeks after I returned from Jerusalem, I met Sister Margaret Walsh. For the previous three years she had been living with two other members of her community in a housing estate in the West Midlands where unemployment was running at 80 per cent, church-going at around 2 per cent; the tenants were mostly West Indian and single-parent families. She said that she had learned more about Christianity in those last three years than in the previous forty, and her teachers were the local tenants. I was intrigued, went, saw, and began to learn too from these people, most of them badly battered emotionally and physically, discounted, caught in the poverty trap, exacerbated for some by their inability to manage their own lives. Yet they could meet together and talk with an openness which is only found in those who have faced the depths of their own helplessness, share with one another in a way in which only the very poor seem capable of sharing, forgive after serious rows and then care for one another with tenderness, sharing with one another not only at parties but also at religious celebrations in the community centre in a spirit which did not divide the sacred from the secular, laughing and weeping at both. They showed me a Jesus living today and still dining with 'prostitutes and sinners'.

So, 'what can we little people do?'

The first thing is to recognise the whole web of assumptions underlying our question. We are assuming that change can only be effected by the wealthy, the powerful and the influential. Faith in the reality of God at work in ourselves and in everything in creation is absent.

The second thing is to begin to recognise just how little we are, for then we shall discover the illusoriness of our value system, of our criteria for success and failure, of our trust in nuclear deterrence as a means of security. To know our littleness we must not 'help' the poor, but make friends with them so that they can help and teach us. This is the hardest lesson to learn because we do not want to see our own wretchedness and nakedness. That is why we shun the poor, assure ourselves that their poverty is their own fault, due to their own fecklessness, call them 'the problem of the underclass', spend vast sums of money, not in inviting them to parties, as Jesus exhorts in the Gospel, or in ensuring that they have adequate food and shelter, but in strengthening our security forces to prevent their rioting. In the Old Testament, it was through the 'Anawim', which means literally, 'the bent-over ones', that salvation was to come.

I had written most of this book before the dramatic events at the end of 1989 when miracles began to happen in Europe. Without bloodshed, apart from Rumania, governments toppled before the spirit of peoples enslaved for over forty years. The end came suddenly and took the world by surprise, but the change began in the minds and hearts of 'little people', like the small peace groups I had met in Yugoslavia, held in subjection for years, but never losing hope or the will to be free.

What can we little people do? Trust in the Spirit that is within us and, in our own hearts, be channels of his peace in our own immediate environment. Each day I shall pray for Christ's peace for every reader of this book and I ask your prayers for me.

On my return from Jerusalem, I visited Ephesus. Everything I have been trying to say in this book is summed up in St Paul's prayer for the Ephesians,

Out of his infinite glory, may he give you the power through his Spirit for your hidden self to grow strong, so that Christ may live in your hearts through faith, and then, planted in love and built on love, you will with all the saints have strength to grasp the breadth and the length, the height and the depth; until, knowing the love of Christ, which is beyond all knowledge, you are filled with the utter fullness of God. Glory be to him whose power working in us, can do infinitely more than we can ask or imagine. (Eph. 3:16–21)